Report of the Inter-agency
Task Force on Financing
for Development

FINANCING FOR DEVELOPMENT: PROGRESS AND PROSPECTS 2018

United Nations
New York, 2018

This report is a joint product of the members of the Inter-agency Task Force on Financing for Development (members are shown on page xi). The Financing for Development Office of the United Nations Department of Economic and Social Affairs serves as the coordinator and substantive editor of the Task Force report.

The online annex of the Task Force (http://developmentfinance.un.org) comprehensively monitors progress in implementation of the Financing for Development outcomes, including the Addis Ababa Action Agenda and relevant means of implementation targets of the SDGs. It provides the complete evidence base for the Task Force's annual report on progress in the seven action areas of the Addis Agenda (chapters III.A–III.G). The report is by necessity more concise and selective, and should thus be read in conjunction with the online annex.

The online annex of the Task Force also covers several key cross-cutting initiatives that build on the synergies of the Sustainable Development Goals in-depth:

- Delivering social protection and essential public services
- Ending hunger and malnutrition
- Closing the infrastructure gap
- Promoting inclusive and sustainable industrialization
- Generating full and productive employment for all
- Protecting ecosystems
- Promoting peaceful and inclusive societies
- Gender equality
- Investing in children and youth
- Addressing the diverse needs and challenges faced by countries in special situations
- Global partnership

Inquiries about the Task Force or its report and online annex can be sent to:

Financing for Development Office
Department of Economic and Social Affairs
2 United Nations Plaza (DC2- 2170)
New York, N.Y. 10017
United States of America
+1-212-963-4598

developmentfinance@un.org

http://developmentfinance.un.org

United Nations publication
Sales no. E.18.I.5
ISBN 978-92-1-101386-3

Foreword

Financing is critical for achieving the Sustainable Development Goals and fulfilling the aims of the Paris Agreement on climate change.

The Addis Ababa Action Agenda provides a framework for financing sustainable development, and stresses the importance of upholding long-standing commitments to Official Development Assistance, which remains a lifeline for many developing countries.

At the same time, we know that Official Development Assistance is part of a wider financing landscape encompassing trade and much else. The Addis Agenda also calls for innovative sources of finance. We must also do more to build up the capacity of Member States to mobilize domestic resources, including through tax reform, good governance and creating an enabling environment for investment and entrepreneurship. But that must be accompanied by a stronger commitment by the international community to fight tax evasion, money laundering and illicit financial flows.

The private sector has a central role to play. The innovations, technologies and global reach of business can galvanize our work for the Sustainable Development Goals. The investment community is also an indispensable partner; pension funds, institutional asset managers, banks and insurers can help to unlock the capital we need.

In this context, the 2018 report of the Inter-Agency Task Force on Financing for Development finds a mixed picture. There are promising examples of reform and gains in advancing the 2030 Agenda for Sustainable Development, underpinned by a broad-based recovery in the world economy. But the pace of change is insufficient, and significant financial, political and environmental risks threaten to derail progress.

The choices we make now on financing will be pivotal. This report puts forward a rich set of options to accelerate our work. I urge all actors to consider them carefully as they implement the Addis Ababa Action Agenda. I will host a High-level Meeting on Finance in New York in September 2018 to review efforts across key international platforms and domestically by Member States.

The world has the resources to deliver, but they are not allocated where they are needed most. Let us align financing behind sustainable development, invest in the 2030 Agenda and ensure a better world for all.

António Guterres
Secretary-General

Preface

In 2017, we witnessed continued progress in implementing the Addis Ababa Action Agenda, supported by a more favourable global macroeconomic environment. Yet, progress was uneven. Significant medium-term risks remain, which, if unaddressed, threaten to undermine sustainable development. This is the assessment put forward in the 2018 report of the Inter-agency Task Force on Financing for Development. To address risks and close implementation gaps, the Task Force lays out a range of policy options and recommendations for corrective action, across the seven action areas of the Addis Agenda.

The report begins its assessment of progress with an analysis of the global macroeconomic context, which sets the economic framework for implementation efforts. After a prolonged period of slow growth, the world economy is experiencing a broad-based upturn, but this cyclical expansion masks significant underlying weaknesses. Most importantly, both public and private investment remain insufficiently aligned with sustainable development, calling for additional policy action to ensure adequate financing of the Sustainable Development Goals (SDGs).

The subsequent thematic chapter explores financing for the five SDGs under in-depth review at the 2018 High-level Political Forum on Sustainable Development: water and sanitation, affordable and clean energy, sustainable cities and communities, sustainable production and consumption patterns, and terrestrial ecosystems. Building on the financing framework laid out in the Addis Agenda, the chapter identifies options for capital structures and financing options for SDG investments in these sectors, depending on the characteristics of the investment and the situation of country. Public and private finance have different strengths and weaknesses, and thus can play different roles in SDG investment.

The remainder of the report discusses progress in the seven action areas of the Addis Agenda and data. The Task Force finds that progress has been made in each Action Area, but also finds that significant implementation gaps remain. The Task Force makes recommendations on options for closing these gaps and addressing new and emerging issues in each Action Area, with additional analysis included in the comprehensive online annex of the Task Force report (http://developmentfinance.un.org). The report also addresses eight new mandates the Task Force received in the intergovernmentally agreed conclusions and recommendations of the 2017 ECOSOC forum on financing for development follow-up, drawing on background research, dedicated technical meetings and engagement with outside experts. We trust that the sound evidence base provided will assist Member States and all other stakeholders as they work toward fully implementing the 2030 Agenda and Addis Agenda to achieve the SDGs.

The production of this report would not have been possible without the cooperation of dozens of departments, agencies, funds, and other organisations that make up the Inter-agency Task Force. The Task Force is emblematic of the new kind of working together the world needs to deliver the SDGs. Greater partnership, an end to siloed thinking, and the recognition of different points of view are essential as the world rises to the challenges set out in the 2030 Agenda.

Liu Zhenmin
Under-Secretary-General for Economic and Social Affairs
United Nations
Chair of the Inter-agency Task Force

Contents

Foreword iii

Preface iv

Overview 1

I.   The global economic context and its implications for the Sustainable
        Development Goals 7
        1. Outlook and risks for the global economy   7
        2. Sources of the global upturn.   10
        3. Challenges to medium-term growth and sustainable development. . .   12
        4. Reorienting policy towards long-term sustainable development   13

II.   Financing investment in selected SDGs 15
        1. Overview   15
        2. Subnational finance   18
        3. Water and sanitation.   22
        4. Energy   28
        5. Terrestrial ecosystem   33

III.A   Domestic public resources. 39
        1. Key messages and recommendations   39
        2. Domestic resource mobilization   41
        3. International tax cooperation   50
        4. Illicit financial flows   52
        5. Expenditure   56

III.B   Domestic and international private business and finance 61
        1. Key messages and recommendations   61
        2. Trends in investment and cross-border capital flows.   63
        3 The investment climate and the domestic enabling environment   64
        4. Aligning the global financial system with long-term investment for
           sustainable development.   65
        5. Financial inclusion   77

Page

III.C   International development cooperation 87

1. Key messages and recommendations 87
2. Trends in international development cooperation. 88
3. Graduation and access to concessional finance. 97
4. Catalytic aid and blended finance. 102
5. Development effectiveness 105

III.D   International trade as an engine for development 111

1. Key messages and recommendations 111
2. Developments in international trade 112
3. The multilateral trading system 115
4. Promoting international trade that is consistent with the SDGs. . . . 117
5. Bilateral and regional trade and investment arrangements 121
6. Domestic enabling environment for trade 124
7. Trade, technology and incomes 125

III.E   Debt and debt sustainability. 127

1. Key messages and recommendations 127
2. Debt trends. 128
3. Borrowing sustainably to advance sustainable development 131
4. Natural disasters, shocks and debt sustainability 135
5. Resolving unsustainable debt situations 136

III.F   Addressing systemic issues 139

1. Key messages and recommendations 139
2. Macroeconomic stability 140
3. Financial regulation 142
4. Shocks financing instruments. 147
5. Institutional and policy coherence at the United Nations. 152
6. Global economic governance 153

Annex: Inventory of quick-disbursing international instruments 155

III.G   Science, technology, innovation and capacity-building 159

1. Key messages and recommendations 159
2. New and emerging technologies and the SDGs 160
3. Impact of new technologies on labour markets and jobs 162
4. New technologies and Financing for Development: opportunities and
   risks in the action areas of the Addis Ababa Action Agenda. 167
5. National and international actions on science, technology and
   innovation 170

Page

IV.   Data, monitoring and follow-up 175

    1. Key messages and recommendations   175
    2. Strengthening data and statistical capacities.   176
    3. Monitoring the financial sector   179

Inter-agency Task Force members

Task Force coordinator and substantive editor

 United Nations Department of Economic and Social Affairs (UN/DESA)

Financing for development major institutional stakeholders

 World Bank Group

 International Monetary Fund (IMF)

 World Trade Organization (WTO)

 United Nations Conference on Trade and Development (UNCTAD)

 United Nations Development Programme (UNDP)

Regional economic commissions

 Economic and Social Commission for Asia and the Pacific (ESCAP)

 Economic and Social Commission for Western Asia (ESCWA)

 Economic Commission for Africa (ECA)

 Economic Commission for Europe (ECE)

 Economic Commission for Latin America and the Caribbean (ECLAC)

United Nations system and other agencies and offices

 Basel Committee on Banking Supervision (BCBS)

 Committee on Payments and Market Infrastructure (CPMI)

 Financial Stability Board (FSB)

Food and Agriculture Organization of the United Nations (FAO)

 Global Environment Facility (GEF)

 International Association of Insurance Supervisors (IAIS)

 International Atomic Energy Agency (IAEA)

 International Civil Aviation Organization (ICAO)

 International Fund for Agricultural Development (IFAD)

 International Labour Organization (ILO)

 International Organization for Migration (IOM)

 International Telecommunication Union (ITU)

 International Trade Centre (INTRACEN)

 Joint United Nations Programme on HIV/AIDS (UNAIDS)

 Office of the High Commissioner for Human Rights (OHCHR)

 Office of the High Representative for the Least Developed Countries, Landlocked Developing Countries and Small Island Developing States (OHRLLS)

 Office of the Secretary-General's Envoy on Youth

 Office of the Special Adviser on Africa (OSAA)

 Organisation for Economic Co-operation and Development (OECD)

 Principles for Responsible Investment (PRI)

 Secretariat of the Convention on Biological Diversity (CBD)

 Sustainable Energy for All (SE4All)

 The Convention on International Trade in Endangered Species of Wild Fauna and Flora (CITES)

 The Global Alliance for Vaccines and Immunizations (GAVI)

 UN Capital Development Fund (UNCDF)

 United Nations Children's Fund (UNICEF)

 United Nations Commission on International Trade Law (UNCITRAL)

 United Nations Convention to Combat Desertification (UNCCD)

United Nations Educational, Scientific and Cultural Organization (UNESCO)

 United Nations Entity for Gender Equality and the Empowerment of Women (UN Women)

 United Nations Environment Programme (UNEP)

 United Nations Framework Convention on Climate Change (UNFCCC)

 United Nations Global Compact

 United Nations High Commissioner for Refugees (UNHCR)

 United Nations Human Settlements Programme (UN-HABITAT)

 United Nations Industrial Development Organization (UNIDO)

 United Nations Office for Disaster Risk Reduction (UNISDR)

 United Nations Office for Project Services (UNOPS)

 United Nations Office for South-South Cooperation (UNOSSC)

 United Nations Office for the Coordination of Humanitarian Affairs (OCHA)

 United Nations Office on Drugs and Crime (UNODC)

 United Nations Population Fund (UNFPA)

 United Nations Research Institute for Social Development (UNRISD)

 United Nations University (UNU)

 United Nations World Food Programme (WFP)

 World Health Organisation (WHO)

 World Intellectual Property Organization (WIPO)

Abbreviations

ADB	Asian Development Bank
ADF	African Development Fund
AfDB	African Development Bank
AfCFTA	African Continental Free Trade Area
AHIDI	African Human and Infrastructure Development Index
AI	Artificial Intelligence
AIIB	Asian Infrastructure Investment Bank
AMF	Arab Monetary Fund
AML	Anti-Money Laundering
ARC	African Risk Capacity
ASEAN	Association of Southeast Asian Nations
B2C	Business-to-consumer
ATI	Addis Tax Initiative
BCBS	Basel Committee on Banking Supervision
BEPS	Base Erosion and Profit Shifting
BIS	Bank for International Settlements
BITS	Bilateral Investment Treaties
CCRIF	Caribbean Catastrophe Risk Insurance Facility
CCyB	Countercyclical Capital Buffer
CDP	Committee for Development Policy
CFT	Counter Financing of Terrorism
CERF	Central Emergency Response Fund
CGAP	The Consultative Group to Assist the Poor
CIAT	Inter-American Center for Tax Administrations
CMIM	Chiang Mai Initiative Multilateralization
CRA	Credit-rating Agency
CRS	Creditor reporting system
COP	Conference of Parties
CPA	Country Programmable Aid
CPIA	Country Policy and Institutional Assessment
CPTPP	Comprehensive and Progressive Agreement for Trans-Pacific Partnership
CTD	Committee on Trade and Development
DAC	Development Assistance Committee
DCD	Development Co-operation Directorate
DCF	Development Cooperation Forum
DDC	Decentralized Development Cooperation
DGI	Data Gaps Initiative
DFIs	Development Finance Institutions
DFQF	Duty-free, Quota-free
ECLAC	Economic Commission for Latin America and the Caribbean
ECOSOC	United Nations Economic and Social Council
EFSD	European Fund for Sustainable Development
EPOC	Environmental Policy Committee
EPG	Eminent Persons Group
ESM	European Stability Mechanism
ESMAP	Energy Sector Management Assistance Program
ESCAP	Economic and Social Commission for Asia and the Pacific
ESG	Environmental, Social and Governance
EU	European Union
EWEs	Early Warning Exercises
FATF	Financial Action Task Force
FDI	Foreign Direct Investment
FIGI	Financial Inclusion Global Initiative

FINRA	Financial Industry Regulatory Authority	**IATT-STI**	United Nations Inter-agency Task Team on Science, Technology and Innovation for the Sustainable Development Goals
FLAR	Fondo Latinoamericano de Reservas		
FOCAC	Forum on China-Africa Cooperation	**IBRD**	International Bank for Reconstruction and Development
FSB	Financial Stability Board	**ICT**	Information and Communications Technology
FTA	Free Trade Agreement		
G20	Group of Twenty	**IDA**	International Development Association
GCF	Green Climate Fund		
GDP	Gross domestic product	**IDB**	Inter-American Development Bank
GEF	Global Environment Facility	**IDFC**	International Development Finance Club
GFAR	Global Forum on Asset Recovery		
GFSN	Global financial safety net	**IEA**	International Energy Agency
GHG	Greenhouse Gas	**IFC**	International Finance Corporation
GIF	Global Infrastructure Facility	**IFFs**	Illicit financial flows
GIFT	Global Initiative for Fiscal Transparency	**IFFIm**	International Financing Facility for Immunization
GIIN	Global Intermediary Identification Number	**IIA**	International Investment Agreement
GLAAS	Global Analysis and Assessment of Sanitation and Drinking-water	**IIF**	Institute of International Finance
		IISS	International Infrastructure Support System
GNI	Gross National Income		
GPEDC	Global Partnership for Effective Development Cooperation	**ILO**	International Labour Organization
		IMF	International Monetary Fund
GRB	Gender-responsive Budgeting	**IRENA**	International Renewable Energy Agency
GPI	Global Partnership Initiative		
G-SIBs	Global systemically important banks	**ISDS**	Investor-state dispute settlement
		ISORA	International Survey on Revenue Administration
G-SIIs	Global systemically important insurers		
		IOTA	Intra-European Organisation of Tax Administration
GSDR	Global Sustainable Development Report		
		IUU	Illegal Unreported Unregulated
GSP	Generalised Scheme of Preferences	**ITC**	International Trade Centre
HAPAs	High access precautionary Arrangements	**ITU**	International Telecommunications Union
HDI	Human Development Index	**LDCs**	Least developed countries
HIPC	Heavily Indebted Poor Countries	**LEI**	Legal Entity Identifier
J-CAP	Joint Capital Markets Program	**LIC DSF**	Low-income Country Debt Sustainability Framework
KYC	Know-your-customer		
IATI	International Aid Transparency Initiative	**LLDC**	Landlocked developing countries
		MCAA	The Common Reporting Standard Multilateral Competent Authority Agreement
IAIS	International Association of Insurance Supervisors		
IASB	International Accounting Standards Board	**MCL**	Moderately Concessional Loan
		MC11	The Eleventh WTO Ministerial Conference
IATF	Inter-agency Task Force		
		MDB	Multilateral Development Bank

MDG	Millennium Development Goal	StAR	Stolen Asset Recovery
MDRI	Multilateral Debt Relief Initiative	STEM	Science, Technology, Engineering and Mathematics
MIDP	Mesoamerican Integration and Development Project	STI	Science technology and innovation
MNE	Multinational Enterprise	STIP	Science, Technology and Innovation Policy
MSMEs	Micro, Small and Medium-sized Enterprises	TFA	Trade Facilitation Agreement
MTRS	Medium-term Revenue Strategies	TADAT	Tax Administration Diagnostic Assessment Tool
NDB	National Development Bank		
NetFWD	Global Network of Foundations Working for Development	TCFD	Task Force on Climate-related Financial Disclosures
NEPAD	The New Partnership for Africa's Development	TED	Total Economy Database
		TFM	Technology Facilitation Mechanism
NGO	Non-Governmental Organizations	TFP	Total Factor Productivity
NPC	Non-Paris Club	TISC	Technology & Innovation Support Center
NTO	Network of Tax Organisations		
OCHA	Office for the Coordination of Humanitarian Affairs	TIPs	Treaties with Investment Provisions
		TISI	Trade and Investment Supportive Institution
ODA	Official Development Assistance		
OECD	Organisation for Economic Co-operation and Development	TOSSD	Total Official Support for Sustainable Development
PFM	Public Financial Management	TRIPS	Trade-Related Aspects of Intellectual Property Rights
PFI	Policy Framework for Investment		
PIFCSS	Program to Strengthen South-South Cooperation	UCLG	United Cities and Local Governments
PPI	Private Participation in Infrastructure	UNCAC	United Nations Convention Against Corruption
PPP	Public-private partnership	UNCDF	United Nations Capital Development Fund
PRGT	Poverty Reduction Growth Trust		
PROFOR	Program on Forests	UNCITRAL	United Nations Commission on International Trade Law
PRI	Principles for Responsible Investing		
PUP	Public-public Partnerships	UNCTAD	United Nations Conference on Trade and Development
QCPR	Quadrennial Comprehensive Policy Review	UN/DESA	United Nations Department of Economic and Social Affairs
RFA	Regional Financial Arrangements		
R&D	Research and development	UNDP	United Nations Development Programme
SCAV	Standing Committee on Assessment of Vulnerabilities	UNDP-UNV	United Nations Development Programme Volunteering and Capacity-building
SCDIs	State-contingent Debt Instruments		
SDG	Sustainable Development Goals		
SDR	Special drawing right	UNDS	United Nations Development System
SIDS	Small island developing States		
SLS	Short-term Liquidity Swap	UNECA	United Nations Economic Commission for Africa
SMEs	Small and medium-sized enterprises		
SNG	Subnational government	UNEP	United Nations Environment Programme
SPIAC-B	Social Protection Inter-Agency Cooperation Board		
SPV	Special Purpose Vehicle	UNESCO	United Nations Educational, Scientific and Cultural Organization

UNFCCC	United Nations Framework Convention on Climate Change	**WEO**	World Economic Outlook
UNODC	United Nations Office on Drugs and Crime	**WEE**	Women's Economic Empowerment
		We-Fi	Women Entrepreneurs Finance Initiative
UNSD	United Nations Statistical Division	**WEPs**	Women's Empowerment Principles
UNOSSC	United Nations Office for South-South Cooperation	**WGP**	World Gross Product
		WHO	World Health Organization
UNTT	United Nations Task Team	**WIPO**	World Intellectual Property Organization
VAT	Value Added Taxes		
VCs	Virtual Currencies	**WTO**	World Trade Organization
VSS	Voluntary Sustainability Standards		

Overview

In 2017, most types of development financing flows increased, amid progress across all the action areas of the Addis Ababa Action Agenda (hereafter, Addis Agenda). These advances were underpinned by a broad-based upturn in the world economy, increased investment and supportive financial market conditions. While not evenly distributed—per-capita growth remains negative or insignificant in many countries where poverty rates are high—the positive momentum is expected to continue and provide a platform for further progress in financing for development and implementation of the Sustainable Development Goals (SDGs).

Yet, the cyclical upturn masks significant weaknesses and medium-term risks. A disorderly tightening of financial conditions, the adoption of inward-looking policies and associated increases in interest rates and debt vulnerabilities, or an escalation of geopolitical tensions could derail development progress. Persistently high levels of inequality pose a challenge to robust growth and sustainable development. Declining private investment in infrastructure and a renewed increase in global carbon emissions in 2017 are stark reminders of the inability, so far, to sufficiently align investment with long-term sustainable development.

If left unaddressed, structural impediments will continue to undermine sustainable development prospects. The current cyclical upturn in the global economy provides an opportunity to focus policymaking on addressing long-standing concerns, and to accelerate the pace of progress towards the SDGs. The Addis Agenda offers a framework for individual actions and international cooperation towards this end. This 2018 report of the Inter-agency Task Force on Financing for Development (hereafter, Task Force) assesses progress and gaps, and provides policy options across its seven action areas which, if implemented, would put the world on a sustained

and more sustainable growth and development path. It also examines the financing challenges to the SDGs under in-depth review in 2018 in order to help assess progress in the means of implementation for goals on water and sanitation, affordable and clean energy, sustainable cities and communities, sustainable production and consumption, and terrestrial ecosystems.

Several overarching messages have emerged from the Task Force analysis:

- **Integrated national sustainable development strategies and financing frameworks must inform policies, plans and project pipelines.** Integrated strategies provide a long-term vision that reaches beyond short-term political cycles and overcomes siloed thinking. Strategies should incorporate medium-term policies, plans and regulatory frameworks, as well as domestic and international financing flows and needs. They should incorporate parameters and incentives to better align the financial system and investment flows with sustainable development. This is critically evident for infrastructure plans and pipelines, where today's investment decisions will lock in development paths until 2030 and beyond. National actions also need to be supported by a global enabling environment that can facilitate long-term and quality investments, particularly in developing countries;

- **Incentives of actors in public and private financial institutions need to be aligned with long-term sustainable development.** Without a long-term investment horizon, certain risks, such as those from climate change, will not be incorporated into decision-making. Incentive structures need to be reviewed across the financial system and aligned with the SDGs;

■ **Public, private and blended financing contribute to financing SDG investments.** Innovative instruments and approaches are rapidly changing the development finance landscape and creating opportunities to scale up the contributions of all sources of financing towards the SDGs. Private finance and investment, public and blended financing all remain indispensable. Project and country characteristics and national policy priorities will determine which financing model is best suited for specific investments, and which actors are best positioned to manage investment risks and provide services equitably and cost-effectively;

■ **Public policies and actions are at the heart of the 2030 Agenda for Sustainable Development.** While public, private and blended finance all play important roles in financing sustainable development, public leadership is indispensable to set rules, provide guidance, promote coherence, and overcome structural constraints that impede sustainable-development-oriented structural transformation.

Three cross-cutting issues are addressed throughout the chapters of this year's report:

■ **New technologies have the potential to support progress across the SDGs and the action areas of the Addis Agenda.** They open new possibilities to address long-standing development challenges across the SDGs, but their transformative power also raises complex challenges and risks, and puts adaptive pressure on economies and societies, including their labour markets. It is critical to make complementary investments, strengthen social protection and set regulatory frameworks so that benefits are shared broadly, and risks to privacy and data protection, financial stability and integrity are addressed;

■ **Gender equality must be addressed at every point in policymaking and programming.** Gender inequalities persist in access to finance, technology, public services, decent jobs, unpaid care and domestic work, participation in policymaking processes and many other areas. Such inequality threatens achievement of the 2030 Agenda for Sustainable Development, but also weakens inclusive growth prospects by denying women opportunities to fully participate in the economy. Gender equality needs to be mainstreamed in fiscal policies, business, access to finance, and development cooperation, and all financing policies need to be monitored and assessed consistently for gender impacts. This also requires increased availability of sex-disaggregated data;

■ **Focus needs to firmly remain on the poorest and most vulnerable, to ensure no one is left behind.** Financing and capacity gaps are greatest in countries with the least ability to close them—in particular, least developed countries and small island developing States. Yet, international support is not sufficient to effectively help these countries meet the SDGs. International commitments for vulnerable countries need to be met, and their interests and concerns considered in international norm-setting and policymaking.

The seven action areas of the Addis Agenda provide the building blocks for implementation of the 2030 Agenda for Sustainable Development and SDG achievement. Task Force recommendations for each of them are described in detail in subsequent chapters. Key overarching messages include the following:

■ **Mobilizing additional domestic public finance and spending it more effectively remains critical.** Effective revenue collection and public service delivery can boost the link between citizen and state, and form the basis of the social contract. The implementation of medium-term revenue strategies can support improved domestic public resource mobilization. International cooperation needs to complement these efforts—by increasing financial support for fiscal capacity-building, and by ensuring developing countries benefit fully from new international standards on tax transparency. New technologies can both increase efficiency in revenue collection and strengthen the fight against illicit financial flows. Improving the alignment of budgets with the SDGs, especially through greater transparency and disaggregation of fiscal data, will further efforts across the 2030 Agenda for Sustainable Development, such as supporting gender equality and implementing universal social protection systems;

- **Achieving the SDGs will require a shift in the financial sector towards long-term investment horizons and sustainability as a central concern of investment decisions.** The momentum around sustainable investment is growing. Yet, long-term investment in sustainable development, especially in countries most in need, remains insufficient. There are both supply and demand constraints to greater private investment. Countries need to strengthen enabling environments, thus reducing investment risks, and develop project pipelines and investable projects. At the same time, incentives along the investment chain need to be aligned with sustainable development to unlock SDG investments. However, short-term horizons in decision-making remain a major obstacle. New technologies can help channel financing to all segments of the economy, including to women, in an inclusive manner. Effective regulation is necessary to monitor systemic or consumer risks that may arise from digitization of finance;

- **Development cooperation remains central to supporting implementation of the agenda; international public finance is increasing, but critical funding gaps remain.** Official development assistance (ODA) providers should continue to increase aid, in particular to vulnerable countries, with a view to meeting commitments they have made. Multilateral development banks (MDBs), development finance institutions and South-South cooperation providers are also scaling up their contributions to the 2030 Agenda for Sustainable Development. Innovative instruments and approaches, such as blended finance, are increasingly deployed to catalyse additional sources of finance to achieve the SDGs. As MDBs and other providers are scaling up the use of such modalities, they should ensure their activities are aligned with existing development effectiveness principles and do not eschew challenging country contexts. Countries most in need and investment areas critical to leaving no one behind should not be neglected, even as development cooperation increasingly targets global challenges. The international community should lend greater support to efforts of countries to manage transitions and graduation, and should consider flexibilities that allow countries access to appropriate sources of financing, depending on country needs and vulnerabilities;

- **Trade policies are increasingly focused on the impact of trade on sustainable development in all its dimensions, reinforcing its ability to serve as an engine for inclusive economic and sustainable growth and poverty reduction.** International trade growth picked up substantially in 2017. E-commerce may provide untapped potential for further enhancing inclusive trade growth in developing countries. An open dialogue is warranted on aligning new trade agreements with the SDGs—for example, by including provisions on gender or labour. Trade finance plays a key role in helping developing countries participate in global trade; it can be enhanced by promoting greater standardization in rules, practices and relevant programmes;

- **Debt risks are increasing, raising the spectre of a renewed cycle of debt crises and economic disruption.** Countries face pressing demands for additional public investments in the SDGs at a time when constraints on further debt financing are likely to become more binding. Stronger consideration could be given to the positive impact of investments in infrastructure and productive capacity on debt sustainability, particularly if risks are carefully and transparently managed. The latter requires better and broader data collection, and improvements in debt management capacities. To lessen the financial stress on countries affected by shocks, the international community should work towards realizing the potential of state-contingent debt instruments. The changing composition of debt in developing countries also calls for a reexamination of creditor coordination mechanisms;

■ **To create fit-for-purpose international rules and institutions for sustainable development, greater focus is needed on prevention, risk reduction and crisis response to address financial and economic vulnerabilities and disasters.** Despite preventative measures, the world regularly experiences shocks that set back development progress. The international monetary and financial system should aim to reduce volatility and contain systemic risks while boosting investment, implying continued vigilance on financial regulation. Self-insurance is costly and often inadequate for developing countries to respond to the most severe shocks. Building incentives for risk reduction into financing instruments can boost investment in prevention, while the international community can increase the efficiency and speed of shocks response by shifting resources from ex post response to ex ante instruments, using both insurance-type mechanisms and pooled funds. Expanding the size of risk pools can increase efficiency, but may require the financial support of donors for those unable to pay;

■ **More and disaggregated data will allow policymakers to make more informed decisions and help them better implement their policies and programmes, but this will require more capacity-building support.** Significant efforts are required to strengthen national statistical capacities, including investment in integrated national systems for gender statistics and better financial sector data to assess financial vulnerabilities. Throughout the chapters there are calls for more data and greater transparency. These efforts should be coordinated and coherent so that transparency efforts are linked, interoperable, and more efficient in providing actionable information.

The Task Force will continue to deepen its analysis on the harnessing of all financing flows, and integration of all policies and plans towards SDG achievement in 2019. Building on findings from this year's report, the 2019 report will seek to draw an integrated picture of the state of sustainable development financing from a country and a global perspective. The analysis will draw on ongoing efforts within the United Nations system and beyond on development finance assessments and integrated national financing frameworks, on road maps for sustainable financial systems, and related analytical work. This holistic approach can support an initial broader stocktaking of progress in implementation of the Addis Agenda for the 2019 ECOSOC Forum on Financing for Development Follow-up (hereafter ECOSOC Forum) and for the High-level Dialogue on Financing for Development of the General Assembly, which will be held in September 2019. In addition to reporting on progress in all action areas of the Addis Agenda, the thematic analysis of the Task Force will consider the 2019 High-level Political Forum theme of "empowering people and ensuring inclusiveness and equality" and the SDGs under in-depth review in 2019.

About this report

The 2018 report of the Inter-agency Task Force on Financing for Development begins its assessment of progress with an analysis of the global macroeconomic context (chapter I), which sets the economic framework for implementation efforts. The thematic chapter (chapter II) explores financing needs, capital structures and financing options in the SDGs under in-depth review at the 2018 United Nations High-level Political Forum on Sustainable Development, namely SDGs 6 (clean water and sanitation), 7 (affordable and clean energy), 11 (sustainable cities and communities), 12 (responsible consumption and production) and 15 (life on land). The chapter builds on both the 2016 report of the Task Force, which laid out this financing framework and highlighted the different roles and mandates of public and private finance, and the 2017 report, which addressed challenges in mobilizing long-term public and private quality investments for sustainable infrastructure.

The remainder of the report (chapters III.A to III.G and IV) discusses progress in the seven action areas of the Addis Agenda: domestic resource mobilization, private finance, international development cooperation, trade, debt, systemic issues and science, technology and capacity-building, as well as data issues. Each chapter begins with a summary that highlights key messages and presents policy options. The necessarily concise assessments in the report are complemented by and should be read in conjunction with the comprehensive online annex of the Task Force report.[1] The annex provides data and analysis for each of the more than 100 clusters of commitments and actions across nine areas covered in the Financing for Development outcomes.

Chapters III.A to III.G also address the eight new mandates that Member States gave the Task Force in the conclusions and recommendations of the 2017 ECOSOC Forum, which were agreed at the intergovernmental level.[2] They called for analysis on social protection and crisis financing; three separate areas of private finance; the catalysing impact of ODA; trade finance; sustainable financial systems; and the impact of new technologies on labour markets. The Task Force carried out background research, held dedicated technical meetings, and engaged outside experts to inform this analysis.[3] The report further benefited from the work of the Intergovernmental Group of Experts on Financing for Development, which was created at the UNCTAD XIV Conference in Nairobi in 2016, and held its first session in Geneva from 8 to 10 November 2017, on the topics of domestic public resource mobilization and international development cooperation.[4]

Member States also invited international regulatory standard-setting bodies to contribute to the work of the Task Force. They join more than 50 United Nations agencies, programmes and offices, the regional economic commissions and other relevant international institutions such as the Organization for Economic Cooperation and Development and the Financial Stability Board. The report and its online annex draws on their combined expertise, analysis and data. The major institutional stakeholders of the financing for development process, the World Bank Group, the International Monetary Fund, the World Trade Organization, the United Nations Conference on Trade and Development, and the United Nations Development Programme take a central role, jointly with the Financing for Development Office of the United Nations Department of Economic and Social Affairs, which also serves as the coordinator of the Task Force and substantive editor of the report.

1   Available from http://developmentfinance.un.org.
2   United Nations, "Report of the Economic and Social Council forum on financing for development follow-up", 8 June 2017, E/FFDF/2017/3. Available from http://www.un.org/ga/search/view_doc.asp?symbol=E/FFDF/2017/3.
3   For additional information on these workstreams and related technical meetings, please refer to the dedicated section on the online annex. Available from https://developmentfinance.un.org/workstreams.
4   United Nations, "Report of the Intergovernmental Group of Experts on Financing for Development on its first session", 21 December 2017, TD/B/EFD/1/3. Available from http://unctad.org/meetings/en/SessionalDocuments/tdb_efd1d3_en.pdf.

Chapter I
The global economic context and its implications for the Sustainable Development Goals[1]

After a prolonged period of slow growth, the world economy is experiencing a broad-based upturn. With headwinds from the global financial crisis and other recent shocks gradually dissipating, economic activity around the world has strengthened considerably. For the first time since 2010, all major economies are expanding in unison, albeit at varying rates. While some downside risks remain, overall, the positive momentum is expected to continue in 2018-2019, with near-term risks to the outlook broadly balanced.

The global recovery is underpinned by increased investment, which accounted for about 60 per cent of the acceleration in global growth. However, this cyclical expansion masks significant underlying weaknesses. The increase in investment follows an extended period of weak investment and low productivity growth, which continues to limit the longer-term potential of the world economy. A disorderly tightening of financial conditions and changes to interest rates in systemically important economies could have spillover effects on exchange rate stability, capital flows and growth, particularly in developing countries. The adoption of inward-looking policies and an escalation of geopolitical tensions could also derail the global recovery.

The improvement in global growth has also not been evenly distributed across countries and regions. Per capita growth remains negative or insig-nificant in many countries where poverty rates are high. Persistent weakness in wages not only contributes to within-country inequality, but also restrains the rebound in aggregate demand. Importantly, the recovery in global growth appears to have been associated with a renewed increase in global carbon emissions, highlighting the importance of ensuring the quality of investment and its alignment with sustainable development.

For policymakers worldwide, the synchronized upturn in growth provides an opportunity to address these and other structural problems that restrain progress towards the Sustainable Development Goals (SDGs). Reorienting policies to tackling these problems can support the cyclical upturn and generate a virtuous circle of inclusive and sustainable growth.

1. Outlook and risks for the global economy

1.1 Global growth: a broad-based cyclical upturn

The world economy is currently experiencing a broad-based cyclical upturn. According to the United Nations *World Economic Situation and Prospects 2018*, global gross domestic product (GDP) growth reached 3.0 per cent in 2017—the highest rate in

---

[1]   This chapter is based on the following reports: *World Economic Situation and Prospects 2018* (United Nations publication, Sales No. E.18.II.C.2); International Monetary Fund (IMF) (2017). *World Economic Outlook, October 2017: Seeking Sustainable Growth* (Washington, D.C., IMF, 2017); IMF, *World Economic Outlook Update, January 2018: Brighter Prospects, Optimistic Markets, Challenges Ahead* (Washington, D.C., IMF, 2018); *Trade and Development Report 2017* (United Nations publication Sales No. E.17.II.D.5); and World Bank, *Global Economic Prospects* (Washington, D.C., World Bank, 2018).

six years and well above the 2.4 per cent recorded in 2016.[2] For the first time since 2010, global growth exceeded rather than falling short of expectations, as the lingering effects of the global financial crisis and other recent shocks, such as the European debt crisis of 2010-2012 and the commodity price collapse of 2014-2016, subsided (see figure 1).

The recovery is underpinned by a rebound in investment, manufacturing activity and international trade. These gains have come against a backdrop of accommodative global financial conditions, rising confidence levels and firming commodity prices. Headline labour market indicators have also shown some improvement, while global inflation has remained subdued. The robust growth momentum is expected to continue in the next two years. In its baseline forecast, the United Nations projects steady global growth of 3.0 per cent for both 2018 and 2019. The International Monetary Fund recently revised its global growth forecasts upwards, expecting slightly stronger growth in 2018-2019 than in 2017.[3] This upward revision partly reflects an expected posi-

tive impact of tax policy reforms on output in the United States of America and its trading partners in the short term.

Roughly two thirds of countries worldwide recorded stronger growth in 2017 than in 2016. The major developed economies are experiencing a synchronized upswing (see figure 2) and several large developing and transition economies have emerged from recession, benefiting from a recovery in commodity prices and investment. East and South Asia continue to strongly expand, accounting for nearly half of global growth in 2017.

Despite the broad-based nature of the upturn, recent economic gains have been unevenly distributed. Per capita GDP declined in four regions (West, Central and Southern Africa and Latin America and the Caribbean) in 2016. Further setbacks or negligible per capita growth are anticipated in these regions and Western Asia, with many countries still suffering from the effects of the commodity price collapse of 2014-2016. These regions are home to more than one third of people living in extreme poverty (earn-

Figure 1
Growth of world gross product, 2011–2019
(*Percentage*)

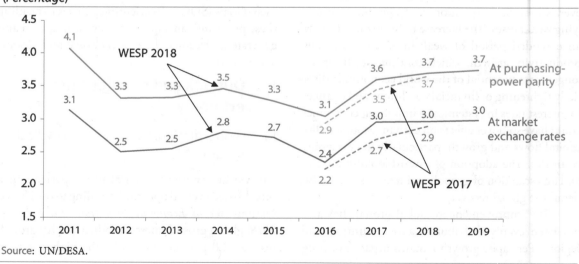

Source: UN/DESA.

2   *World Economic Situation and Prospects 2018*, p. vii. The 3.0 per cent growth is based on at-market exchange rates. When adjusted for purchasing power parity (PPP), global output is estimated to have risen by 3.6 per cent in 2017, up from 3.1 per cent in 2016 (UN, 2018). These figures are broadly in line with the estimates by other Task Force members. IMF (2018) estimates that global growth at PPP exchange rates accelerated to 3.7 per cent in 2017 from 3.2 per cent in 2016.

3   International Monetary Fund (2018) forecasts global growth of 3.9 per cent in both 2018 and 2019 (using PPP exchange rates).

Figure 2
Contributions to change in world gross product growth by component, 2017
(Percentage)

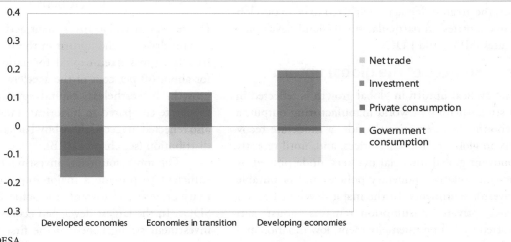

Source: UN/DESA.

ing $1.25 per day or less). While the recent strengthening of commodity prices, along with a supportive macroeconomic environment, should support growth over the next two years, the recovery will likely be slow and fragile.

For almost all least developed countries (LDCs), the SDG target of at least 7 per cent GDP growth per annum remains elusive. As a group, LDCs are estimated to have grown by 4.8 per cent in 2017, a moderate improvement over the previous years. Average growth is projected to strengthen further to 5.4 per cent in 2018 and 5.5 per cent in 2019, with an increasing number of countries expanding by at least 5 per cent. Despite the improved prospects, LDCs continue to face large investment gaps, including for poverty alleviation, sustainable energy, public service delivery, information and communication technologies (ICT), and climate change adaptation.

1.2. Significant downside risks in the medium term

Risks to the outlook appear to be broadly balanced in the short term, but remain skewed to the downside in the medium term. Positive financial market conditions mask lingering risks and vulnerabilities.

The prolonged period of abundant global liquidity and exceptionally low borrowing costs has led to an increase in global debt levels, with financial vulnerabilities emerging in both developed and emerging economies (see chapter III.E). Financial markets appear highly susceptible to shifting expectations about monetary tightening of major central banks. Changes in investors' perception of market risk could trigger a sharp correction in asset prices and a disorderly tightening of global financial conditions,[4] with a sharp reversal of portfolio flows to developing countries.

Downside risks to the global economic outlook also stem from the growing discontent with globalization and a further rise in inward-looking policies. Given the linkages between trade, investment and productivity growth, an increase in trade barriers and a move towards a more fragmented international trade landscape could hinder a stronger and more sustained revival of global growth. A failure to make growth more inclusive could increase the pressures for inward-looking policies. The medium-term global prospects are further clouded by non-economic factors, such as geopolitical tensions, and political uncertainty. The number, scale and geographic span of weather extremes continues

---

4   The global stock market rout seen in early February 2018 illustrates this vulnerability, although the ripple effects on other countries and asset markets have so far been limited.

to rise as global temperatures increase at an unprecedented pace. While losses and damage resulting from climate change impact all nations and all people, the greatest damage is expected to be in developing countries, in particular small island developing States (SIDS) and LDCs.

2. Sources of the global upturn

The cyclical upturn in global growth is reflected in a strengthening of world manufacturing output, a rebound in international trade, a moderate recovery in global commodity prices, and, until recently, buoyant global financial markets, underpinned by accommodative monetary policies and favourable investor sentiments. In the major developed economies, private consumption remains robust, supported by falling unemployment, low inflation and easy financing conditions. In developing regions, growth has been supported by an improvement in both domestic and external demand conditions. The increase in commodity prices, particularly of energy

and metal, has lifted export revenues and alleviated fiscal pressures for commodity exporters.

2.1 Rebound in investment

The revival in global investment activity has been a main driver of the upturn in the world economy. In 2017, gross fixed-capital formation accounted for about 60 per cent of the acceleration in global growth. Nevertheless, capital spending remains moderate compared to historical standards; this is also reflected in record share buy-backs and dividend distribution (see chapter III.B).

For most countries, investment is not (yet) sufficient to provide a major impetus to productivity growth and towards the achievement of the SDGs. In the largest developed economies, private investment strengthened in the first half of 2017 (see figure 3). Investment in machinery and equipment contributed significantly to investment growth, which, if sustained, could underpin stronger productivity growth over the medium term. Among

Figure 3

Average annualized change in private investment, by asset type, in constant prices, 2010–2017
(*Percentage*)

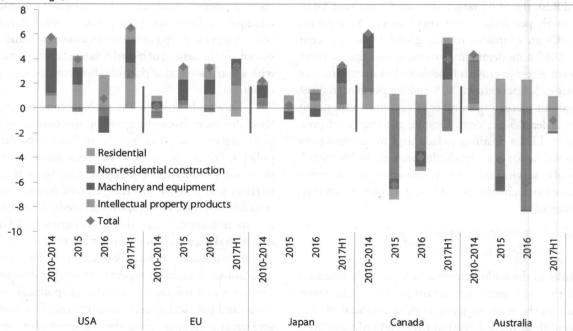

Source: UN/DESA, based on data from the United States Bureau of Economic Analysis, Eurostat, Statistics Canada, Cabinet Office of Japan, Australia Bureau of Statistics.
Note: Data for the EU and Japan include public sector investment.

Figure 4

Average year-on-year change in gross fixed capital formation, in constant prices, 2010–2017
(Percentage)

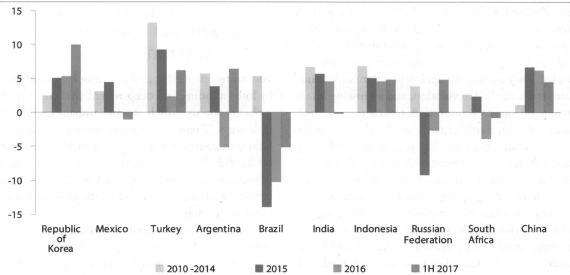

Source: UN/DESA, based on data from OECD Quarterly National Accounts, United Nations Statistics Division National Accounts Main Aggregates Database, CEIC, Project LINK.

developing countries and economies in transition, investment dynamics have differed considerably (see figure 4). Following the sharp realignment in commodity prices in 2014, global investment in natural resources collapsed, weighing on investment growth in commodity-exporting countries. By contrast, investment in East Asia has remained relatively strong, as Governments continue to embark on large infrastructure projects. Private investment activity has picked up in the region, particularly in the export-oriented sectors. In South Asia, public investment in infrastructure has also remained strong.

Looking ahead, a sustained improvement in the global macroeconomic conditions should support a continued recovery in investment activity. Nevertheless, several headwinds may restrain the strength of the rebound. These include elevated uncertainty surrounding the direction of international trade policy and the pace of monetary tightening by the major central banks. In addition, high levels of debt and longer-term financial fragilities weigh on investment prospects in several large developing economies. Finally, there are questions about the quality of investment. Sustainable development calls for high quality and long-term productive

investment that bolsters decent work, sustainable industry and infrastructure.

2.2 Productivity growth

The tentative revival in global investment marks an important step towards a more entrenched recovery in global productivity growth. Stronger investment in productive assets would help improve efficiency, alleviate structural bottlenecks, and strengthen resilience to shocks, thus contributing to a rise in countries' longer-term growth potential.

Global productivity growth has picked up at a moderate pace. Following growth of only 1.3 per cent in both 2015 and 2016, global labour productivity is estimated to have increased by 1.9 per cent in 2017. The recent upturn in productivity growth has been broad based across developed, developing and transition economies (see figure 5). For the first time since 2011, all regions experienced positive labour productivity growth in 2017.

It is, however, unclear whether the recent improvement in productivity growth can be sustained. For developed economies, the period since the global financial crisis has been characterized by exceptionally slow labour productivity growth.

Much of this weakness has been attributed to sluggish private and public investment, due to subdued demand, fiscal austerity, fragile bank balance sheets, and elevated policy uncertainty over the period. However, productivity growth in developed economies has been on a downward trend since the 1970s and 1980s, suggesting that structural factors are also at play. They include an ageing population, waning gains from the ICT revolution, and a growing financialization of the economy. A return to sustained labour productivity growth in developed economies of about 2 per cent—as seen in the 1990s and early 2000s—will therefore likely remain elusive if far-reaching policy reforms are not enacted.

In the developing economies, average productivity growth has improved, but with significant variation across regions. Despite a modest recovery, productivity growth in Africa and Latin America and the Caribbean remains subdued and far below the Asian economies. The sharp deceleration in total factor productivity growth in the post-crisis period suggests that developing countries have been experiencing slower efficiency gains and technological absorption. This is due to both cyclical factors, such as the decline in commodity prices and weak developed-market demand, and structural influences, such as slower trade integration and less dynamic economic transformation processes.

3. Challenges to medium-term growth and sustainable development

The more optimistic global outlook is dampened by long-standing and deep-rooted challenges in the global economy, which remains unbalanced in multiple ways. There is increasing recognition that the failure to address rising inequality and environmental degradation, if left unaddressed, will have destabilizing effects on political, social and environmental systems and undermine long-term growth and sustainable development.

From a socioeconomic perspective, high or rising levels of economic inequality that prevail in many parts of the world economy pose a fundamental challenge to robust growth, poverty reduction and sustainable development. Inequality in income and wealth often goes hand-in-hand with other forms of inequality, such as political inequality, health inequality and inequality in opportunities, threatening prospects for social cohesion. There is widespread evidence that the economic gains of the

Figure 5

Labour productivity growth in developed versus emerging and developing economies, 1990–2017
(*Percentage*)

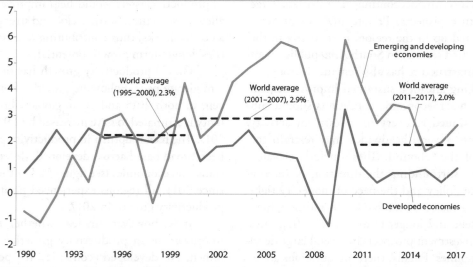

Source: UN/DESA based on data from The Conference Board's Total Economy Database (TED), November 2017 update.

past few decades have disproportionately gone to a small minority.[5] Within-country income inequality increased sharply in many economies, as average wage growth has often not kept up with productivity growth and most of the wage gains have gone to the highest-earning workers. Although technological advances have played a role in these developments, it is ultimately socioeconomic institutions and policies (e.g., decline in the unionization rates, rising market concentration and the increased influence of the financial sector) that drive these outcomes.[6] Labour markets across the world also remain divided along gender lines. High inequality in turn weakens aggregate demand, and can also lead to lower investment in education and health, impairing long-term growth.

The return to stronger economic growth in 2017 has been accompanied by a renewed rise in global emission levels. According to preliminary data, the level of global carbon dioxide emissions from fossil fuel combustion and cement production increased by about 2 per cent last year, after having remained flat between 2013 and 2016.[7] Hopes that global emissions had peaked and would enter a period of steady decline appear to have been premature.

Coping with climate change is one of the fundamental challenges of the twenty-first century. While global in nature, its adverse consequences are concentrated in developing countries, and particularly in the LDCs and SIDS. In areas with hot climates, higher temperatures reduce agricultural output, lower productivity of workers, slow the rate of capital accumulation, and damage health.[8] These countries are also most exposed to natural disasters, which are increasing in frequency. Poor households appear to be particularly vulnerable to the effects of climate change. Developing countries will require large-scale investment to build resilient infrastructure, expand safety nets and adopt new technologies—all of which entails significant spending needs. So far, however, the international financial system is not allocating sufficient financial resources towards long-term, low-carbon and sustainable development.

4. Reorienting policy towards long-term sustainable development

As global economic output gains momentum, the need to focus policy on crisis mitigation and short-term macroeconomic stabilization has eased. This creates greater scope to reorient policies towards addressing fundamental weaknesses in the world economy. The Addis Ababa Action Agenda, which provides a comprehensive framework for ensuring that investments are long-term oriented and that growth is inclusive and sustainable, speaks to these structural challenges. The rest of this report will highlight progress and implementation gaps in each of the Addis Agenda's action areas, and puts forward recommendations to put the global economy on a more sustained, sustainable and inclusive growth path, and to achieve the SDGs.

Chapter II focuses on infrastructure financing challenges in several SDG investment areas, including water, energy and ecosystems. In delineating the different roles and contributions of policy and public and private financing, the chapter emphasizes that SDG investment must be inclusive and leave no one behind, support a transition towards environmentally sustainable growth paths, and contribute to a rise in long-term sustainable growth potential.

5   The recently released *World Inequality Report 2018* (World Inequality Lab, 2017, p. 11) finds that between 1980 and 2016, the top 1 per cent of the world population captured 27 per cent of total income growth—twice as much as the bottom 50 per cent. Available from http://wir2018.wid.world/files/download/wir2018-full-report-english.pdf.
6   *Trade and Development Report 2017.*
7   Global Carbon Budget 2017. Global Carbon Project. Available from http://www.globalcarbonproject.org/carbon-budget/17/files/GCP_CarbonBudget_2017.pdf.
8   IMF. *World Economic Outlook, October 2017.*

Chapter II
Financing investment in selected SDGs

1. Overview

The Addis Ababa Action Agenda (hereafter, Addis Agenda) calls for increased investment in sustainable and resilient infrastructure, including the areas of energy, water and sanitation for all, as prerequisites for achieving the Sustainable Development Goals (SDGs). Closing the global infrastructure gap has become a major priority for the international community. Several new initiatives have been launched, including the Global Infrastructure Forum called for in the Addis Agenda, other infrastructure platforms and facilities, and new development banks and finance institutions. Yet, major challenges remain to scale up SDG investments in infrastructure and beyond. To support countries in this effort, this chapter examines the SDG financing challenges under in-depth review at the 2018 United Nations High-level Political Forum on Sustainable Development, namely SDGs 6 (clean water and sanitation), 7 (affordable and clean energy), 11 (sustainable cities and communities), 12 (responsible consumption and production) and 15 (life on land).[1]

While the financing models for each of these SDGs draws on all seven chapters of the Addis Agenda, a key question underlying many of the international debates is what roles public, private and blended financing should play. The Addis Agenda stresses that all sources of financing are needed and that they are complementary, with different objectives and characteristics making them more or less suitable in different contexts and sectors. The Addis Agenda also underlines the potential of blended finance instruments, while calling for careful consideration of their appropriate structure and use.

Because the sectors covered in this chapter in large part address public services and goods, national and subnational public authorities are ultimately responsible for service delivery. Public policies and actions must thus be the driving force. An examination of the SDG sectors under review highlighted several policy priorities.[2] These include:

- **Enhancing institutional and regulatory frameworks** Strong institutions and the rule of law are the starting point for effective economic governance. They need to be coupled with transparent, consistent and quality regulatory frameworks to guide private operators in each sector, manage natural monopolies, encourage innovation, limit red tape, and promote universal access to infrastructure services. Without this enabling environment, investment risks will remain particularly high, and neither public nor private financing or operation is likely to satisfy public need in a cost-efficient manner. A stable international macroeconomic environment is also required to support sustainable long-term investments in the targeted sectors (see chapter III.F);

- **Developing infrastructure plans** Plans should integrate financing frameworks and align with country development strategies.[3] They should provide a long-term vision (beyond the political cycle), include adequate

---

1   Responsible consumption and production is treated as a cross-cutting issue throughout the different sections of this chapter, where applicable.

2   On this topic, see also *World Investment Report 2014. Investing in the SDGs: An Action Plan* (United Nations publication, Sales No. E.14.II.D.1). Available from http://unctad.org/en/PublicationsLibrary/wir2014_en.pdf.

3   According to the Global Infrastructure Hub's Infra Compass, only 25 out of a sample of 48 countries have a national or subnational infrastructure plan (data accessed on 13 February 2018).

stakeholder consultations, and incorporate climate impact and resilience as well as gender assessments. They should also serve to coordinate across sectors, given synergies and interconnections (e.g., hydropower plants impact energy, water and ecosystems);

- **Translating plans into quality project pipelines** This calls for sufficient human and financial resources, adequately prepared projects, and effective procurement and frameworks for public-private partnerships (PPP), as applicable. In this context, Governments can benefit from multilateral development bank platforms that support the development of replicable and scalable infrastructure projects, such as SOURCE and the Global Infrastructure Facility (GIF);[4]

- **Strengthening public finance** Equity, social inclusion and other public good considerations provide a rationale for public engagement through direct financing, subsidies, guarantees, or other incentives and/or regulation. However, in many countries, public balance sheets and fiscal space are constrained, and debt sustainability is a major concern. This underscores the need for boosting public financial resources, both domestically (largely through improved taxation) and internationally (through official development assistance (ODA)). South-South cooperation and other official development finance can play complementary roles (see chapter III.A, III.C, and III.E);

- **Mobilizing the private sector** The private sector may be involved in the ownership, operation and finance of projects, depending on country and sector priorities (with most deals focused on finance or operation, and not on privatization per se). While the private sector can bring cost-efficient solutions, it is also often associated with higher financing costs because most investors demand a competitive return for the risk they assume.

To effectively contribute to many SDGs, private financing flows need to be stable and long-term oriented (see chapter III.B);

- **Getting prices right** Where socially feasible, price signals can address externalities ("polluter pays principle") and support sustainable consumption and production patterns—for example, through carbon pricing or phasing out harmful subsidies, taking fully into account the specific needs and conditions of developing countries and minimizing possible adverse impacts on their development in a manner that protects the poor and the affected communities, as called for in the Addis Agenda;

- **Strengthening international cooperation** Developing countries need significant capacity-building support to make progress in these areas and create institutions capable of delivering the ambitious SDG agenda (see chapter III.C).

These policy priorities can guide stakeholders as they scale up SDG financing. Previous Inter-agency Task Force reports have also highlighted several factors to consider in determining combinations of private and public ownership, operation and financing of projects, including (i) whether investments can be sufficiently profitable to compensate private investors for the risks they bear; (ii) whether investments produce goods or services that can be effectively supplied by the market, or whether they have public-good properties (including positive or negative externalities) that require public involvement; (iii) whether public intervention is warranted for social equity reasons; and (iv) whether private investors can bring efficiency gains through the profit incentive.

For example, investments in ecosystems will largely be publicly financed owing to the public-good nature of the sector, although private initiatives sometimes play a role, often through philanthropy or impact investing[5] (see chapter III.B). Private

---

4   SOURCE is a joint initiative of multilateral development banks to develop sustainable, bankable and investment-ready infrastructure projects (https://public.sif-source.org/). The Global Infrastructure Facility (GIF) supports Governments in bringing well-structured and bankable infrastructure projects to market (http://www.globalinfrafacility.org/).

5   That is, private investors who seek to have a positive social or environmental impact alongside their profit.

financing is most likely to be appropriate in sectors where projects can generate sufficient returns, such as in the energy sector, although with public oversight and often public support. The use of private finance is more challenging in areas where equity considerations and large financing gaps reduce profit prospects—such as water, where various financing models have been utilized (see figure 1, which provides a rough breakdown of the roles of public and private financing across sectors, each of which depends on an overall enabling environment).

As noted above, the domestic and international enabling environments are critical factors for investment. When the perceived risk of project failure is high, the cost of private finance, in particular, is likely to be prohibitive. Financing strategies need to consider how to avoid locking in high financial costs that reflect domestic risks for the entire duration of infrastructure projects (often 20 years or more). This is particularly relevant for countries that are in the process of strengthening institutions and thus reducing risks. Development banks could assist countries in building such financing strategies. This also underscores the importance of public finance, either through direct financing or blending strategies (see chapter III.C). However, blended strategies can also create contingent liabilities that need to be carefully managed (see chapter III.E).

The scale of financing in these sectors requires mobilizing both domestic and international sources. International financing is often a critical complement to domestic resources, but might generate currency risks that are difficult to manage at a country level. This calls for examining whether global approaches allowing the diversification of currency risks could be developed, by development banks, for instance.

To examine how public and private firms can contribute in the sectors under review, it is also important to better understand the sources of cash flows that maintain operations and cover financing costs. They can come from three main sources: (i) users (tariffs), (ii) public authorities (taxes) and transfers from national to subnational governments or (iii) external partners (see table 1). These sources of cash flow provide the basis to mobilize repayable finance, including concessional and non-concessional finance, necessary for realizing the required investments in these sectors. Table 1 lists examples of these different financing sources across the SDG sectors under review.

These initial considerations provide a general framework for understanding the capital structure of some SDG investments. However, further analysis of sector specificities is needed to better understand possible financing options and the practical reality of each sector.

Figure 1
Continuum of public and private finance

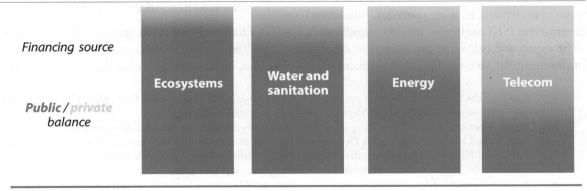

Source: UN/DESA.

Table 1
Examples of cash flow sources per sector

Type of cash flow	Examples of cash flows in highlighted sectors			
	Subnational finance	Water and sanitation	Energy	Terrestrial ecosystem
Tariffs / user fees / user investment	• Fees (e.g., for public transport / trash collection / parking)	• User investment (e.g., toilets or boreholes) • Fees to water utilities	• User investment (e.g., clean cooking fuels / solar panels) • Fees to energy utilities/ energy service companies • Savings on energy bills (energy efficiency)	• Payment for ecosystems services • Green commodities • Biodiversity offsets
Taxes / public subsidies/ domestic transfers	• Local taxes (e.g., property taxes) • Transfers from central Governments	• Transfers from central Governments • Targeted subsidies	• Public subsidies (e.g., feed-in tariff premium) • Tax breaks for energy efficiency • Carbon credits	• Budget allocation • Agricultural subsidies with biodiversity goals
Grants (donor assistance / philanthropy)	• External grants (e.g., to public transport systems)	• Viability gap funding in water projects	• Technical assistance for energy audits	• Grants channelled through NGOs • REDD +

Source: UN/DESA.

2. Subnational finance

SDG 11 aims to make cities inclusive, safe, resilient and sustainable in a context of unprecedented urban growth. In 2015, close to 4 billion people—54 per cent of the world's population—lived in cities, and that number is projected to increase to about 5 billion people by 2030.[6] In the least developed countries (LDCs), the proportion of urban population is expected to increase from 31 per cent in 2014 to 49 per cent in 2050.[7] Such rapid growth demands significant investments at the subnational level, including in housing, public transport, water, and waste management. In some countries, subnational governments (SNGs) already contribute significantly to financing and delivering infrastructure, accounting for nearly 40 per cent of public investment.[8] It is

estimated that more than 70 per cent of infrastructure will be built in urban areas, and that by 2030 these investments could be greater than the $50 trillion value of all the infrastructure in the world today.[9] However, subnational governments, especially second-tier cities, face considerable challenges in mobilizing adequate revenue to meet recurrent expenditures and make long-term investments in support of inclusive and sustainable local development. LDCs face the steepest challenges. Addressing these challenges requires a better understanding of the financing options available to SNGs.

2.1 Characteristics of subnational finance

SNGs have to finance their operational expenditures as well as a range of investments. Their financing sources include local taxes and user fees;[10] trans-

6   Report of the Secretary-General on progress towards the Sustainable Development Goals (E/2017/66). Available from http://www.un.org/ga/search/view_doc.asp?symbol=E/2017/66&Lang=E.

7   Daniel Platz and others, "Financing sustainable urban development in the least developed countries" (New York, United Nations Financing for Development Office of the Department of Economic and Social Affairs and the United Nations Capital Development Fund, 2017). Available from http://www.un.org/esa/ffd/wp-content/uploads/2016/09/Financing-Sustainable-Urban-Development-in-LDCs.pdf.

8   Based on a sample of 90 countries in 2013. Organization for Economic Cooperation and Development (OECD) and United Cities and Local Governments (UCLG), *Subnational governments around the world: structure and finance* (Paris and Barcelona, 2016).

9   Cities Climate Finance Leadership Alliance, "State of city climate finance 2015" (New York, 2015).

10   User fees include parking fees, business licences, trash collection fees, or other charges (fees imposed on market vendors for using public space, charges from taxi stalls or bus terminals). These fees often make up the bulk of own-source revenues in poorer developing countries that have very limited taxing authority.

ferred national or state revenues; and borrowing from public and private lenders. Transfers from a higher level of government are typically the most significant source in this category, underscoring the importance of effective national/subnational interfaces.

The projects needing finance have varying cash flow profiles, which influences the kind of financing they can use. While revenue-generating investments (e.g., public transport systems) are more suitable for borrowing, social investments, like school buildings, are more likely to be financed through transfers or tax financing. Subnational governments' creditworthiness also affects the types of instruments available, with stronger entities being capable of accessing capital markets. Table 2 provides a framework to assess the range of finance options available to SNGs.

2.2   Action areas

Action areas for subnational financing include raising domestic revenues through user fees and taxes—including defining the most appropriate types of taxation for SNGs—and fostering sustainable access to long-term finance.

Reforms and actions will, however, depend on specific country conditions such as the existing experience of a country with decentralization, the legal systems in place, and the levels of institutional development and capacity.

2.2.1 Promoting revenue raising authorities

In many countries, SNGs have limited fiscal authority and capacity to raise their own revenues. Intergovernmental transfers are dominant because national Governments have an inherent advantage in revenue generation. Nonetheless, SNGs are often in a better position to plan and manage a range of local public services in a more holistic manner, since local governments are more likely to think about the linkages between service sectors than national Governments, where sectoral ministries tend to focus on the services with which they are directly concerned. The ability of SNGs to raise resources depends on the extent to which they have adequate fiscal powers and the capacity and incentives to use them. This requires both a clear *de jure* legal framework as well as *de facto* autonomy and independence at appropriate levels. One lesson from experiences with subnational taxation is that it is important not to let sources of revenue or some types of taxes create disproportionate administrative costs compared to the collected revenues.

Empowering subnational authorities

As noted above, two common revenue sources for subnational governments are user fees and local taxes. User fees help to establish accountability for service delivery, although they can also render some services too expensive for the poor. Regarding taxes, surcharges and property taxes are particularly useful on the subnational level.

Surcharges (known as piggyback taxes) allow SNGs to add a usually small but sometimes significant percentage onto the same tax base and through the same collection system as taxes at the national level (e.g., sales and income taxes), thus exploiting more efficient centralized revenue administration. As such, they are easier to implement than other forms of taxation.

Table 2
Illustrative financing arrangements by type of investment and SNG creditworthiness

Type of investment	SNG income level/creditworthiness		
	Low	Medium	High
Self-financing	Mix of loans (possibly subsidized) and transfers	Mix of loans (possibly subsidized) and bonds (if feasible)	Mix of bonds and loans
Partially revenue generating	Mix of loans (likely subsidized) and transfers	Mix of loans (possibly subsidized) and transfers	Mix of loans (possibly subsidized) and transfers (if justified)
Non-self-financing/ social purpose	Transfers only	Mix of loans (likely subsidized) and transfers	Mix of loans (possibly subsidized) and transfers (if justified)

Source: Paul Smoke, "Policies, reforms and strategies for enhancing subnational development finance", paper commissioned by United Cities and Local Governments, United Nations Capital Development Fund and UN-HABITAT for the expert group meeting of the Inter-agency Task Force on Financing for Development on subnational finance, United Nations Headquarters, 29 November 2017.

Property taxes are harder to avoid than many other types of taxes because real estate is not moveable. However, property taxes require development of a cadastral system for tracking ownership, along with continued updating of real estate valuations.

Capitalizing on the revenue potential of municipal assets

SNGs should consider whether they could better utilize the real estate they own and enhance the performance of utilities and commercial assets they control. Land is one of the most valuable municipal assets and SNGs may use land-value capture mechanisms as a financial tool, in particular for cities. These mechanisms follow the basic logic that enhanced accessibility to new infrastructure, such as mass transit systems, adds value to land and real estate. As this value premium results from public investments, SNGs should try to capture the surplus by using taxes or other mechanisms. Land exchange or land concessions need to be carefully managed to ensure transactions remain in the public interest. Also, environmental considerations need to be factored in, as "undeveloped lands" may provide important ecosystem services. In this respect, transparency around land ownership and permits for development is paramount to avoiding conflicts of interest and corruption.

2.2.2 Strengthening institutional frameworks for national/subnational interface

To make subnational finance a powerful instrument of development, strengthening the coherence and collaboration between central and subnational authorities is critical. Subnational development finance does not exist in a vacuum and there are a number of fundamental conditions that must be in place or developed over time: [11]

- SNGs cannot play a developmental role unless they are empowered to act autonomously. A good institutional framework is expected to include **formal and clear assignment of functions and revenue generation responsibility** as well as systems and processes to support implementation;

- SNG operations should be sufficiently **transparent and accountable**. This includes downward accountability to citizens through elections and non-electoral means, and upward accountability to ensure that basic financial management procedures are followed and legitimate national goals and standards adhered to;

- SNGs need **the capacity and incentives to function effectively** (for example, to strengthen SNG financial and asset management systems and administer SNG taxes and fees);

- **Intergovernmental transfers should be made more predictable and transparent**. Stability will help local authorities to plan while reasonable flexibility on the use of transfers will allow SNGs to respond to local needs;

- Transfers should **contribute to global, national, and local development goals**, such as reducing disparities among SNGs and creating incentives to focus on SDGs. For example, it is possible to incorporate gender-equality objectives into the system of transferring national funds to lower levels of government in order to stimulate local governments' commitment to incorporating gender-oriented goals in public policies.

2.2.3 Fostering access to sustainable long-term finance

Borrowing can be challenging for many SNGs. Capital markets in many developing countries are underdeveloped, and many SNGs are not creditworthy, so interest rates charged by domestic and international lenders are often unaffordable. The World Bank estimated that less than 20 per cent of the largest 500 cities in developing countries are deemed creditworthy in their local context, severely constricting their capacity to finance investments in public

---

11   On this topic, see also Paul Smoke, "Policies, reforms and strategies for enhancing subnational development finance", paper commissioned by UCLG, the United Nations Capital Development Fund (UNCDF) and UN-HABITAT for the expert group meeting of the Inter-agency Task Force on Financing for Development on subnational finance, United Nations Headquarters, 29 November 2017.

infrastructure, with only a fraction of the creditworthy cities able to issue municipal bonds.[12] Despite challenges, there are means to promote and support SNG access to long-term finance. Many countries have developed, or are developing, SNG borrowing and fiscal responsibility frameworks, which aim to provide a foundation for credible borrowing. Table 3 presents a variety of instruments, ranging from public to private, which SNGs may use, depending on national and local conditions and levels of investor confidence.

International public finance

Multilateral and national development banks can lend more widely to SNGs through innovative and responsible instruments (e.g., innovative credit enhancement for subnational loans and reduction of foreign exchange risks). Other initiatives are also desirable, such as means to improve the access of SNGs to climate-change financing mechanisms to facilitate investments in resilient and sustainable infrastructure. Development cooperation among SNGs, also known as decentralized development cooperation (DDC), is also emerging.[13] From 2005 to 2015, DDC volumes grew by 1 per cent per year to $1.9 billion in 2015 and represents 6 per cent

of bilateral ODA among members reporting on these volumes.[14]

Enhancing access to commercial finance

As noted above, a sound legal framework, careful planning, transparency, good governance, and financial sustainability are prerequisites to enabling SNG borrowing capacity. SNGs may create a separate legal entity, such as a special purpose vehicle (SPV), to borrow money for public infrastructure investments; the vehicle might have a higher credit rating than the SNG, since ownership of the municipal quality assets—such as public land and shares of public utilities—are typically transferred to it. The risk, however, is that these entities accumulate unsustainable amounts of debt and evade public oversight. Hence, transparency is critical to ensuring that debt levels are carefully monitored (see chapter III.E). Also, the level of sovereign guarantee provided by the national authorities for any subnational government borrowing should be made explicitly clear.

Ultimately, and with the right conditions in place, SNGs may be able to access capital markets and issue municipal bonds. Development banks can support municipalities in this process by issuing

Table 3
Subnational lending mechanisms / external source revenue

Management and finance	Ownership			
	Government agency	Government owned	Mixed public-private	Private entity
Lead institution	Ministry of Finance or local government	Development bank, fund or utility	Development bank or fund	Commercial banks, financial markets, private investors
Source(s) of finance	National budget or external donors	National budget, SNG contributions, external donors or financial institutions	National budget, SNG contributions, private investors, depositors, external investors	Private finance

Source: Paul Smoke, "Policies, reforms and strategies for enhancing subnational development finance", paper commissioned by United Cities and Local Governments, United Nations Capital Development Fund and UN-HABITAT for the expert group meeting of the Inter-agency Task Force on Financing for Development on subnational finance, United Nations Headquarters, 29 November 2017.

---

12   See http://www.worldbank.org/en/topic/urbandevelopment/brief/city-creditworthiness-initiative and Daniel Platz and others, "Financing sustainable urban development in the least developed countries".

13   Decentralized development cooperation (DDC) is defined as aid provided by the public sector other than the central government to developing countries.

14   Organization for Economic Cooperation and Development, *Decentralized Development Co-operation: Financial Flows, Emerging Trends, and Innovative Paradigms* (Paris, OECD Publishing, forthcoming).

guarantees that can help lower the cost of financing and/or lengthen the maturity of issuances.

Public-private partnerships (PPPs)

Public-private partnerships (PPPs) could potentially help SNGs secure expertise and funds from the private sector, particularly for revenue-generating projects. City-level PPPs are common in sectors such as public transport, water and housing. However, PPP projects tend to be complex and local authorities often lack the necessary capacity to both negotiate PPP deals and effectively regulate private operators. At the central level, many Governments have created PPP units to address this issue. Reinforcing the linkages between the central PPP unit and SNGs is a way to better support local authorities in their PPP projects.

Safeguards need to be in place to ensure the fiscal sustainability of these projects and preserve public interests, while guaranteeing access for the more vulnerable to public services. Enhancing the transparency of these deals should help strengthen accountability. A higher level of disclosure in PPP projects should also go hand in hand with more disclosure of publicly financed infrastructure projects (actual costs vs. budget), as this will support decision-making between PPP and traditional procurement in the future.

3. Water and sanitation

SDG 6 aims to achieve universal, equitable and affordable access to safely managed water, sanitation and hygiene. In contrast to the Millennium Development Goals, which focused on basic water supply and sanitation, SDG 6 is broader, aiming for safe and affordable drinking water and adequate sanitation and hygiene. It also covers water-use efficiency and integrated water resource management (including the need to protect and restore water-related ecosystems, which can provide water retention and purification services, and can present low-cost alternative solutions).[15] The table below lays out different service delivery options by subsector.

Financing needs to meet SDG 6 are considerable. The World Bank estimates that global total capital costs of achieving universal access to safely managed water and sanitation services and hygiene are $114 billion annually (or three times the historical financing trend), with needs well above average in sub-Saharan Africa and Southern Asia.[16]

The Global Analysis and Assessment of Sanitation and Drinking-water (GLAAS) 2016/2017 country survey estimates that 66 per cent of financing for water, sanitation and hygiene originates from household sources via tariffs and self-supply (e.g., household investments in toilets and wells). The

Table 4
Typical solutions by subsectors

	Water	Sanitation	Irrigation
Urban	Piped supplies (i.e., water distribution network) plus unregulated providers for the poor, unserved by public utilities	Networked sanitation (i.e., toilets connected to sewers) plus on-site sanitation in cities with no or limited sewer networks	
Rural	Piped and non-piped supplies (e.g., boreholes, rainwater, packaged water)	On-site sanitation (e.g., toilets connected to septic tanks or pit latrines)	Irrigation systems (mainly for agriculture purposes)

Source: UN/DESA.

---

15 The upcoming *United Nations World Water Development Report 2018* will focus on nature-based solutions for water and showcase the importance of considering fully nature-based solutions (in parallel with alternative approaches) in water management policy and practice. See https://en.unesco.org/events/launch-world-water-development-report-2018.

16 The $114 billion figure represents a capital cost and does not include operation and maintenance costs. See Guy Hutton and Mili Varughese, "The costs of meeting the 2030 Sustainable Development Goal targets on drinking water, sanitation, and hygiene" (Washington, D.C., World Bank, 2016). Available from https://openknowledge. worldbank.org/bitstream/handle/10986/23681/K8632.pdf?sequence=4).

remainder comes through government taxes, external ODA and voluntary grants, as well as repayable finance such as loans.[17]

Figure 2
Financing sources for water, sanitation and hygiene

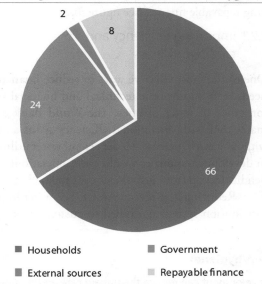

■ Households ■ Government
■ External sources ■ Repayable finance

Source: UN-WATER and the World Health Organization, "Financing universal water, sanitation and hygiene under the Sustainable Development Goals: UN-Water Global Analysis and Assessment of Sanitation and Drinking-Water (GLAAS 2017 Report)" (Geneva, World Health Organization, 2017). Note: Figure is based on data for 25 countries.

3.1   Sector characteristics

Several key characteristics shape service provision in the water sector:

- **Natural monopoly characteristics** It is not economical to lay competing sets of pipes for water and sanitation network infrastructure, which severely limits competitive pressures on providers. For basic services, such as wells or on-site sanitation, households themselves are the primary investors;

- **Capital intensities** The network infrastructure also makes the sector capital intensive, with high-up front investment needs;[18]
- **Local provision** Water and sanitation services are usually locally provided, with limited options for wider-scale networks, so that service provision is often set up at the municipal level. Thus, the creditworthiness of local utilities determines the feasibility of raising private finance. For households and communities, small-scale financing options are necessary;
- **Equity considerations** Equity considerations severely limit the ability to apply cost-recovery tariffs for water services. Access to water and sanitation has to be provided to all households independent of their ability to pay. As a result, public subsidies are usually required, such as reduced tariffs and block tariffs structures (i.e., highly subsidizing the first few cubic meters to cover basic needs). Low-income households not connected to utility networks tend to have higher costs than wealthy people who are connected. Similarly, the financial burden is higher for rural citizens in sanitation as they do not benefit from public investment in urban sewerage systems;
- **Gender equality considerations** Even though lack of access to water affects all, women and girls are often the most affected as the primary users, providers and managers of water in their households. Where running water is unavailable at home, women and girls travel long distances to meet household water needs. Lack of adequate sanitation facilities may expose women and girls to illness, and to safety risks and violence at school, at work and in their communities— hampering their ability to learn, earn an income and move freely (see box 1);[19]

---

17   UN-WATER and the World Health Organization, "Financing universal water, sanitation and hygiene under the Sustainable Development Goals: UN-Water Global Analysis and Assessment of Sanitation and Drinking-Water (GLAAS 2017 Report)" (Geneva, World Health Organization, 2017).

18   World Panel on Financing Water Infrastructure, "Financing Water for All" (2003). Available from https://www.oecd.org/greengrowth/21556665.pdf.

19   UN Women, *Turning Promises into Action: Gender Equality in the 2030 Agenda for Sustainable Development* (New York, UN Women, 2018).

- **_Health considerations_** Clean water prevents the occurrence of water-borne diseases and the associated health care costs;
- **_Cash flows_** In this sector, cash flows come from tariffs and user self-investments; taxes levied by local and national governments and provided to the sector as grants or subsidies; and transfers from external sources (e.g., donor assistance and philanthropy), which come in different forms with different agendas, and generally cannot be broadly used the way taxes and tariffs are. Transfers can also include cross subsidies where a service provider uses revenues from more affluent areas to subsidize less affluent ones.

3.2 Financing options

Equity considerations severely limit the ability to increase tariffs and fees.[20] The most recent GLAAS country survey found that in more than half of all countries, household tariffs are insufficient even to cover operation and maintenance costs.[21] To address the financing gap in the sector, utilities will have to combine different strategies, such as raising revenue sources for utilities, improving efficiency and tapping repayable finance (see figure 3).

3.2.1 Improving efficiency and creditworthiness

One of the most effective ways to reduce financing needs is to improve the technical and financial performance of water utilities. The World Bank estimates that with operational efficiency gains alone, without a tariff increase, 65 per cent of water utilities in developing countries would cover operational expenditures, up from just 15 per cent today.[22]

Reducing non-revenue water (i.e., water in the distribution system not billed to customers or lost

---

Box 1

Integrating gender equality into WASH (water/sanitation/hygiene)

Water and sanitation is an area where basic infrastructure development can reduce the unpaid care and domestic work burdens for women and girls. Globally, it is estimated that women and girls spend 200 million hours per day gathering water.[a] Additionally, the distance to the water supply can put women and girls at risk of violence. Therefore, "policy-makers must embed WASH in plans and budgets with interconnected objectives, such as health, nutrition and education. Cross-referencing between sectors will ensure all are better placed to reach their goals."[b] Ensuring water and sanitation policies and programmes are designed and implemented in a gender-responsive manner presents an opportunity to reduce and redistribute women's unpaid care and domestic work, as well as improving health and education outcomes. This requires that water programmes reflect the integral roles of women and girls as providers, users and managers of water.

Gender-responsive budgeting can strengthen the capacity of sector ministries as well as local governments to conduct gender analysis and integrate gender priorities in water and sanitation policies, plans and programmes. These efforts also require the active participation of women in all stages of planning and budgeting decisions. For example, UN-Women has supported women's engagement in local councils to advocate for their priorities on water quality and access to be reflected in plans and budgets. This has contributed to greater prioritization of these issues and increased resource allocations for water service delivery, with tangible benefits to women, girls and entire communities.

a United Nations Children's Fund, "Collecting water is often a colossal waste of time for women and girls", press release. Available from https://www.unicef.org/media/media_92690.html.

b WaterAid, "How to reach everyone with safe water and sanitation by 2030" (London, WaterAid, 2018). Available from https://washmatters.wateraid.org/sites/g/files/jkxoof256/files/How to get water and sanitation to everyone by 2030_0.pdf.

---

20   Organization for Economic Cooperation and Development, *Meeting the Challenge of Financing Water and Sanitation: Tools and Approaches*, OECD Studies on Water (Paris, OECD Publishing, 2011). Available from https://www.pseau.org/outils/ouvrages/ocde_meeting_the_challenge_of_financing_water_and_sanitation_2013.pdf. Whereas tariffs accounted for 90 per cent of funding in France, they only raised 30 per cent of funds in Mozambique and 10 per cent in Egypt.

21   UN-WATER and the World Health Organization, "Financing Universal Water, Sanitation and Hygiene under the Sustainable Development Goals".

22   World Bank Group and United Nations Children's Fund, "Sanitation and water for all: how can the financing gap be filled?" A discussion paper. World Bank, (Washington, D.C., March 2017).

Figure 3
Cost, funding and financing sources in the water and sanitation sector

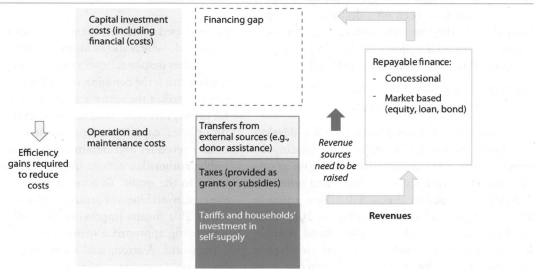

Source: UN/DESA, Organization for Economic Cooperation and Development, Meeting the Challenge of Financing Water and Sanitation: Tools and Approaches, OECD Studies on Water (Paris, OECD Publishing, 2011).

through leaks) can boost operational revenues while decreasing capital expenditures. Reducing leaks also contributes to the objective of more sustainable production as less water needs to be introduced in the systems. Using local technology and ensuring timely maintenance can improve cost efficiency. Similarly, organizational improvements, such as enhanced labour productivity and higher collection rates, impact the performance of utilities.

Introducing and monitoring key performance indicators can be a way to trigger efficiency gains. For efficiency reasons, some countries have also delegated water services to private operators via PPPs and management contracts. These operators are incentivized to improve performance to generate profits. Other countries choose to maintain local control of service provision to have greater control over service provision and ensure universal access. Public-public partnerships (PUPs), such as partnerships among different public water utilities to exchange best practices and technical expertise, have also been established to enhance efficiency.

Sector regulation should contribute to reinforce accountability frameworks and clarify the roles and responsibilities of the different stakeholders.

For instance, distinguishing sector oversight from service provision is usually required to better align incentives and provide the necessary autonomy for service providers. Water regulation, which addresses elements such as tariffs, service quality standards, competition, consumer protection and pro-poor regulation, need to be transparent and applied independently of political interferences. Sector reforms are often the first step required to enable repayable finance.

3.2.2 Raising revenue sources for utilities

Another effective way to close the financing gap is to increase levels of public finance. This has the added benefit of demonstrating the Government's commitment to improving the sector's financial viability, which ultimately creates the condition for commercial finance. Recognizing this, countries have increased their budgets for water, sanitation and hygiene at an average annual rate of about 4.9 per cent over the last three years. However, the GLAAS 2016/2017 country survey shows that 80 per cent of countries have reported that the increase is still insufficient to meet nationally defined targets for those services.[23]

---

23   UN-WATER and the World Health Organization, "Financing Universal Water, Sanitation and Hygiene under the Sustainable Development Goals".

In some countries, international transfers help fill this gap, although ODA grants for water supply and sanitation have been on a declining trend, particularly over the last several years. ODA commitments reached $3.8 billion in 2013, but dropped to $2.5 billion in 2016 (in constant prices).[24]

3.2.3 Tapping concessional loans and market-based/commercial finance

The bulk of repayable finance for developing countries has traditionally been lending by development finance institutions. While grants have decreased recently, ODA loans and other official flows increased to almost $10 billion a year in 2015-2016, from a base of $6 billion in 2007-2008 (see figure 4). While this is a positive trend, it might have currency risk implications for developing countries if these loans are in hard currency. Also, total borrowing from these institutions remains small relative to the annual requirements in the sector, which exceed $100 billion. To significantly expand investment, utilities will need to increasingly tap commercial sources of finance, particularly domestic finance, where feasible, to avoid creating currency-exchange risks.

Explore the full continuum of commercial finance solutions

In developed countries, the water sector is perceived as low risk, which allows utilities to attract commercial lenders despite relatively low returns. In developing countries, the combination of low and uncertain returns makes the sector a challenging proposition for private investors. Without some level of certainty on utilities' capacity to implement tariff revisions, collect revenues and obtain regular funding from public authorities, private investors are unlikely to invest in the sector. To access commercial markets, the creditworthiness of utilities needs to be strengthened. This means improving their efficiency and developing appropriate institutions and regulatory frameworks. A strong and independent regulatory body could provide confidence to investors, while well-managed fiscal positions could help reassure investors about the capacity of public authorities to support the sector.

While utilities/municipalities are often the largest borrowers, several other types of entities borrow to finance water services:

Figure 4
Trends in official development assistance loans and other official flows to water and sanitation
(*Billions of United States dollars, 2-year average commitment, constant 2015 prices*)

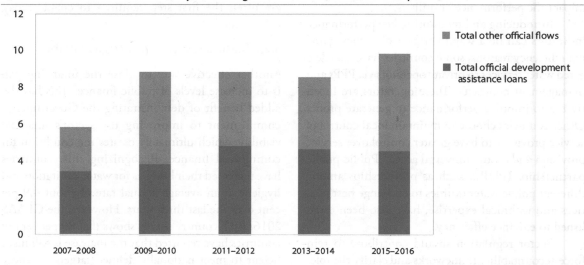

Source: OECD Creditor Reporting Systems. Available from https://stats.oecd.org/Index.aspx?DataSetCode=CRS1# (accessed on 23 January 2018).

---

24   Organization for Economic Cooperation and Development, Creditor Reporting System, OECD.Stat. Available from https://stats.oecd.org/Index.aspx?DataSetCode=CRS1 (accessed on 23 January 2018).

- **Households** may access microfinance for investment in water connections and vendor finance for purchasing toilets. This may be more economical than relying on water merchants on a daily basis. However, this requires having access to small and affordable loans that spread the upfront cost over time, especially those that minimize transaction and opportunity costs, such as through digital payment plans;
- **Small-scale independent providers** may offer solutions to unserved communities. They include pushcart vendors and water kiosks, which operate typically in the informal sector. This creates challenges to ensure service quality and avoid excessive rates. These providers nevertheless fill a gap in the absence of adequate service provided by public utilities. To operate and expand their businesses, they also need to access finance;
- **Communities and medium-sized entrepreneurs** also play a significant role in the sector. For example, in sanitation, community-based

organizations can manage public toilets while private operators may provide fecal sludge management services, such as latrine pit or septic tank emptying. Similarly, access to piped water can be provided through community taps or standpipes. Development partners, including non-governmental organizations (NGOs), can provide support to facilitate access to commercial finance for communities through capacity-building.

The figure below outlines the types of financial instruments that can access different borrowers.

In addition to lending, the private sector can also provide equity investments. Many water utilities are traded on stock exchanges around the world, with the market capitalization of these companies estimated to exceed $1 trillion.[25]

Develop an incremental approach through blending strategies

To access commercial finance, borrowers need to be creditworthy, implying that utilities operating

Figure 5
Options for commercial finance

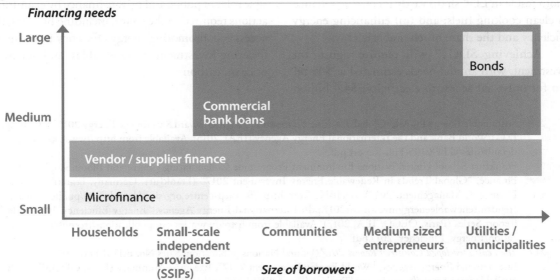

Source: Adapted from a presentation delivered by Joel Kolker, Lead Water and Sanitation Specialist, World Bank, at the technical meeting of the Inter-agency Task Force on Financing for Development, 1 December 2017.

25   Summit Water Capital Advisors, "The case for water equity investing" (La Jolla, California, 2017). Available from http://www.summitwatercapital.com/media/1019/case-for-water-equity-investing-2017-a021317.pdf.

at a loss have to initially rely on grants as a source of finance, but could progressively access concessional and commercial finance once their performance improves.

Blending strategies can support this transition. These strategies use public resources to leverage additional finance. They share risks, soften lending terms, and support project development through technical assistance and capacity-building. They also help local banks become more familiar with lending to the water sector, and reduce risk perceptions through pilot projects. For example, the World Bank has been providing funds to local banks in Kenya to introduce loans, combined with output-based subsidies, to water utilities for projects in underserved rural and urban areas. Blending strategies are also attractive if the use of such instruments leads to greater transparency, accountability and efficiency gains in utilities.

4.   Energy

SDG 7 aims to ensure access to affordable, reliable, sustainable and modern energy for all. Achieving this goal requires (i) providing electricity to the remaining 15 per cent of the world population without access (1 billion people, more than half of whom reside in LDCs); (ii) vastly increasing reliance on clean cooking fuels; and (iii) enhancing energy efficiency and the share of renewable energy.

Achieving SDG 7 will require significant investment, with annual needs estimated at $45 billion for universal access to electricity; $4.4 billion for clean cooking; between $442 and 650 billion for achieving the transition towards renewable energy compatible with climate goals; and $560 billion for energy efficiency.[26] In all cases, investment needs considerably exceed current spending (e.g., renewable power capacity and energy efficiency investments amounted to $242 billion and $231 billion in 2016, respectively).[27] The investment costs for universal access to modern energy in LDCs alone are on the order of $12 billion to $40 billion per year from now until 2030.[28]

Historically, public utilities have generated and distributed electricity and funded their operation and capital investments from end-users (retained earnings from tariffs), subsidies by the public sector, and, in developing countries, through development assistance. In recent decades, many countries, particularly developed countries, have increased private sector participation in the sector, primarily in electricity generation (since transmission and distribution networks have natural monopoly characteristics).[29] Decentralized energy solutions, such as mini-grids and off-grids, also rely primarily on private investments, either from enterprises or households directly.[30]

The following sections aim to unpack the possible roles of public and private finance by examining actions required in the sector, including bridging the access gap, promoting energy efficiency investments, fostering investments in renewables, and putting a price on carbon.

26   Sustainable Energy for All, "Global Tracking Framework. Progress toward Sustainable Energy 2015" (Washington, D.C., World Bank and the International Energy Agency (IEA), 2015). Available from http://www.se4all.org/sites/default/files/GTF-2105-Full-Report.pdf.

27   Frankfurt School-United Nations Environment Programme Collaborating Centre and Bloomberg New Energy Finance, "Global Trends in Renewable Energy Investment 2017" (Frankfurt, Germany, Frankfurt School of Finance & Management, 2017). Available from http://fs-unep-centre.org/sites/default/files/publications/global-trendsinrenewableenergyinvestment2017.pdf; International Energy Agency, "Energy Efficiency 2017", Market Report Series (Paris, OECD/ IEA, 2017). Available from http://www.iea.org/publications/freepublications/publication/Energy_Efficiency_2017.pdf.

28   *The Least Developed Countries Report 2017* (United Nations publication, Sales No. E.17.II.D.6, 2017).

29   International Energy Agency, "World Energy Investment 2017", Executive Summary (Paris, OECD/IEA, 2017). Available from https://www.iea.org/Textbase/npsum/WEI2017SUM.pdf.

30   Mini-grids are defined as localized power networks, usually without infrastructure to transmit electricity beyond their service area, while off-grid systems are not connected to a grid and typically power single households. Decentralized systems include both (International Energy Agency, "Energy Access Outlook 2017", World Energy Outlook (WEO) series, (Paris, OECD/IEA, 2017). Available from https://www.iea.org/publications/freepublications/publication/WEO2017SpecialReport_EnergyAccessOutlook.pdf.

4.1 Bridging the access gap: clean cooking fuels and access to electricity

More than 3 billion people use polluting cooking fuels, such as wood and charcoal, primarily in rural areas and poor urban neighbourhoods.[31] The health impacts of these fuels can be particularly devastating for women and children, who usually spend more time in the home. Likewise, in terms of issues such as deforestation and CO_2 emissions, environmental externalities are large. The social cost is estimated at $123 billion annually,[32] far above the investment needed to achieve clean cooking.

Providing universal access to electricity is achieved either through a power grid connected to large power plants, or via decentralized systems. Almost all of those who gained access to electricity from 2000 to 2016 did so through grid connection, yet decentralized systems are estimated to be the most cost-effective solution for over 70 per cent of those expected to gain access to electricity in rural areas by 2030.[33] Such distributed solutions rely primarily on private investments and third-party ownerships (e.g., energy services companies and households).

Bridging the access gap, both for clean cooking fuels and electricity, necessitates tackling affordability constraints of poorer households. While these households are already dedicating significant resources to pay for lighting and cooking fuels, many are unable to finance capital investments for modern solutions, such as solar panels or improved cookstoves. This is particularly true for women, who still have less access overall to financial assets, which further constrains their ability to purchase these energy solutions.[34]

While commercial banks are reluctant to lend to low-income households, alternatives exist such as pay-as-you-go systems, third-party ownership models, or microloans. Technology is making these solutions more efficient, for instance, through remote metering and online payments that reduce transaction costs, improve collection rates, and align interests of companies and consumers.

Consumer finance lets borrowers spread costs over time, although regular payments from households are still required. Hence, affordability also rests on the capacity to reduce the cost of sustainable solutions. Providing better access to finance is a way to support entrepreneurs in developing cost-efficient solutions. For example, in many parts of the world, the cookstove and fuels market remains fragmented and dominated by artisanal and semi-industrial solutions provided by small and medium-sized enterprises, which often suffer from limited access to capital. Addressing this challenge could allow these companies to develop their businesses, innovate, and eventually provide better performing and more affordable solutions. Likewise, energy enterprises providing off-grid solutions may struggle to mobilize financing, as this market segment has only received a small share of overall development financing for electricity access.[35] Another key aspect in the pursuit and development of effective and sustainable solutions is the further involvement of women, who have positively influenced the market as clean energy entrepreneurs.[36]

There is a role for the public sector, including for development finance institutions, to improve access to finance and support market development, through performance-linked subsidy approaches, for instance.

---

31   Report of the Secretary-General on progress towards the Sustainable Development Goals (E/2017/66). Available from http://www.un.org/ga/search/view_doc.asp?symbol=E/2017/66&Lang=E.

32   Venkata Ramana Putti and others, "The state of the global clean and improved cooking sector", Energy Sector Management Assistance Program (ESMAP) Technical Report No. 007/15 (Washington, D.C., World Bank, 2015). Available from https://openknowledge.worldbank.org/bitstream/handle/10986/21878/96499.pdf.

33   International Energy Agency, "Energy Access Outlook 2017".

34   Globally, only 9.6 per cent of females borrowed from a financial institution in 2014 compared to 11.8 per cent for males (World Bank, Global Financial Inclusion database). Available from http://databank.worldbank.org.

35   See, for example, Sustainable Energy for All, "Energizing finance. Scaling and refining finance in countries with large energy access gaps", Energizing Finance Report Series (Vienna and Washington, D.C., 2017). Available from http://www.se4all.org/sites/default/files/2017_SEforALL_FR4_PolicyPaper.pdf.

36   Anita Shankar, "Strategically engaging women in clean energy solutions for sustainable development and health" (New York, Global Sustainable Development Report (GSDR) Brief, 2015). Available from https://sustainabledevelopment.un.org/content/documents/631479-Shankar-Women_in Clean Energy_Solutions.pdf.

There may also be a need for targeted subsidies for the poorest consumers and for female-headed households, although the sustainability of these schemes should be carefully assessed. Public authorities should raise awareness regarding the benefits and feasibility of sustainable solutions. For example, despite the benefits of switching fuel for cooking, lack of public awareness prevents a wider adoption of cleaner solutions, such as improved cookstoves or modern fuel stoves (e.g., LPG and electric). Anecdotal evidence suggests that a majority of rural wood collectors in Africa and Asia are willing to purchase improved cooking appliances once they become aware of the benefits.[37]

4.2   Promoting energy efficiency investments through regulation

Enhancing energy efficiency reduces the need for added generation capacity and improves energy security, while also contributing to the objectives of more sustainable consumption and production. Investments in this sector cover a wide range of activities, with the building sector receiving the most, followed by transport and industry.[38] These investments can be self-financing since they generate cash flows from savings on energy bills. However, payback periods can typically be long, making investments sensitive to financing costs and energy prices. Additional market failures also impede investment. For example, the absence of information about the energy performance of buildings prevents buyers from incorporating this into their investment decisions and denies owners an incentive for making necessary improvements. Regulation can address some of these issues, through minimum energy-efficiency standards in building codes, for instance.

4.3   Fostering investments in renewables

Power generation assets typically last for a few decades, and today's investments lock in decisions for the future. It is therefore critical to fast-track the transition towards renewables.

4.3.1 The economics of renewables

The economics of renewables are changing rapidly, providing additional momentum for the sector, with the cost of solar PV and wind now within the cost range of fossil fuels.[39] The decline in prices has been associated with a surge of investments, which increased six-fold between 2005 and 2015, before falling somewhat in 2016. Yet, 2016 was a record year in terms of installed renewable capacity, which represented about 60 per cent of the net power-generating capacity added that year.[40] The growth in investments was particularly strong in large emerging economies such as China.

Mechanisms to encourage renewable energy investments include tax incentives and feed-in tariffs. As the price difference between technologies decreases and, in some cases, is eliminated, the need for such mechanisms will decline, as will the associated regulatory and political risks. This should allow countries to envisage more ambitious targets for renewable energy (e.g., by requiring a higher percentage of power generated from renewables and/or auctioning larger amounts of generation capacity from renewables).

The growing share of project finance structures over time, as opposed to on-balance sheet finance by utilities, also suggests that banks are becoming more comfortable with the risk of lending to large renewable projects.[41] The rise of green bonds should provide additional financing to the sector (see chapter III.B).

However, despite the sharp drop in costs, investments in renewables remain more expensive than fossil fuel alternatives in many situations. There is thus a continued need for the public sector to support the energy transition, including through development banks. Regulatory improvements, such as enhancing contract enforcement and facilitating permit issuance, can be more cost effective than

---

37   Venkata Ramana Putti and others, "The State of the Global Clean and Improved Cooking Sector".
38   International Energy Agency, Energy Efficiency 2017.
39   See International Renewable Energy Agency (IRENA) LCOE 2010-2016. Available from http://resourceirena.irena. org/gateway/dashboard/index.html?topic=3&subTopic=1057, accessed 15 March 2018.
40   Frankfurt School-United Nations Environment Programme Collaborating Centre and Bloomberg New Energy Finance, "Global Trends in Renewable Energy Investment 2017".
41   Ibid. Project finance accounted for 14 per cent in 2004 compared to 46 per cent in 2016.

using public capital. Specific issues related to the transition—stranded assets, or newly arising challenges with higher market penetration of renewables, such as storage costs and possible baseload issues—would also need to be addressed.

4.3.2 Enhancing the risk-return profile of renewable investments

Similar to the water sector, there is a wide range of ownership models for energy projects, from pure public to pure private. One goal of the ownership structure is to allocate risks to the parties best able to manage and control them. An ideal risk allocation would allow a project to achieve cost-efficient service delivery, and positively influence the project costs and feasibility (see box 2). Governments can use additional policy and financing instruments to further address mismatches between ideal and actual risk allocation, including through blended finance mechanisms,[42] although care should be taken not to build up unsustainable contingent liabilities or take on risks that cannot be managed.

One example of private involvement in power generation is the independent power producer model. In this model, a private consortium builds, operates and maintains a power plant and sells the electricity generated to an off-taker, generally a state-owned utility, via a power purchase agreement.[43] Private investors are generally well placed to manage operational and construction risks because shareholders will exert pressure on the management to limit costs and delays. In contrast, policy risks are typically better understood and managed by public entities.[44]

The ideal risk allocation also depends on the nature of the energy technology. For example, private investors in combined cycle gas turbine are in a strong position to hold price and curtailment risks due to the technology's flexibility.[45] However, onshore wind investors have limited ability to manage these risks—a possible argument for the public sector to take it on. The ideal risk allocation might also differ across countries. Currency risk is high in countries where long-term local currency loans are not available, while this is less of an issue in countries where capital markets are well developed.

4.4 Putting a price on carbon

As noted at the start of this chapter, externalities, like carbon emissions, are side effects of business activity that are not incorporated into private returns. Carbon pricing transfers the cost burden to those responsible for emission, thus driving efficiency improvements and supporting the renewable transition. There are two main carbon-pricing mechanisms. *Emission-trading schemes* set a cap on the level of emissions, and issue a limited number of permits to emitting companies. Those exceeding their allocation buy permits from those achieving carbon reduction, thus setting a price on carbon. This creates a market price for greenhouse gas (GHG) emissions. The second mechanism is a *carbon tax*, which sets a price on carbon, although without specifically defining emission reduction targets.

As of 2017, 42 countries and 25 subnational jurisdictions (cities, states, and regions) are putting a price on carbon, with the value of these mechanisms reaching $52 billion (an increase of 7 per cent over 2016).[46] However, the vast majority price carbon at less than $10/tCO_2$, far below the international recommendation of at least $40-80/tCO_2$ by 2020

---

42   Will Steggals, David Nelson and Gaia Stigliani, "Financing clean power: a risk-based approach to choosing ownership models and policy/finance instruments", Climate Policy Initiative Working Paper (Climate Policy Initiative, September 2017). Available from https://climatepolicyinitiative.org/publication/financing-clean-power-risk-based-approach-choosing-ownership-models-policy-finance-instruments/.

43   Power purchase agreements aim to provide certainty regarding the project revenues and make the project financially viable.

44   For example, policy changes impacting the project revenues or costs, such as reduction in subsidies.

45   Curtailment occurs when power plant operators are requested to reduce their output, for instance when transmission lines are congested or when there is an excess of supply. This results in foregone earnings, particularly for renewables that do not save on fuels.

46   Richard H. Zechter and others, "State and Trends of Carbon Pricing 2017", Working Paper (Washington, D.C., World Bank, Ecofys and Vivid Economics, November 2017). Available from http://documents.worldbank.org/curated/en/468881509601753549/pdf/120810-REVISED-PUB-PUBLIC.pdf.

and $50-100/tCO2 by 2030.[47] This implies that the cap is set too high, so that there is too much supply. However, political will to tighten the cap on emissions, and thus raise costs for companies, appears to be limited. Geographical coverage also remains limited as existing initiatives only cover 15 per cent of global GHG emissions. Extending these initiatives and raising carbon prices would generate hundreds of billions of dollars, while driving economic actors towards more sustainable consumption and production.

Some companies and development banks utilize internal carbon pricing to guide their decisions. Over 1,300 firms use or are planning to use

---

Box 2
Risk premium for renewable energy investment

Private investors' decision-making is based on an evaluation of returns compared to risks. Investments face a variety of risks, each of which can be valued and quantified. Expected returns need to compensate investors for the total risk of the project (with the extra return called the risk premium). The risk premium is generally a bit less than the sum of the individual risks, due to diversification. The figure below illustrates different project risks for an investment in utility-scale renewable energy in a developing country. Since the cost of financing represents a significant share of renewable energy project costs, reducing risk premiums should make these projects more competitive vis-à-vis fossil fuel solutions. In the example, the risk premium (before government intervention) is about (or a bit less than) 9 per cent (i.e., the sum of the individual risk factors), with transmission risk and geopolitical risk being the most significant. After government interventions, the net risk premium is reduced to 5.8 per cent, reflecting the risk factors in the Lebanese market. Policymakers can target these risks with public instruments, for example via streamlining processes for permits, or including "take-or-pay" clauses to address transmission risks.[a]

a   This means the generator is paid for potential rather than actual output and does not suffer if the grid operator is not capable of absorbing the power generated.

Figure 2.1
Equity financing cost (Solar PV)— example from Lebanon
(Percentage)

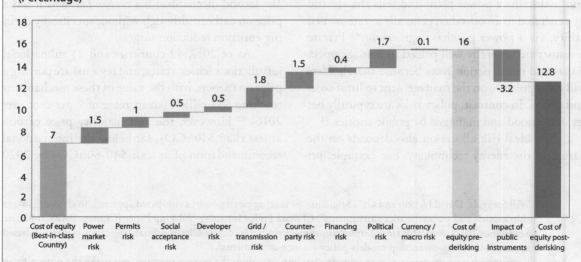

Source: Oliver Waissbein and others, "Derisking renewable energy investment (New York, United Nations Development Programme, April 2013). Available from http://www.undp.org/content/undp/en/home/librarypage/environment-energy/low_emission_climateresilientdevelopment/derisking-renewable-energy-investment.html.

---

47   Joseph E. Stiglitz and others, "Report of the high-level commission on carbon prices", Carbon Pricing Leadership Coalition (Washington, D.C., World Bank, 29 May 2017). Available from https://static1.squarespace.com/static/54ff9c5ce4b0a53decccfb4c/t/59b7f2409f8dce5316811916/1505227332748/CarbonPricing_FullReport.pdf.

Box 3
The World Bank's carbon shadow price

The World Bank recently introduced the application of a shadow price of carbon in the economic analysis for all International Bank for Reconstruction and Development (IBRD)/International Development Association (IDA) projects in key high-emitting sectors. The application of a shadow carbon price contributes to greater transparency and consistency regarding the climate impacts of World Bank's projects, thereby allowing better decision-making by the Bank and its clients. The World Bank 2017 Guidance Note on Shadow Price of Carbon recommends the use of a *low* and *high* estimate of the shadow carbon price starting at $40 and $80 (undiscounted, real values), respectively, per ton of CO2e in 2020, rising to $78 and $156 per ton of CO2e by 2050.[a] The use of a low and high carbon shadow price reflects the uncertainty linked to the unpredictability of future socioeconomic and technological trends as well as the need to consider the country context.

a   World Bank, "Guidance note on shadow price of carbon in economic analysis" (Washington, D.C., World Bank, 12 November 2017). Available from http://pubdocs.worldbank.org/en/911381516303509498/2017-Shadow-Price-of-Carbon-Guidance-Note-FINAL-CLEARED.pdf.

---

this mechanism in the coming two years.[48] Box 3 illustrates how the World Bank is applying internal carbon pricing in its operation.

5.   Terrestrial ecosystem

SDG 15 aims to protect, restore and promote sustainable use of terrestrial ecosystems, sustainably manage forests, combat desertification, halt and reverse land degradation, and halt biodiversity loss. Healthy ecosystems provide humanity with services fundamental to well-being. Biodiversity underpins the resilience of ecosystem services, which provide food and clean water, buffer the impact of climate change, control the outbreak of diseases and support nutrient cycling. There are several intergovernmental processes that contribute to these objectives, such as the Convention on Biological Diversity, the United Nations Convention to Combat Desertification, and the United Nations Forum on Forests.

Yet progress in preserving and sustainably using ecosystems and biodiversity is uneven. The

pace of forest loss has slowed and improvements continue to be made in managing forests sustainably and in protecting areas that are important for biodiversity. However, declining trends in land productivity, biodiversity loss, and poaching and trafficking of wildlife remain serious concerns.[49] Women, particularly those from landless and land-poor households, are among the most affected by these trends. Due to their lack of access to private land, poor rural women depend more than men on common pool resources, such as forests, and their responsibility for meeting household food and fuel needs means that they are particularly affected by the depletion of natural resources.[50]

Financing needs for preserving ecosystems range from $150 billion to $400 billion annually, while current financing is estimated at roughly $50 billion annually.[51,52] Financing needs projections include activities for restoring ecosystems or establishing protected areas; administrative resources to manage such programmes; and compensation pay-

---

48   Richard H. Zechter and others, "State and Trends of Carbon Pricing 2017".

49   Report of the Secretary-General on progress towards the Sustainable Development Goals (E/2017/66). Available from http://www.un.org/ga/search/view_doc.asp?symbol=E/2017/66&Lang=E.

50   UN Women, *Turning Promises into Action.*

51   CBD High-level Panel, *Resourcing the Aichi biodiversity targets: a first assessment of the resources required for implementing the strategic plan for biodiversity 2011-2020. Second report of the high-level panel on global assessment of resources for implementing the strategic plan for biodiversity 2011-2020* (Montreal, Canada, Secretariat of the Convention on Biological Diversity, 2014). Available from https://www.cbd.int/financial/hlp/doc/hlp-02-report-en.pdf.

52   Current financing estimates are from 2010 to 2015. See United Nations Development Programme, "The 2016 BIOFIN workbook: mobilizing resources for biodiversity and sustainable development", The Biodiversity Finance Initiative (New York, United Nations Development Programme, 2016). Available from http://www.biodiversityfinance.net/sites/default/files/content/publications/undp-biofin-web_0.pdf.

ments for income foregone for actions to conserve biodiversity (e.g., incentive payments for sustainable agriculture and land purchases). It is projected that only a minority of the identified investment needs will be covered through dedicated nature conservation budgets, which make up only about 20 per cent of the estimated total global resources required.[53]

The challenge is to increase available resources—first and foremost from public sources but also by generating revenues from other sources of funding—and realigning existing expenditures towards more sustainable practices. These measures would in turn reduce needs by avoiding future costs.

5.1   Sector characteristics

In contrast to water and energy, ecosystem protection has public-good characteristics in that beneficiaries cannot be separated from non-beneficiaries and charged accordingly. Investments in ecosystem protection thus usually offer little opportunity for profit. When profit opportunities exist, such as sustainable farming, returns typically are not competitive with alternative use of land. Yet, once ecosystems are degraded below a certain threshold, their restoration becomes costly, if not impossible, and the services provided must be replaced at high cost. Moral entreaties to guard the biosphere are typically not sufficiently effective; only policy prohibitions and incentives are reliable—and even then, there will often be strong incentives to bypass regulation (e.g., illegal logging).

5.2   Financing options

Financing for ecosystem protection comes overwhelmingly from public sources, either domestic budgets or through international support, such as ODA. Some Governments also offer public subsidies with biodiversity goals.[54] Another financing source

Figure 6
Annual biodiversity finance by mechanisms estimated for 2010
(*Billions of United States dollars*)

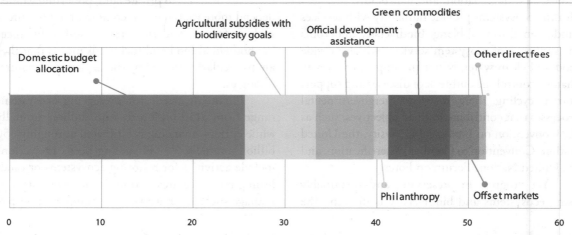

Source: Adapted from Charlie Parker and others (eds.), The Little Biodiversity Finance Book (Oxford, United Kingdom, Global Canopy Programme, 2012) and "The 2016 BIOFIN workbook: mobilizing resources for biodiversity and sustainable development" The Biodiversity Finance Initiative (New York, United Nations Development Programme, 2016). Available from http://www. biodiversityfinance.net/sites/default/files/content/publications/undp-biofin-web_0.pdf.

---

53   CBD High-level Panel, *Resourcing the Aichi biodiversity targets*.

54   However, agricultural subsidies in OECD countries potentially harmful to the environment (e.g. market price support and output-based payments) largely exceed subsidies with biodiversity goals. Although on a declining trend, the former stood at about $130 billion per year in 2012-2014 according to the OECD. See "Draft agenda and issues. Meeting of the Environmental Policy Committee (EPOC) at Ministerial level 28-29 September 2016", OECD Conference Centre (Paris, OECD, 2016). Available from https://www.oecd.org/environment/ministerial/agenda/ENV-Ministerial-Agenda-Issues-2016.pdf.

is philanthropy, which provides around $2 billion to the sector and finances the work of civil society organizations active in the sector (e.g., World Wildlife Fund, The Conservation Fund).

There are also market mechanisms that create funds for the sector. Green commodities, such as certified agriculture and timber markets, are gaining traction and foster sustainable production. Direct revenues for biodiversity activities, including offset markets and fees for ecosystem services, provide the rest of the financing (see figure 6).

5.2.1 Mobilizing additional resources

National budget allocations

Budget allocations have increased for biodiversity-related public expenditures; however, the trend needs to be solidified and further broadened.[55] At the national level, Governments should develop coherent plans to preserve ecosystems, which should be embedded in broader national development planning and budgeting processes. The development of such plans is a key goal of the biodiversity finance initiative BIOFIN, managed by the United Nations Development Programme, and also responds to the targets for resource mobilization for implementing the Strategic Plan for Biodiversity 2011-2020 and its Aichi Biodiversity Targets.

Scaling up ODA resources

In 2014, the Parties to the Convention for Biodiversity decided to double biodiversity related financial aid to developing countries through 2020, and while some countries have reached this target, collectively, donors still fall short.[56] This trend is mirrored in forestry-specific ODA, which has increased over the last 15 years, but has plateaued since 2012 (see figure 7).

Different mechanisms are available to channel additional concessional resources. In particular,

Figure 7

Official development assistance commitments to forestry and environment protection
(Billions of United States dollars, (constant 2015 price))

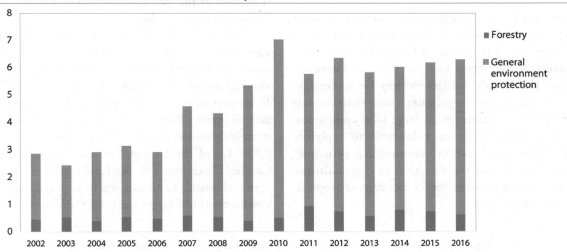

Source: OECD Creditor Reporting Systems. Available from https://stats.oecd.org/Index.aspx?DataSetCode=CRS1#.

---

55 Convention on Biological Diversity, "Analysis of the information provided through the financial reporting framework and of methodological information and definitions as provided by parties (UNEP/CBD/COP/13/11/Rev1). Available from https://www.cbd.int/doc/meetings/cop/cop-13/official/cop-13-11-rev1-en.doc.

56 Convention on Biological Diversity, "Draft global monitoring report on financing for biodiversity". Available from https://www.cbd.int/doc/meetings/sbi/sbi-01/information/sbi-01-inf-46-en.doc.

REDD+,[57] which features in article 5 of the Paris Agreement of the United Nations Framework Convention on Climate Change, enables developing countries to receive payments proportional to the reduction of their greenhouse gas emissions from slowing deforestation and forest degradation against a pre-agreed deforestation baseline scenario. REDD+ breaks down into three phases:

(i)   Readiness (capacity-building and preparation of a national REDD+ strategy);
(ii) Transition (demonstration activities and piloting);
(iii) Implementation (results-based payments).

Phases one and two have entirely depended on upfront funding, usually in the form of ODA, while phase-three funding is delivered once countries show evidence of emissions reductions from forests and land use. After almost a decade of working on phases 1 and 2 of REDD+, in October 2017 phase 3 started in earnest with a $500 million pilot programme approved by the Green Climate Fund on REDD+ results-based payments.[58]

Monetizing externalities

Payments for ecosystem services have often been branded as the solution for "internalizing externalities" in this sector, although to date, only small-scale payments have been made. However, some larger-scale initiatives may be underway. For instance, under pressure from environmental NGOs and consumers, large food companies have begun committing voluntarily to applying the "zero-deforestation" commodity principle, in recognition of the fact that key agricultural commodities account for 71 per cent of tropical deforestation.[59]

Biodiversity offsets follow the same concept as carbon offsets to combat global warming, but compensate biodiversity impacts associated with economic development (e.g., habitat banks in the United States of America). Tax policies are another tool that can increase resources while raising relative prices of activities that negatively impact ecosystems—for instance, with taxes on fuels, pesticides and the use of natural capital, such as timber.

Tapping investors

Although still small, there is also increasing interest in mobilizing financing for ecosystem projects through development banks and impact investors. An example is the first-loss guarantees and subordinated loans provided by the Global Environment Facility (GEF) for land restoration projects in Latin America under the Risk Mitigation Instrument for Land Restoration. The instrument combines a GEF investment of $15 million to leverage $120 million of co-financing (including loans from the Inter-American Development Bank and equity investments from impact investors) by reducing the projects' perceived risks. This financial instrument aims to bring low productivity land into production, such as for increased ecosystem services and high-value forest products.

The 2017 Global Impact Investing Network annual survey estimates that around $4.5 billion of assets are allocated to the forestry and timber sector, although mainly in Canada and the United States.[60] To support sustainable land use, the Land Degradation Neutrality Fund was launched in 2017 at the thirteenth session of the Conference of the Parties (COP 13) of the United Nations Convention to Combat Desertification. The fund is privately managed and intends to raise capital from public and private investors (the target size is $300 million). It will

57   The United Nations Framework Convention on Climate Change defines REDD+ as "reducing emissions from deforestation and forest degradation and the role of conservation, sustainable management of forests and enhancement of forest carbon stocks in developing countries" (see http://unfccc.int/land_use_and_climate_change/redd/items/7377.php).

58   Green Climate Fund, "GCF in brief: REDD+". Available from https://www.greenclimate.fund/documents/20182/194568/GCF+in+Brief+-+REDD%2B/6ad00075-1469-4248-a066-8a8e622edacd.

59   Sam Lawson and others, "Consumer goods and deforestation: an analysis of the extent and nature of illegality in forest conversion for agriculture and timber plantations", Forest Trends Report Series (Washington, D.C., Forest Trends, September 2014). Available from http://www.forest-trends.org/documents/files/doc_4718.pdf.

60   See https://thegiin.org/assets/GIIN_AnnualImpactInvestorSurvey_2017_Web_Final.pdf.

invest equity and junior debt in profit-generating sustainable land management and land restoration projects worldwide.[61] Given that it is looking for investments that are profit generating, one challenge will be to develop enough investment proposals that create cash flows together with measurable conservation impact.

Scaling up also requires facilitating the identification of sustainable projects. In this respect, the Climate Bonds Initiative is developing standards for bond issuers looking to finance land-use projects, such as afforestation. Establishing recognized standards should reduce transaction costs for investors (see chapter III.B).

5.2.2 Realigning expenditures and activities

Aligning private investments with sustainable development

Aligning existing private finance flows with sustainable development is critically important for ecosystem preservation. For example, while a considerable amount of private money flows into the forest sector, it often contributes to unsustainable models, and funds to protect ecosystems are concentrated in some regions. In 2011, annual total private forest plantation in developing countries was estimated at $1.8 billion, with 83 per cent in Latin America, but only 1 per cent in Africa.[62] Addressing the sector challenges requires shifting from unsustainable to sustainable practices and changing the economic drivers. For instance, landowners will continue to clear natural forest if they can convert it to more lucrative agricultural production. Land-use regulation and public

ownership is a way to address this issue. Public policies can also promote corporate sustainability, including reporting on environmental, social and governance impacts to enhance accountability of private companies. In addition, development finance institutions can make their financing conditional on following strict environmental standards.[63] These actions need to be complemented by measures addressing the economic drivers behind unsustainable practices, such as externalities and harmful financial incentives.

Transforming the incentive structure

"Green commodities" have proven their capacity to change behaviours. In this model, consumers pay a price premium for goods that are produced sustainably—for example, products that are certified compliant with sustainability standards by a third party through labelling. Forest product certification labels such as FSC and PEFC[64] are just two examples. Based on the zero-deforestation principle, initiatives are underway to apply similar mechanisms to food products conducive to tropical deforestation, such as soy, beef and palm oil.

Public policies should be designed to favour long-term conservation objectives over short-term exploitation. Subsidies to sectors such as soy, beef or palm oil dwarf public financing for preventing deforestation and forest degradation (see figure 8). Eliminating, phasing out or reforming harmful subsidies, in line with Aichi Biodiversity Target 3, would reduce incentives for unsustainable production patterns. Some of these subsidies could also be redirected to ecosystem conservation activities.

61   For more information, see http://www2.unccd.int/sites/default/files/relevant-links/2017-09/LDN%20Fund%20brochure%20-%20Aug2017.pdf.

62   Tuukka Castrén and others, *Private Financing for Sustainable Forest Management and Forest Products in Developing Countries: Trends and drivers* (Washington, D.C., Program on Forests (PROFOR), 2014).

63   Addis Ababa Action Agenda para. 17. Available from http://www.un.org/esa/ffd/wp-content/uploads/2015/08/AAAA_Outcome.pdf.

64   FSC stands for Forest Stewardship Council and PEFC for Programme for the Endorsement of Forest Certification.

Figure 8
Agricultural subsidies versus forest finance
(*Millions of United States dollars*)

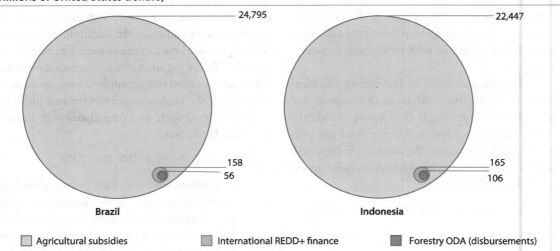

Brazil — 24,795 — 158 / 56

Indonesia — 22,447 — 165 / 106

☐ Agricultural subsidies   ☐ International REDD+ finance   ■ Forestry ODA (disbursements)

Source: B. Singer, "Financing sustainable forest management in developing countries: the case for a holistic approach" International Forestry Review, vol. 18, No. 1 (2016) pp. 96–109; and Will McFarland, Shelagh Whitley and Gabrielle Kissinger, "Subsidies to key commodities driving forest loss: implications for private climate finance", Working Paper (London, United Kingdom, Overseas Development Institute, March 2105).

Note: Annual subsidies to specific agricultural commodities (beef and soy in Brazil; palm oil and timber in Indonesia) compared to annual international REDD+ finance and forestry ODA in Brazil and Indonesia (gross disbursements, all donors, constant prices) for the period 2009-2012 in millions of United States dollars.

Chapter III.A
Domestic public resources

1. Key messages and recommendations

Domestic public finance is essential to providing public goods and services, increasing equality, supporting macroeconomic stability and achieving the Sustainable Development Goals (SDGs). Public finance encompasses raising revenue, budgeting its use, and spending on public programmes and investment. All parts of the process should aim to align with country priorities and the sustainable development agenda.

Tax structures affect society and the economy in many ways beyond a narrow public financing focus. Efforts to strengthen progressivity of fiscal systems, as called for in the Addis Ababa Action Agenda (hereafter, Addis Agenda), help tackle inequalities. Taxes also set incentives (e.g., for private investment, environmental sustainability, improving health outcomes) and affect many other concerns central to the achievement of the SDGs. To address the broad effects of the tax system, *the Inter-Agency Task Force on Financing for Development (hereafter, Task Force) continues to recommend whole-of-government approaches to tax policy and administration.* In the experience of Task Force members, preparing medium-term strategies for tax system reform can help sharpen political will, improve the societal ownership of reforms, and drive the capacity-building needed to deliver them. *Domestic public resource mobilization can be improved with the implementation of medium-term revenue strategies (MTRS).*

MTRS should be seen as part of overall public financial management, with the impact of taxation and revenue analysed in the context of the allocation of public expenditure. Effectiveness and efficiency in revenue collection and public service delivery can boost the link between citizen and State by enhancing accountability and strengthening the social contract.

Gender equality must be addressed in policymaking and programming to build governance systems that are responsive to all citizens. *Governments should conduct comprehensive gender impact analysis of fiscal systems, not only of individual taxes, to ensure that revenue and expenditure are more gender responsive and promote gender equality.* These require analytic capacity and sex-disaggregated socioeconomic and fiscal data. Regional and international tax cooperation bodies can support knowledge transfer and capacity strengthening of Governments. *Guidelines and methodologies for MTRS, tax policy assessment frameworks, and tax administration diagnostic tools should incorporate gender.*

Conflict-affected countries have unique challenges and fiscal systems are a keystone of efforts to rebuild the social contract and establish trust and accountability between citizens and States. Many conflict-affected countries rely on trade taxes as a significant source of revenue; accordingly, *it is important to develop strong customs administration and enforcement mechanisms while working to diversify the tax base.*

Taxes on harmful and unhealthy products such as tobacco, alcohol and sugar-sweetened beverages have potential to raise revenues in addition to changing incentives and behaviour, thus improving the overall health of populations. *There is therefore a double win for society to impose such taxes to achieve health and revenue objectives.*

The digitalization of business and finance has potential for improving tax revenue collection, but the pace of technology innovation could also outstrip the ability of Member States to monitor tax avoidance and evasion. *Application of technology to tax administration, including tax enforce-*

ment, can make more information available and enable revenue authorities to widen the tax base, identify and mitigate compliance risks, more effectively identify and prosecute evaders, and ultimately provide deterrence and stimulate voluntary compliance.

The Addis Agenda calls for taxes to be paid where economic activity occurs and value is created. However, digitalization of business models makes this more difficult because the value of intangibles and the location of value creation are hard to define and measure. *As new rules are agreed in relation to the digitalization of the economy, the Task Force reiterates the principle in the Addis Agenda that efforts in international tax cooperation should be universal in approach and scope and should fully take into account the different needs and capacities of all countries.*

Significant progress has been made to address the international dimensions of taxation. International tax cooperation has led to the implementation of new international standards on tax transparency, including automatic sharing of information by tax authorities. *More work needs to be done to enable developing countries to benefit from the norms, especially the poorest countries.* Last year, the Task Force recommended a *thorough analysis of the implications for sustainable development of international tax reforms.* Such analysis has begun but remains incomplete, with some of the necessary data not yet available.

Official development assistance (ODA) in support of domestic resource mobilization remains small. As agreed in the Addis Agenda, *donors should continue to increase their contributions to revenue mobilization capacity-building, and do so in line with the recommendations on enhancing the effectiveness of external support in building tax capacity in developing countries set out by the Task Force in 2017.*

Task Force members, for their part, will continue to strengthen collaboration, including through the joint United Nations, World Bank, International Monetary Fund (IMF), and Organization for Economic Cooperation and Development (OECD) Platform for Collaboration on Tax. The role of regional tax organizations is also vital. Sharing experiences plays a key role in developing common positions and holds potential for regional cooperation on tax incentives and harmonization of standards. Member States recognized this role last year in the 2017 ECOSOC Forum on Financing for Development Follow-up, meanwhile regional tax organizations are strengthening their global network to enable broader sharing of experiences. *Continued strengthening of existing regional tax organizations, and establishing them in regions without such organizations, will contribute to inclusive tax cooperation.*

The Task Force recognizes the damage done by illicit financial flows (IFFs) and the interest of Member States in combatting this scourge. The Task Force will continue providing component-by-component and channel-by-channel estimates of the value of such flows. Many of the reforms being discussed through international tax cooperation will contribute to preventing IFFs. In addition to the role of technology in strengthening tax administration, *technological advances can also assist Member States to combat IFFs through improved customs administrations, application of anti-money laundering rules, and operation of beneficial ownership registries and financial supervision.* Whole-of-government approaches take on additional significance because combatting IFFs, such as goods trade mis-invoicing, requires cooperation among many different agencies and ministries.

Technological advances also pose risks related to IFFs. The potential for anonymity with the use of new technologies such as blockchain and digital currencies can heighten the risk of illicit finance. *Member States can strengthen regulations on markets that are contributing to the illicit movement of resources.* International cooperation on the return of stolen assets is mandated by the United Nations Convention Against Corruption. *More investment can be made in the human and technical resources necessary to speed up assets return.*

Expenditure and budgeting needs to be effective and aligned with national and global priorities. Data and transparency are necessary on the expenditure side of public finance for delivery of accountable public services and sustainable development. *Stronger implementation of transparency and public participation in the budgeting process can improve the effectiveness of public finance.*

Gender-responsive budgeting can strengthen coherence between government budgets and gender equality objectives by identifying key gender equality goals, allocating appropriate funding and designing tax systems with gender equality in mind. Member States have committed to implement policies and legislation that promote gender equality and the empowerment of all women and girls at all levels. *Member States can use public financial management institutions to operationalize gender-responsive fiscal policies and should measure their progress in doing so.*

Last year the Task Force provided a deeper analysis of financing of universal social protection systems. Building universal social protection systems has synergies with other social policies, as well as additional benefits, such as helping improve tax administration and delivering emergency assistance in response to shocks.

Finally, the Addis Agenda emphasises that national development banks (NDBs) can play a vital role in financing sustainable development. *More in-depth study is warranted of how NDBs can adopt prudential risk management frameworks that align their activities with long-term investment and all three dimensions of sustainable development.*

2. Domestic resource mobilization

2.1 Trends and revenue targets

The Addis Agenda recognizes that domestic public resources are first and foremost generated by economic growth. The particularly weak global growth of 2016, as noted in chapter I, was reflected in the resource mobilization data of some countries. Median tax/gross domestic product (GDP) ratios continued to increase in small island developing States (SIDS) and in middle-income countries, although at a slower rate, with a median ratio of 17.9 per cent (see figure 1). For least developed countries (LDCs), median tax revenue declined in 2016 to 13.3 per cent of GDP. Of the 42 LDCs with reported data, 19 increased their tax-GDP ratios in 2016. Large gaps remain between LDCs, middle-income countries and countries in developed regions, with the 2016 gaps rising to levels not seen since 2008.

The composition of tax revenues also differs between developed and developing countries. Corporate and trade taxes constitute a much higher proportion of revenues in developing countries than in developed countries (see figure 2). Although resource-rich countries rely less on income and consumption taxes as a source of revenue, the institu-

Figure 1
Median tax revenue, 2000–2016
(*Percentage of GDP*)

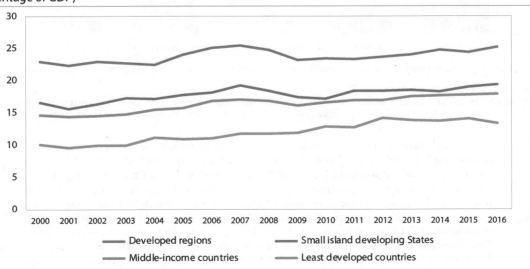

Source: IMF, World Revenue Longitudinal Dataset.

tional framework for taxation remains important. Commodity exporters are sometimes exposed to higher fiscal risks because of the high volatility of revenues associated with resource extraction and the propensity towards boom-bust economic cycles.[1] Taxation also has important positive effects on governance.[2]

Developed countries continue to have greater proportions of personal income and goods and services taxes. The value of goods and services taxes collected by developing countries has generally increased over the past decade, particularly in LDCs, as shown in figure 3. The increasing reliance on these types of indirect taxes has important implications for the progressivity of tax systems.

2.2 Tax administration

During 2017, the 2016 International Survey on Revenue Administration (*ISORA*) was completed with 135 tax administrations participating.[3] The survey found that while 91 per cent of tax administrations have strategic plans, only 64 per cent publish them. In terms of autonomy of tax authorities, 73 per cent have authority over their own internal structure, and 64 per cent have authority over their internal budget. Over 91 per cent of revenue administrations provide tax policy advice to their Governments.

The Tax Administration Diagnostic Assessment Tool (TADAT) is designed to provide an assessment of the health of key components of a

Figure 2
Median tax revenue by type of tax, 2015
(*Percentage of GDP*)

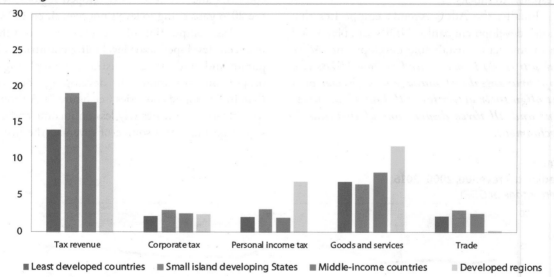

■ Least developed countries   ■ Small island developing States   ■ Middle-income countries   ■ Developed regions

Source: IMF, World Revenue Longitudinal Dataset.
Note: Because the database has a low number of observations for some of the tax breakdowns for 2015, there is considerable uncertainty associated with this analysis. There were 10 or fewer observations for SIDS, and only 10 or 14 observations for LDCs.

1   International Monetary Fund, "Macroeconomic Policy Frameworks for Resource-Rich Developing Countries" (Washington D.C., 2012). Available from https://www.imf.org/external/np/pp/eng/2012/082412.pdf.
2   See, inter alia, Adrian Gauci and John Robert Sloan, "From Consumer to Citizen Building a society contract for transformation through direct taxation", paper presented at African Economic Conference (Addis Ababa, 2017).
3   This was the first survey for the International Survey on Revenue Administration (ISORA) partners (Centro Interamericano de Administraciones Tributarias (CIAT), the International Monetary Fund (IMF), Intra-European Organisation of Tax Administrations (IOTA) and the Organization for Economic Cooperation and Development (OECD)) to jointly gather tax administration data through a single, shared, online survey. Aggregated data from this survey round is available to the public, while participating tax administrations may access country level data. The ISORA 2018 will be launched in May 2018 with a simplified and shortened questionnaire to make it easier for tax administrations to complete. Available from https://data.rafit.org.

Figure 3
Median goods and services tax revenue, 2000–2015
(*Percentage of GDP*)

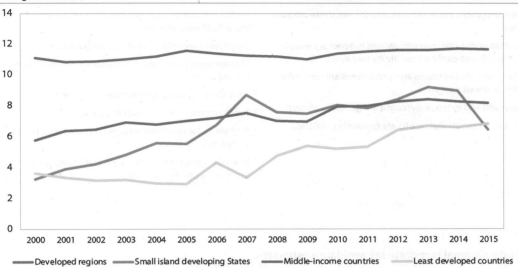

Developed regions   Small island developing States   Middle-income countries   Least developed countries

Source: IMF, World Revenue Longitudinal Dataset.
Note: Because the database has a low number of observations for 2015, there is considerable uncertainty associated with that year's data.

country's system of tax administration. This framework is focused on the nine key performance areas that cover most tax administration functions, processes and institutions. As at end-February 2018, 53 TADAT assessments have been conducted, with 36 in middle-income countries, and 2 for subnational authorities. Developed countries are also conducting the exercise. At least eight national level assessments are planned or in progress, with a further two subnational assessments planned. As shown in table 1, some patterns, gaps, and policy recommendations emerge from the assessments, recognizing that tax administration maturity levels vary from country to country. Hosting a TADAT assessment can help revenue authorities plan reforms that enhance effectiveness, efficiency and accountability.

2.3   Tax avoidance and tax evasion

A barrier to greater domestic resource mobilization is a high and persistent level of tax evasion and avoidance that undercuts public revenues. Some global estimates of international corporate tax avoidance were presented in the 2017 Task Force report and

a number of new or updated studies have been released, as shown in table 2.

In Africa, the large share of subsistence and smallholder agriculture in the economy and employment results in narrow tax bases, reducing the potential of tax collection. In some countries, the political and economic elite remain outside the tax base. The informal sector, which contributes to a large part of GDP in some countries (particularly in Africa), also may not be taxed, although many in this sector are in extreme poverty.

In Latin America and the Caribbean, the Economic Commission for Latin America and the Caribbean (ECLAC) estimates that tax non-compliance is equivalent to 2.4 per cent of GDP for value-added taxes (VAT) and 4.3 per cent for income tax, worth a combined total of $340 billion in 2015.[4] Estimates of VAT point to an average evasion rate of roughly 28 per cent, with evasion of income tax estimated to be more severe, averaging 50 per cent of income tax receipts (as compared to theoretically generated tax collections), although there is significant heterogeneity at the national level. Evasion rates are estimated

---

4   *Economic Survey of Latin America and the Caribbean: The 2030 Agenda for Sustainable Development and the challenges of financing for development* (United Nations publication, Sales No. E.16.II.G.3).

Table 1

Emerging patterns from completed TADAT assessments

Tax administration strengths that stand out	Prominent areas needing attention
• Tax administrations strive to bring into the net those who are outside it. • Information about taxpayer obligations is generally wide in scope, current and easily accessible by taxpayers. • Dispute resolution processes and procedures are generally available and well designed. • Internal audit and external oversight are generally strong. • Financial and operational results are generally published.	• Data is unreliable—a major crosscutting weakness that impacts all outcome areas. • Taxpayer registration databases are inaccurate. • Management practices for compliance and institutional risk are weak. • On-time filing and payment rates are poor. • Tax debt management practices are weak. • Wait times for resolving taxpayer disputes are unnecessarily long. • Revenue accounting systems are inefficient; size of suspense accounts is often unknown.

Source: IMF.

Table 2

Select international corporate tax avoidance estimates

Estimate provider	Date of publication	Volume of tax loss	Underlying data
OECD Economics Department Working Paper (Johansson, Skeie, Sorbe, & Menon)	2017	$100 billion – $240 billion in 2014	Firm-level corporate financial information databases
WIDER Working Paper (Cobham & Janský)	2017	$500 billion annually	Country-level statutory tax rates and corporate income tax revenues
IES Working Paper (Janský, & Palanský)	2017	$150 billion – $188 billion annually	Foreign direct investment data and reported rates of return

Source: Inter-agency Task Force on Financing for Development, UN/DESA.

to be higher for corporate than for personal income tax, and within personal income, much higher for self-employed persons than employees.

2.4 Tax reform and medium-term revenue strategies

Experience shows that progress in reforming revenue administrations and reducing evasion is achievable. Common elements of success include aligning administrative reforms with policy changes, and capacity-building to support both administrative reforms and policy changes. As many of these changes may encounter powerful opposition and political interference, sustained political commitment at the highest level and strong leadership of the revenue administration are essential.

In 2017, the Task Force encouraged the adoption of country-owned MTRS, which set out an overall four-year (or longer) plan for the development of the revenue system. This approach—which covers tax policy, law and administration—considers not only administrative issues such as efficiency in tax collection, but also the distributional implications of the tax system and potential reforms, including the fiscal space these reforms create for public spending aligned with the sustainable development agenda. It can also help gather political support for reform within countries and provide a mechanism to facilitate improved donor coordination. The MTRS approach can also help shape and improve the relationship between citizens and their Governments through stakeholder engagement, which can build broad social and political commitment to the tax system and its reform. Already in 2017, three Member States have committed to developing a full-fledged MTRS.

2.5 Digitalization and taxation

The intersection of tax policy and tax administration with the digitalization of the economy can be characterized as a series of small innovations being patched onto an institutional framework that is not sufficiently updated to take advantage of the opportunities or counter the risks presented.

Automated information systems can improve compliance, widen the tax base, and enable revenue authorities to more quickly and easily identify and mitigate risks related to tax avoidance and evasion, staff, technology and processes. Other possible benefits include improving government service delivery and levelling the playing field for taxpayers. They can also make enforcement more effective by enabling revenue authorities to share information across borders. For example, one estimate of seven major developing and emerging economies finds that digitizing payments can lead to direct savings between 0.8 and 1.1 per cent of GDP on an annual basis, with about 0.5 per cent of GDP accruing to government.[5]

Greater access to information and enhanced digital systems and processing capabilities open new options for policymakers. Digital information affords better enforcement of existing rules; while access to richer information can drive improvements in the rules themselves. For example, tax liabilities could be based on a taxpayer's lifetime income and wealth, rather than current yearly income, which would arguably lead to a fairer distribution of tax burdens. Digital systems also offer potential new roles for consumers and third parties in facilitating enhanced compliance—including through the emerging peer-to-peer economy.[6]

At the same time, some analysts have suggested that because the opportunities for tax avoidance associated with the scale of growth in online business may be putting so much pressure on current tax arrangements, fundamental changes in the international tax system are needed to ensure efficiency and fairness across countries in the allocation of taxing rights. From the perspective of international corporate tax policy, the issue of how to treat cross-border digital transactions has become highly contentious.[7] There are several key features of archetypal "digital companies" that provide challenges for current norms of international corporate taxation: sales with little or no physical presence; heavy reliance on intangible assets; and "user-generated value".[8] The issue of permanent establishment, in particular, has sparked concerns. Under existing rules, digital companies often have no liability to pay income tax in jurisdictions where they have users and customers, because those rules require some form of physical presence for a set period of time. This has opened a broader debate on the allocation of taxing rights and attribution of income between the residence and source countries. There is also disagreement on how user-generated value should affect taxing rights. Digital economy business models make heavy use of data to realize profit, while users of online services generate information that has commercial value. Much of the data collected is extremely valuable, but there is no agreement on whether, or how, to attribute value to the creation and use of data. The lack of a universal tax standard opens the possibility for fragmentation in approaches to this issue across jurisdictions but also creates incentives towards unilateral action to counter risks to the tax base.

There are different views on how to adapt international tax rules to the digitalization of the economy.

---

5   Sanjeev Gupta and others, "Digital Revolutions in Public Finance" (International Monetary Fund, 2017). Available from http://www.elibrary.imf.org/view/IMF071/24304-9781484315224/24304-9781484315224/24304-9781484315224.xml.

6   Ibid.

7   For a deeper discussion of these issues please see a background paper written for the UN Committee of Experts (E/C.18/2017/CRP.22) and the Organization for Economic Co-operation and Development Base erosion and profit shifting (OECD BEPS) Action Plan report on Addressing the Tax Challenges of the Digital Economy, available from https://www.oecd.org/tax/addressing-the-tax-challenges-of-the-digital-economy-action-1-2015-final-report-9789264241046-en.htm.

8   Digital economy business models do bear significant resemblance to those in the services sector. The taxation of cross-border services provision has been grappling with many of the same issues as now face taxation of the digital economy activities. Many multinational enterprises that are involved in the production and trade of merchandise also use intra-group transactions on services and other intangibles, which has been a significant source of base erosion and profit shifting activity. See Organization for Economic Co-operation and Development Base erosion and profit shifting (OECD BEPS) Action Plan report on Transfer Pricing. Available from https://www.oecd.org/tax/aligning-transfer-pricing-outcomes-with-value-creation-actions-8-10-2015-final-reports-9789264241244-en.htm.

Some experts doubt the desirability or even the possibility of ring-fencing digital companies for the purpose of designing special tax treatment. However, in recent policy debates, other experts have raised the prospect of tax rules that would be restricted to specific business lines. The United Nations Committee of Experts on International Cooperation in Tax Matters has established a subcommittee to consider necessary revisions in the United Nations Model Double Taxation Convention as well as to provide revised guidance. The Task Force on the Digital Economy, which is now a subsidiary body of the OECD-housed Inclusive Framework on Base Erosion and Profit Shifting (BEPS), is examining the tax challenges of digitalization; it is anticipated that the Inclusive Framework on BEPS will release an interim report on the findings by the end of April 2018, with a final report by 2020. The European Commission is waiting for that interim report and, if it does not include satisfactory proposals, may propose its own measures. Any changes to the provisions of either the United Nations or OECD model conventions as a result of this work will not automatically change the existing base of over 3,000 tax treaties or domestic practices unless Member States take action to incorporate them.

2.6   Gender and tax

Both the 2030 Agenda for Sustainable Development and the Addis Agenda include commitments to increasing investments in gender equality and women's empowerment. Taxes are a primary source of financing public services, which are of particular importance to women because they can reduce unpaid care and domestic work.

Gender bias in taxation, while an outgrowth of broader bias in society, also reinforces persistent inequalities. Explicit gender bias is the existence of specific provisions in tax law or regulations that impose different rules on men and women. Implicit bias is the existence of provisions in tax law or regulations that consistently have different impacts on men and women. Tax and domestic resource mobilization policies can reinforce and/or perpetuate discrimination in ways that undercut women's access to decent paid work and income security; reinforce women's role in providing unpaid care; and limit women's access to productive assets, wealth and other economic opportunities. For example, a tax that directly or indirectly discourages women from seeking formal employment can threaten women's income and participation in the labour force.

As shown in figure 3, developing countries have seen a rising amount of revenue as a share of GDP raised through goods and services taxes, which includes VAT.[9] Given women's overrepresentation in low-income groups, they bear disproportionate burdens of indirect taxes and consumption taxes. Recent research has also looked into the range of other ways that authorities raise revenue, including presumptive taxes[10] and fees, particularly those assessed at the subnational level.[11] These may also have implicit gender bias and subnational authority efforts to raise own-source revenue should take this into account (see chapter II).

Tax systems and tax policy can be used as powerful tools in addressing inequality, including gender inequality. To be gender responsive, tax policies and the tax mix adopted by a Government can be structured in a progressive manner and designed to reduce implicit bias. A gender analysis of personal income tax should consider four main issues: (i) insufficient tax relief for minimum basic living costs; (ii) the impact of shifts to flat-rate personal taxation;[12] (iii) joint taxation of adult couples; and (iv) the tying of social benefits to income. Overall, however, there is very little internationally comparable sex-disaggregated data on tax system performance and impacts, underscoring the need for more

---

9   Kathleen Lahey, "Gender, Taxation, and Equality in Developing Countries: Issues and Policy Recommendations" (New York, UN-Women, forthcoming).

10   Presumptive taxation involves the use of indirect means to ascertain tax liability, which differs from the usual rules based on the taxpayer's accounts. Examples include flat taxes on informal traders in markets.

11   For a summary, see Anuradha Joshi, "Tax and Gender in Developing Countries: What are the Issues?", ICTD Summary Brief Number 6 (2017). Available from http://ictd.ac/publication/7-policy-briefing/161-ictd-sumbrief6.

12   Over 40 countries at all levels of development have adopted flat-rate personal income tax laws. Women are often negatively affected by the move to flat-rate income tax structures, because this typically results in an increased rate for those with the lowest incomes.

sex-disaggregated data on fiscal systems (see also chapter IV).

2.7 Revenue systems in the context of conflict

Countries experiencing situations of conflict and violence face some of the most pressing challenges to achieving the SDGs.[13] The Task Force has previously noted that there is increasing evidence that countries with tax revenues below 15 per cent of GDP have difficulty funding basic state functions. An IMF study of conflict-affected countries shows that the average tax revenue-to-GDP ratio in 39 States[14] was below 14 per cent during 2005-2014 compared to 19 per cent in other developing countries.[15]

Research conducted in the last two decades points to weak institutional development, particularly in terms of legitimacy, approaches, and practices in conflict-affected countries. In conflict-affected situations, citizens typically have no or low trust in state institutions. The overarching goal is to stop or prevent violence and restore citizen trust. To achieve this goal, legitimacy is important. Redistributive institutions (e.g., revenue, expenditure, and social transfer entities) can help create incentives for individuals, groups and Governments to refrain from using violence. Increasing the mobilization of domestic resources can enhance accountability and thereby state-building, particularly if such efforts are explicitly linked to the provision of public goods.[16] Developing fiscal capacity is particularly important for conflict-affected countries, as the functioning of other State institutions, and the resultant service delivery, depend on the ability to finance them. Yet, tax and other revenue-raising functions tend to receive less attention compared to the attention paid to political institutions by the international community.

Mobilizing greater tax revenue depends on efficient and effective domestic tax administrations, which are frequently not present in conflict-affected situations. Often, an approach other than "best practice" is required in conflict-affected states. Policymakers may need to develop implementable second-best solutions.[17] In this regard, as shown in figure 4, conflict-affected countries rely more on trade taxes as a source of revenue, and are less diversified than non-conflict affected countries. Considerable attention is often paid to reforming the tax administration in conflict-affected countries, while customs administration is considered secondary. One general lesson from international organization experience is that more attention needs to be paid to reforming and strengthening customs administration and enforcement—especially when revenue from taxes at the border is significant.[18] Improvements to customs administration are also critical to contribute to global public goods in many areas, such as mitigating corruption, combatting money-laundering and terrorist financing, combatting drugs and human trafficking, protecting the environment, and trafficking of cultural property, among others.

2.8 Tax and health

Health services have a public-goods nature and in most countries public finance is central to the goal

---

13 There is no clear-cut categorization or definition in the United Nations system to describe which countries are conflict-affected. To help guide its own work, the World Bank Group and other multilateral development banks created a Harmonized List of Fragile Situations. This global common framework is broadly recognized, and the 2018 List classifies 36 countries as being in such situations. The number of countries experiencing conflict may be higher, as countries undergoing subnational-level conflict are not included in the List.

14 The International Monetary Fund (IMF) study was conducted using the IMF definition of "fragile states". This defines fragile states as having either weak institutional capacity as measured by the World Bank's Country Policy and Institutional Assessment (CPIA) score (average of 3.2 or lower) and/or experience of conflict (signalled by the presence of a peacekeeping or peacebuilding operation in the most recent three-year period).

15 The tax ratio excludes extractive industry royalties and other similar non-tax revenue. See International Monetary Fund, "Building Fiscal Capacity in Fragile States", Policy Paper (Washington, D.C., 2017).

16 International Bank for Reconstruction and Development/ World Bank, *World Development Report: Governance and the Rule of Law* (Washington, D.C., 2017). Available from http://www.worldbank.org/en/publication/wdr2017#.

17 International Monetary Fund, "Building Fiscal Capacity in Fragile States", Policy Paper (Washington, D.C., 2017); World Bank Group, *World Development Report: Governance and the Rule of Law* (Washington, D.C., 2017).

18 International Monetary Fund, "Building Fiscal Capacity in Fragile States", Policy Paper (Washington, D.C., 2017).

of achieving universal health coverage (SDG target 3.8). The Addis Agenda notes that, in addition to their revenue-raising function, taxes can be used to change incentives and behaviour. For example, taxes on tobacco, alcohol and sugar-sweetened beverages can potentially reduce consumption of these items, compensate society for increased health-system costs, and increase resources for the health sector. Excise taxes for tobacco control are most frequently used. Different types of excise structures, based on either quantities or value, are applied to tobacco products (see figure 5). Additionally, 35 countries have complex systems, with different (tiered) taxes that are applied to the same product based on sometimes minor differences in product characteristics, which opens loopholes for industry tax avoidance. The World Health Organization (WHO) recommends tobacco tax reforms that close loopholes by implementing single-rate, specific excise taxes that are frequently adjusted upwards. Currently, only 16 countries have automatically adjusted specific excise taxes (see figure

6). WHO recommends that best practice is to have total taxes make up more than 75 per cent of the retail price of cigarettes, although only 32 countries are currently meeting this practice (see figure 7).

Earmarking is increasingly used as a tool for domestic resource mobilization for health and as an instrument of public health policy—often to advance national health priorities. From a fiscal management perspective, hard earmarking (i.e., tying revenue streams to specific purposes and programmes) is not desirable, but earmarking often has political value for policymakers. Softer earmarking (i.e., tying revenue streams to broader expenditure and having more flexible revenue-expenditure links) has been used in some countries as an effective compromise between better public financial management and the need to establish funding for health systems.[19] Fiscal space for health can be expanded even in the absence of new revenue sources through sectoral reallocations and greater efficiency.

Figure 4
Revenue composition in conflict-affected and other developing countries (including grants), 2005–2013
(Percentage of total revenue)

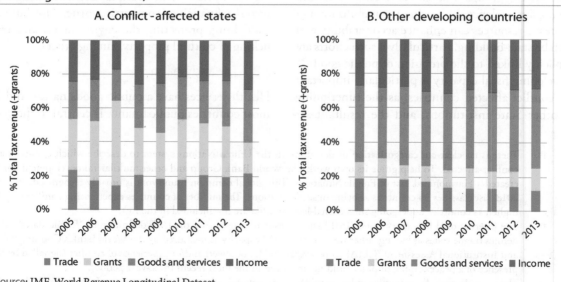

Source: IMF, World Revenue Longitudinal Dataset.
Note: Chart shows data for 38 states considered "fragile" by the IMF, and 93 other developing countries.

19   For further details see Cheryl Cashin, Susan Sparkes and Danielle Bloom, "Earmarking for health: From theory to practice", Health Financing Working Paper No. 5 (Geneva, WHO, 2017).

Figures 5 and 6
Tobacco excise tax structures, 2016 and **Tobacco tax structure good practices, 2016**
(*Number of countries*)

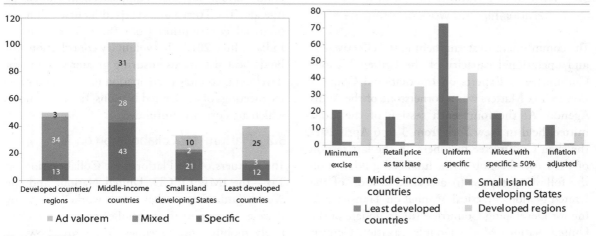

Source: WHO.
Note: Based on 172 countries levying an excise tax. Excludes countries with no excise, with no data reported in 2016, or where tobacco sales are banned. Minimum excise and retail price as tax base based on 108 countries with either ad valorem or mixed tax structures. Mixed with specific greater than 50 per cent based on 61 countries with mixed tax structures. Inflation adjusted based on 126 countries with either specific or mixed tax structures.

Figure 7
Total tax on cigarettes, 2016
(*Number of countries*)

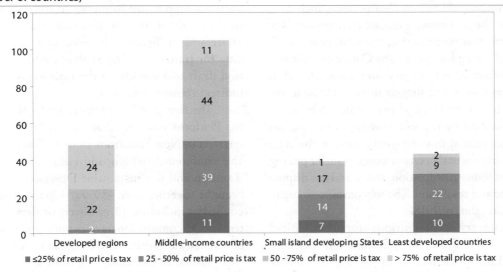

Source: WHO.

3. International tax cooperation

3.1 New United Nations Tax Committee membership and work programme

The commitment to strengthening the effectiveness and operational capacity of the United Nations Committee of Experts on International Cooperation in Tax Matters was a cornerstone of the Addis Agenda. At the fourteenth session of the Committee, held in New York from 3 to 6 April 2017, the then Committee members, in the last session of their membership term, finalized guidance on the following topics: (i) a revised edition of the United Nations Practical Manual on Transfer Pricing for Developing Countries; (ii) an update of the United Nations Model Double Taxation Convention between Developed and Developing Countries (the United Nations Model); and (iii) a new United Nations Handbook on the Taxation of the Extractive Industries.

The fifteenth session of the Committee, held in Geneva from 17 to 20 October 2017, was the first meeting of the new membership of the Committee, with a greatly improved gender balance in comparison with previous memberships. For the first time, the Committee elected co-chairpersons, including, again for the first time, a female chairperson. The main focus was on preparing the work programme for the following four years. The Committee formed eight subcommittees to carry work forward, including one to review and suggest improvements to the Committee's practices and procedures. Key issues to be taken up by the subcommittees include tax challenges related to the digitalization of the economy, environmental taxation issues, transfer pricing, extractive industries taxation issues, and tax dispute avoidance and resolution. The subcommittees began meeting in January 2018.

Voluntary contributions for the United Nations Trust Fund for International Cooperation in Tax, which was set up to help developing countries actively participate in the discussion of tax issues, have been called for by the United Nations and the United Nations Tax Committee since the Trust Fund's establishment in 2006. The call for contributions was also emphasized in the Addis Agenda. The Trust Fund received its first voluntary financial contribution from the Government of India in June 2017. This voluntary contribution will be dedicated towards ensuring greater support for developing-country participation in the subcommittee meetings of the United Nations Tax Committee, which are currently unfunded.

3.2 Platform for Collaboration on Tax

The partners of the Platform for Collaboration on Tax—the IMF, OECD, United Nations and the World Bank Group—have each worked for many decades to support their member countries to effectively mobilize tax revenues. There are, however, opportunities for deeper collaborative work through the Platform.

In 2017, the Platform produced a note on progress made in the implementation of the recommendations included in its 2016 joint report on mechanisms to help ensure effective implementation and funding of technical assistance programmes. The concept of MTRS, outlined above, was put forth in those two reports, with Platform partners supporting countries in implementation in 2017. The Platform also issued a toolkit for addressing difficulties in accessing comparable data for transfer-pricing analyses, and a consultation draft of a toolkit on the taxation of offshore indirect transfers of assets.

The first global conference under the aegis of the Platform was hosted at United Nations Headquarters in New York from 14 to 16 February 2018. The conference, which addressed the theme of "Taxation and the Sustainable Development Goals," brought together over 450 participants from 106 countries, including 18 ministers or deputy ministers and 33 commissioners or deputy commissioners of revenue authorities. The Platform issued a conference statement, including 14 specific actions for the Platform to take forward.[20]

---

20   The World Bank Group, "Platform Partners' Statement at the Closing of the Conference", 16 February 2018. Available from http://www.worldbank.org/en/news/statement/2018/02/16/platform-for-collaboration-on-tax-first-global-conference-on-taxation-and-sdgs.

3.3 Progress on tax transparency, BEPS implementation, and other initiatives

International tax cooperation revolves around international legal agreements that specify what may be taxed by which jurisdiction and how those jurisdictions will cooperate and share information. These legal agreements can be bilateral or multilateral, and can cover a variety of areas. Table 3 summarizes the number of countries that participate in some of the key multilateral legal instruments as well as different forums for cooperation and standards implementation. Tax information exchange is critical, as greater information allows tax authorities to better enforce tax rules and collect more revenue. Agreements listed in table 3 facilitate tax administrations to learn about taxpayers' offshore assets and about the activities of multinational enterprises (MNEs).

A key milestone was passed in 2017, as 49 jurisdictions began exchanging information under the Automatic Exchange of Information standard, which requires tax authorities to automatically exchange financial account information of non-residents with the tax authorities of the account holders' country of residence. A further 53 jurisdictions will start such exchanges in 2018. However, there is a systemic imbalance in application of these norms, as developing countries are not participating for a variety of reasons. For example, actual exchange of country-by-country information on MNEs requires activation through a bilateral matching process, more than 1400 of which have now been activated. Of these, only 477 involve middle-income countries, and no LDCs have any matches. The agreed policy recommendations from the November 2017 meeting of the UNCTAD Intergovernmental Expert Group on Financing for Development emphasize the need for enhanced developing-country participation in current initiatives to improve international tax cooperation.[21]

To discourage hiding of income and wealth, countries are implementing stronger rules on the disclosure and exchange of beneficial ownership[22] information. This is an area with low compliance, even among the jurisdictions that have signed up to global standards. While the European Union has proposed reforms to its anti-money laundering rules that will advance the collection and sharing of beneficial ownership in that region,[23] LDCs and middle-income countries currently have no way to automatically receive such information. This leaves opportunities for tax avoidance and evasion through the use of shell companies, trusts and other opaque financial structures.

3.4 Regional organizations and capacity-building

Regional tax organizations play a vital role in sharing experiences and analyses that are relevant for the contexts of their members. Regional organizations have also come together in the Network of Tax Organisations (NTO), which was created to provide a forum for cooperation and coordination between member organizations, strengthen institutional capacities, and enhance the efficiency and effectiveness of tax administrations worldwide. The heads of the nine participating tax organizations came together in February 2018 for the first NTO Strategy Planning Workshop and will meet again in May 2018 to formalize their enhanced cooperation. The members represent tax administrations in Africa, the Caribbean, members of the Commonwealth, Europe, Francophone countries, Islamic countries, Latin America, the Pacific and West Africa.

Intergovernmental organizations hold a variety of training programmes to build the domestic revenue mobilization capacity of countries that need assistance. The IMF provides technical assistance to approximately 100 countries every year. The United Nations capacity-development programme on

---

21 Trade and Development Board Intergovernmental Group of Experts on Financing for Development, "Financing for development: Issues in domestic public resource mobilization and international development cooperation", 10 November 2017. Available from http://unctad.org/meetings/en/SessionalDocuments/IGE_FfD_1st_session_Agreed_Policy%20_Recommendations.pdf.

22 The beneficial owner of an entity is the natural person that ultimately owns or controls that entity. It also includes those persons who exercise ultimate effective control over an entity.

23 European Commission, "Strengthened EU rules to prevent money laundering and terrorism financing", 15 December 2017. Available from http://ec.europa.eu/newsroom/just/item-detail.cfm?item_id=610991.

Table 3

Participation in international tax cooperation instruments, 2018

(Number of countries)

Instrument/Institution	Total membership	Middle-income countries	Least developed countries	Small island developing States
MCAA Common Reporting Standard — *on financial account information*	98	27	0	17
MCAA exchange of country-by-country reports — *related to MNE activity*	68	18	2	4
Mutual Assistance Convention — *for exchange of tax information on request*	117	42	3	18
Automatic Exchange of Information Standard — *for exchange of tax information between countries*	102	29	1	24
Global Forum — *OECD-housed body for review of implementation of tax transparency standards*	149	63	17	31
Multilateral Instrument on BEPS — *to implement agreed standards for reducing base erosion and profit shifting*	90	31	2	8
Inclusive Framework on BEPS Implementation — *OECD-housed body for review of implementation of BEPS Action Plan*	112	42	10	15

Source: OECD.

international tax cooperation focuses on training developing-country tax administrators in the application of international tax standards, including the outputs of the United Nations Tax Committee. The Tax Inspectors Without Borders initiative, which is jointly operated by the OECD and the United Nations Development Programme (UNDP), supports countries in building tax audit capacity. Tax audits conducted under the initiative to date have resulted in increased tax collection of $328 million. The OECD Global Relations programme provides training events on a range of issues, primarily on international tax cooperation, but also including tax administration issues. The OECD also provides bilateral technical assistance in transfer pricing and other BEPS-related actions in about 20 countries a year. The Global Forum provides assistance to developing countries on all aspects of the international tax transparency standards.

Overall, ODA to domestic resource mobilization reported in the OECD/Development Assistance Committee (DAC) creditor reporting system rose from $181 million, representing 0.15 per cent of DAC members' ODA commitments in 2015, to $288 million, or 0.23 per cent of commitments in 2016.[24] The Addis Tax Initiative was launched in July 2015, and commits donor countries to doubling the resources they provide for capacity-building on tax. Its first monitoring report, published in June 2017, reported the baseline for measuring success at $224 million in support of domestic revenue mobilization in developing countries in 2015.[25]

4. Illicit financial flows

While improved tax administration and better tax policies at the domestic level are essential, IFFs represent a major obstacle to efforts to mobilize domestic resources for sustainable development. Member States expressed their deep concern about IFFs and have repeatedly called for greater international cooperation to combat IFFs.[26] They have also pledged to deter, detect, prevent and counter corruption, and increase transparency and promote good governance for their citizens. Although there remains no inter-

---

24   The large rise was predominantly the result of two very large projects initiated by a single donor.

25   Due to technical problems in recoding the 2015 ODA data under the new code for projects related to domestic resource mobilization, some Addis Tax Initiative (ATI) development partners were unable to report all their related activities in time to the OECD/DAC. The ATI monitoring report thus includes more projects than were recorded in the OECD/DAC creditor reporting system.

26   A/RES/72/207.

governmental agreement on the definition of the term, the Task Force's schematic representation of the components and channels of IFFs remains a useful approach to the topic. Combatting IFFs generally has several elements, including estimation of the volume of IFFs, improvement of policies and enforcement capacity, and return of stolen assets. At the United Nations General Assembly in January 2018, Member States called for the next President of the General Assembly to convene "a high-level meeting on international cooperation to combat illicit financial flows and strengthen good practices on assets return to foster sustainable development".[27] Building on the FfD Forum, this event could provide a venue for a deeper stocktaking.

4.1   Volume estimates

Different components of IFFs are not directly comparable and aggregation of IFF estimates across channels and components could result in double counting. In 2017, the Task Force recommended component-by-component and channel-by-channel analysis and estimation of IFFs. In line with this recommendation, the Task Force will continue to provide summaries of the channel-specific and component-specific estimates, which can be helpful to Member States in designing enforcement and policy responses. The UNCTAD Intergovernmental Expert Group on Financing for Development stressed "the need for transparent and comprehensive statistical indicators to estimate and typify illicit financial flows" and "the importance of continued efforts to ensure effective country-by-country reporting of relevant data".[28]

In 2017, the United Nations Office on Drugs and Crime (UNODC) and UNCTAD — the joint custodian agencies of SDG indicator 16.4.1, which covers IFFs — developed a programme of coordinated actions to develop, review and test a statistical methodology to estimate the volume of IFFs. In December 2017, an expert group meeting divided the statistical work into two subgroups, one focussed on the estimation of IFFs related to activities in illegal markets and one focussed on estimation related to abusive tax practices. In addition, a subgroup was proposed to estimate IFFs related to corruption. As part of this programme, a testing of the statistical measure will initially be conducted in four countries in Latin America, with selected countries in Africa to follow.

Goods trade mis-invoicing is one type of IFF, which involves transactions being manipulated for the purposes of evading tariffs, circumventing capital account rules or financial regulations, or other illicit motives. Several United Nations regional commissions have estimated goods trade mis-invoicing, using different methodologies tailored to their regions' needs (see figure 8, figure 9 and figure 10). Recent research work has also focussed increasingly on using national-level trade data to estimate goods trade mis-invoicing.[29] Caution must be exercised when interpreting these estimates as mismatches between import and export figures may be due to factors other than illicit transactions, such as data-entry mistakes, missing data due to reimports, time differences between goods departure and arrival, and other factors; however, the patterns can be indicative of areas and sectors where Governments may want to focus enforcement attention.[30] The estimates also do not capture all types of mis-invoicing — falsified invoicing where the invoices match at both export and import, for example. The full value of an illicit flow also does not always equate with the domestic public resource impact.

27   Ibid.

28   Trade and Development Board Intergovernmental Group of Experts on Financing for Development, "Financing for development: Issues in domestic public resource mobilization and international development cooperation", 10 November 2017. Available from http://unctad.org/meetings/en/SessionalDocuments/IGE_FfD_1st_session_Agreed_Policy%20_Recommendations.pdf.

29   See background paper for the December 2017 expert group meeting on IFFs estimation, Expert Consultation on the SDG Indicator on illicit financial flows. Available from https://www.unodc.org/documents/data-and-analysis/statistics/IFF/Background_paper_B_Measurement_of_Illicit_Financial_Flows_UNCTAD_web.pdf.

30   For a detailed discussion see, Céline Carrère and Christopher Grigoriou, "Can Mirror Data Help To Capture Informal International Trade?", Policy Issues in International Trade and Commodities Research Study Series No. 65 (Geneva, UNCTAD, 2014). Available from http://www.unctad.org/en/PublicationsLibrary/itcdtab65_en.pdf.

As shown in the Task Force's 2017 schematic, IFFs are often held as offshore wealth. While estimation of offshore wealth holding is difficult because of the secrecy afforded in many jurisdictions, new data is improving the accuracy of estimates. Previous estimates were largely based on global extrapolations from a dataset of foreign holdings of financial wealth in a single popular wealth-management jurisdiction. New estimates take advantage of the decision by a number of financial centres to authorize the Bank for International Settlements to publish data of their banks' cross-border liabilities disaggregated by the jurisdiction of the counterparty. One study estimates that, as of October 2017, 10 per cent of world gross product is held as private offshore financial wealth.[31] However, there is currently insufficient data to determine what volume of this wealth is being disclosed correctly to tax authorities.

Figure 8

Asia-Pacific regional goods trade mis-invoicing, 2016

(*Billions of United States dollars*)

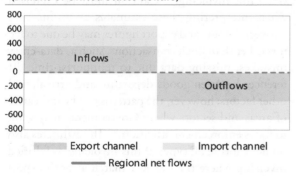

Source: ESCAP calculations.
Note: Chart shows the aggregated bilateral differences between export and import values at product level (Harmonized System six-digit codes) for 86 per cent of export lines and 75 per cent of import lines where matching was possible for 31 jurisdictions within ESCAP Member States. Special administrative regions of China are treated as separate jurisdictions.

Figure 9

Estimates of gross outflows from goods trade mis-invoicing, Latin America and the Caribbean, 2000–2015

(*Billions of United States dollars*)

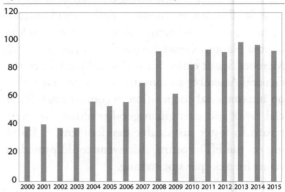

Source: ECLAC calculations.
Note: Chart shows the aggregated gross outflows for bilateral differences between export and import values at product level (Harmonized System six-digit codes) for 33 ECLAC Member States. Results are inversely weighted for differences in volume of goods to correct for inadvertent misreporting.

Figure 10

Estimates of net outflows from goods trade mis-invoicing, African countries, 2000–2015

(*Billions of United States dollars*)

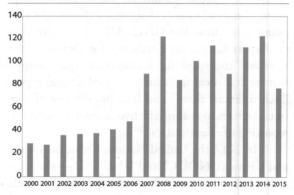

Source: UN/ECA calculations.
Note: Chart shows the aggregated net outflows for bilateral differences between export and import values at sector level (Global Trade Analysis Project 57 sectors) for 49 jurisdictions within ECA Member States, in 2016 prices. The Southern African Customs Union is treated as a single entity.

31   Annette Alstadsæter, Niels Johannesen, and Gabriel Zucman, "Who Owns the Wealth in Tax Havens? Macro Evidence and Implications for Global Inequality", NBER Working Paper No. 23805 (September 2017). Available from https://www.nber.org/papers/w23805.

4.2 Policy advances and the role of technology

Tackling IFFs more effectively will not only bolster domestic resource mobilization, but will also help build trust and confidence in the fairness of the tax, legal and financial systems, the efficiency of law enforcement, and in government as a whole. It can also contribute to better security outcomes. There are multiple efforts to combat IFFs which span from international information sharing to joint interdictions. Many of the tax transparency reforms being introduced, discussed above, will be relevant for tracking and stopping IFFs. In particular, strengthened beneficial ownership registries and mechanisms to share that information will be critical to penetrating the trusts, shell corporations and other financial vehicles used to hide IFFs and their resulting assets.

The World Bank is developing an IFFs risk assessment framework to help countries direct policy and enforcement actions. A model is under development that tests the association of IFFs with policy variables relating to incentives of economic actors to generate IFFs, state capacity to address IFFs, and democratic accountability. Once validated, the model will be used to separate countries into categories of high, medium, and low exposure to illicit financial inflows and outflows. The World Bank intends to pilot test the assessment framework by mid-2018. The OECD along with three countries also launched the Pilot Africa Academy Programme for Tax and Financial Crime Investigation at the G20 Africa Conference, held in Berlin from 12 to 13 June 2017. This initiative aims to provide demand-driven training addressing the specific needs of African countries in tackling IFFs.

New technologies and innovation are altering the landscape for IFFs. While relatively closed financial systems of previous generations made large-scale transfers of resources easier to track, the more open systems of recent times can enable hidden and secret transactions. The anonymity and cross-border reach of virtual currencies (VCs) raise concerns.[32] Transactions recorded in the public ledger of a VC cannot always authoritatively be traced back to real-world identities, owing to user anonymity and anonymizing service providers. This means that VCs can be used to conceal or disguise illicit origin, use or transfer of funds. These vulnerabilities are not only theoretical, but have been exploited in practice. VCs are often the "currency" of choice in cyber-related criminal activity and in illicit virtual markets for contraband, arms and other goods. The Financial Action Task Force has called for regulation of exchanges on which VCs can be exchanged for regulated fiat currencies, as a way to limit the use of VCs for IFFs. In 2017, a number of Asian countries that had hosted significant VC operations and exchanges announced new regulations or the intention to do so.

At the same time, technology can also enable better enforcement. As the regulatory environment catches up to the innovations, digital technologies allow rapid processing of large data sets, which can assist in identifying and pursuing illicit transactions. For example, the Legal Entity Identifier (LEI) system, which assigns each distinct legal entity a unique 20-character identifier to enable easier tracking of transactions and counterparty exposures, has the potential to assist in conducting due diligence and reduce compliance costs (see chapter III.F). To achieve these benefits, solutions need to be widely adopted by industry participants, with appropriate support by public authorities.

4.3 Asset recovery and return

As noted in the 2017 report of the Task Force, efforts to recover stolen assets are part of the overall effort to combat IFFs. The term "stolen assets" is used to describe the proceeds of corruption that have been transferred abroad. Their recovery and return is provided for in the United Nations Convention Against Corruption (UNCAC) and is included in the Addis Agenda and the 2030 Agenda for Sustainable Development. Return of stolen assets is different from and cannot substitute for any other types of financial flows.

Collecting and publishing data on the volume of assets seized, confiscated and returned or disposed of is complex from both a statistical and a policy point of view. Member States' statistical systems do

---

32   This section draws heavily from Dong He and others, "Virtual currencies and beyond: initial considerations", International Monetary Fund Staff Discussion Note, SDN/16/03 (January 2016).

not necessarily produce internationally comparable data over time. Weaknesses in national statistics systems were one of the most frequently identified challenges in country reviews in the first cycle of the Implementation Review Mechanism of UNCAC.

The joint World Bank/UNODC Stolen Asset Recovery (StAR) Initiative works with developing countries and financial centres to prevent the laundering of the proceeds of corruption and to facilitate more systematic and timely return of stolen assets. The StAR Asset Recovery Watch database contains information on 240 past and current asset recovery cases involving corruption. A database on settlements in cases of transnational bribery, contains information on over 500 settlements.

Since the last Task Force report, there has been a broad range of policy initiatives in this area. Non-binding guidelines, validated at an expert group meeting held in Washington, D.C. in December 2017, will be submitted to the Asset Recovery Working Group in June 2018 for consideration and possible submission to UNCAC signatories. The Global Forum on Asset Recovery (GFAR), which was a major commitment of the 2016 London Anti-Corruption Summit, took place in December 2017 and focused on the recovery of assets stolen from Nigeria, Sri Lanka, Tunisia and Ukraine. The co-hosts, the United Kingdom of Great Britain and Northern Ireland and the United States of America, plus the four focus countries issued a statement that welcomed the GFAR Principles for Disposition and Transfer of Confiscated Stolen Assets in Corruption Cases.[33]

5. Expenditure

5.1 SDG budgeting

The 2030 Agenda for Sustainable Development and the Addis Agenda called for Governments to report on their spending and progress towards the achievement of the SDGs. The Addis Agenda commits countries to increase transparency and equal participation in the budgeting process. In the outcome document of the 2017 FfD Forum, Member States recognized the importance of better disaggregation of budget and expenditure data at the national and subnational levels, including by sex, to improve tracking of spending related to the Sustainable Development Goals and efforts to improve gender equality, accountability and transparency, with increased capacity-building for countries that need assistance.

While the IMF and partners have set principles for fiscal transparency through the Global Initiative for Fiscal Transparency (GIFT),[34] there are not yet any associated assessment frameworks. The broadest regular measure of budget transparency and accountability around the world is the Open Budget Survey conducted by the civil society organization International Budget Partnership. The 2017 Open Budget Survey[35] found that, for the first time in a decade, budget transparency has fallen globally, with the decline concentrated in sub-Saharan Africa. The survey also found that only 26 of the covered 115 countries provide sufficient budget information that would enable all stakeholders to track development spending.

The basic information needed to track sectoral spending on specific SDGs at the national level are frequently unavailable, because budget frameworks are not yet designed to capture this information. According to the Open Budget Survey, less than half of countries use functional classification in their budget reports, which would enable tracking of spending in critical sectors such as health, education and disaster risk reduction. Some 59 per cent of countries make data available on actual spending against the budget during implementation, but only 45 per cent make available data on final spending against the budget. Further, 74 per cent of those surveyed do not yet provide expenditures disaggregated by sex, age, income, or region, making it difficult to determine whether the poor, the vulnerable or those furthest behind are benefitting from public

---

33   World Bank, "Global Forum on Asset Recovery Communique" (December 2017). Available from https://star. worldbank.org/star/sites/star/files/20171206_gfar_communique.pdf.

34   See http://www.fiscaltransparency.net/.

35   International Budget Partnership, "The Open Budget Survey 2017" (2017). Available from https://www.internationalbudget.org/open-budget-survey/.

expenditure. Another channel to promote accountable expenditure is public participation, and tested mechanisms for enabling citizen participation exist. The Open Budget Survey conducted its assessment of public participation in the budget based on the GIFT principles, and found that over 80 per cent of countries have at least one participation mechanism, but the vast majority of these national measures were not considered to be strongly inclusive or well-structured.

5.2   Gender-responsive budgeting

Gender-responsive budgeting (GRB) can influence how fiscal policy is designed and implemented. Well-designed gender budgets can improve the efficiency and equity of the overall budget process by integrating gender analysis into policies, plans and programmes. GRB can generate essential data on the gender gaps in services, the priority needs and the potential gender impacts of different actions. This analysis enables programmes to be designed and delivered in ways that respond to the priorities of women and men and can be particularly important in sectors that deliver critical services such as water and sanitation (see chapter II). The IMF 2016 research survey on gender budgeting identified that 23 of the 62 countries in the survey had prominent gender-budgeting efforts, while a further 37 had some gender-budgeting efforts. Two thirds of the countries with prominent efforts linked their gender budgeting goals to the Millennium Development Goals or other national development plans.

The development of systems to track gender equality allocations is an important step in bridging policy commitments and implementation. Comprehensive systems to track gender equality allocations can capture data on the extent to which budget allocations are matched to priority actions and support national efforts to better target resources to address gender gaps.

As reported in 2017, UN Women, together with UNDP and the OECD, has developed the methodology for SDG indicator 5.c.1, which aims to measure government efforts globally to track budget allocations for gender equality and make data publicly available. Following pilot testing in 15 countries, the final methodology was endorsed by a subgroup of the United Nations Statistical Commission, setting an international standard for GRB. Starting in 2018, efforts will focus on supporting countries to report against the indicator.

5.3   Social protection finance update[36]

In the Addis Agenda, Member States committed to establishing a new Social Compact to provide (i) fiscally sustainable and nationally appropriate social protection systems and measures and (ii) essential public services for all (education, health, water, sanitation and other services). The 2017 outcome of the ECOSOC Forum on Financing for Development Follow-up encouraged support for capacity-building to help countries, according to their needs, to design and implement nationally appropriate social protection systems, and asked the Task Force to lay out domestic and international funding sources for social protection and quick-disbursing instruments (see also chapter III.F). As part of that work, the Task Force's social protection cluster coordinator, the International Labour Organisation (ILO), prepared a paper on social protection financing, in consultation with Social Protection Inter-Agency Cooperation Board (SPIAC-B), building on the 2017 report of the Task Force. The paper found that resources for social protection are available in some countries, but more needs to be done, including in helping countries set up social protection systems, including floors, in accordance with SDG 1.3. Such systems would serve multiple purposes, such as developing human capital, promoting growth and political stability, and can be utilized during economic shocks and disasters.

Figure 11 presents regional data public expenditures on social protection, excluding health, as a percentage of GDP for 2015 or latest available year. There are large regional differences in the proportion of resources allocated to social protection, reflecting significant gaps at both country and regional levels. For example, African countries' average spending on

---

36   This section is based on a longer paper prepared by the International Labour Organization. Available from https://developmentfinance.un.org/sites/developmentfinance.un.org/files/files/policy-briefs/Social%20protection%20FfD%20Final%20Jan18.pdf.

social protection is only 4.5 per cent of GDP. Countries in the LDCs and SIDS groupings also have low expenditure, with respective averages of 3.0 per cent of GDP and 1.9 per cent of GDP. Differences between countries, even within the same region or subregion, are also significant, as can be seen by the dispersion of countries within each region shown in figure 12.

Domestic financing represents the main source of resources for social protection systems in both developed and developing countries. As discussed in the 2017 Task Force report, social contributions (employers and workers contributions to social security) play an important role in financing public social protection, although, as shown in figure 13, such contributions must be combined with tax revenues in order to fully meet the funding needs of comprehensive social protection systems.

Domestic resources are supplemented by international assistance with the role of ODA for social protection especially critical in LDCs. Between 2010 and 2015, the disbursed ODA to social protec-

tion varied between $1.9 billion and $2.6 billion, as shown in figure 14, accounting for about 2 per cent of total ODA. [37]

Other sources of finance for social protection may also be considered, to complement but not replace ODA and domestic sources, as discussed in the 2017 Task Force Report and the ILO paper.

5.4   National development banks

National development banks (NDBs) are a critical part of the Addis Agenda. As noted in the Addis Agenda, one role of NDBs is to address market failure. While NDBs have an effective sovereign guarantee, they often borrow from capital markets, and thus need to signal to the markets that they are effectively managing their risks. Indeed, given that they, in essence, represent contingent liabilities of the State, it is critical that their risks are prudently managed. Some NDBs have started using the standardized models for managing risk at commercial banks, which are promoted by the Basel Committee (see chapter III.F). Yet those standards give higher capital

Figure 11

Public social protection expenditure (excluding health), by region and country category, latest available year

(Percentage of GDP)

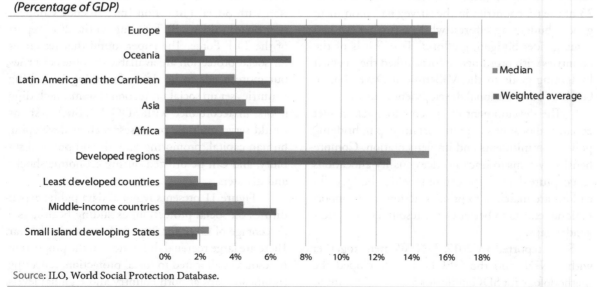

Source: ILO, World Social Protection Database.

---

[37]   Measured using the OECD/DAC CRS code 16010, which includes ODA for the following areas: Social legislation and administration; institutional capacity-building and advice; social security and other social schemes; special programmes for the elderly, orphans, the disabled, street children; social dimensions of structural adjustment; unspecified social infrastructure and services, including consumer protection.

costs to activities perceived to be of higher risk—which are often precisely those that are of public interest, where NDBs are expected to operate, such as in infrastructure, SME financing, or innovation—thus raising costs of lending in these areas. By using commercial bank risk management models, NDBs make it more costly to serve a different role in the economy than private banks. It would be useful if there was a specialized risk management framework for NDBs that, if followed, could demonstrate that the bank is managing risk prudentially while incentivizing them to lend in ways that are more aligned with sustainable development. More research on this is warranted.

Figure 12
Public social protection expenditure (excluding health), by region, latest available year
(Number of countries)

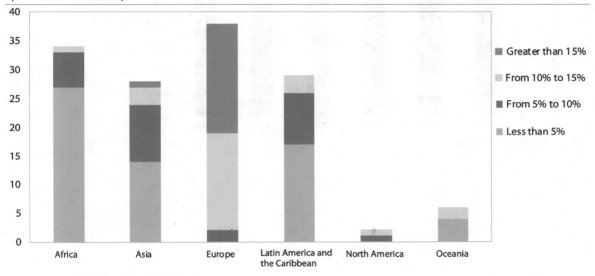

Source: ILO, World Social Protection Database.

Figure 13
Share of social contributions in social protection expenditure, 2015
(Percentage)

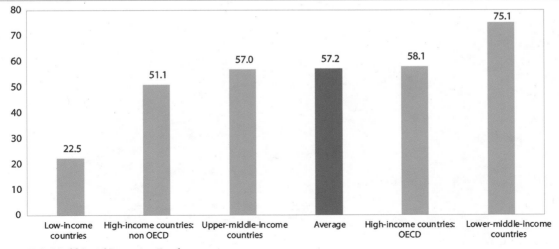

Source: ILO, World Social Protection Database.

Figure 14
Official Development Assistance disbursements for social protection, 2010–2016
(Millions of United States dollars, percentage of gross national income)

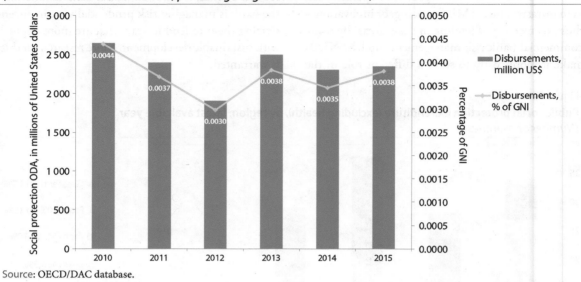

Source: OECD/DAC database.

Domestic and international private business and finance

1. Key messages and recommendations

Private investment and business activity is integral to development and job creation. The Addis Ababa Action Agenda (hereafter, Addis Agenda), calls on businesses to apply their creativity and innovation to solving sustainable development challenges, and invites them to engage as partners in implementation of the sustainable development agenda.

Two years into the 2030 Agenda for Sustainable Development, the momentum around sustainable investment is growing[1] and private companies are progressively recognizing that sustainability can foster long-term value. Indeed, the 2030 Agenda creates enormous opportunities for commercial finance and investment. The Business and Sustainable Development Commission found that achieving the Sustainable Development Goals (SDGs) could unlock $12 trillion in market opportunities across just four sectors: food and agriculture; cities; energy and materials; and health and well-being.[2]

Yet, while investment picked up in 2017, long-term investment in sustainable development, especially in some developing countries (such as least developed countries (LDCs), landlocked developing countries (LLDCs) and small island developing States (SIDS)), remains insufficient; and despite a global consensus on the need to increase investment in infrastructure in particular, private participation in infrastructure has fallen each year since the Addis Agenda was adopted in 2015.[3]

Public policies set the enabling environment and the regulatory framework for private sector investment and activity. The Monterrey Consensus tasked Member States of the United Nations with building transparent, stable and predictable investment climates, and many countries have made great strides in this area, though gaps still remain. *Developing countries should continue to work to build competitive business environments, and develop project pipelines and investible projects, supported by international cooperation and capacity development, especially for vulnerable countries including LDCs, LLDCs and SIDS.*

In the Addis Agenda, countries also underscored the importance of better aligning business activities and investment decisions with sustainable development objectives. Investment in the SDGs requires long-term investing. Indeed, without a long-term perspective, certain risks, such as climate risks, will not be priced into private decision-making. One of the greatest challenges policymakers face in raising resources for sustainable development is how to address excessive short-term-oriented decision-making.

Achieving the SDGs will require a shift to a long-term investment horizon, with sustainability as a central concern. *Governments can explore ways to incentivize institutional investors to take a long-term approach, including by reviewing*

1   See for example, the Dutch SDG investing and the CEO of BlackRock's note on contributing to society. Available from https://www.sdgi-nl.org/ and https://www.blackrock.com/corporate/en-no/investor-relations/larry-fink-ceo-letter.

2   Business Commission on Sustainable Development, "Ideas for a Long-Term and Sustainable Financial System", (2017). Available from http://s3.amazonaws.com/aws-bsdc/BSDC_SustainableFinanceSystem.pdf.

3   World Bank, Private Participation in Infrastructure database. Available from http://ppi.worldbank.org/.

regulatory frameworks.[4] The Inter-agency Task Force on Financing for Development (hereafter, Task Force) found that proper interpretation of fiduciary duty of institutional investors with long-term liabilities would include a focus on the long-term, and would incorporate all factors (including environmental, social and governance (ESG) indicators) that have a material impact on returns, as these will drive the long-term performance of investments.

Asset owners can take the lead in aligning their incentives with long-term investment, such as by linking compensation to longer-term returns; also, rating agencies, consultants and advisors can support investors by evaluating risks and returns over the long-term. *The United Nations, in collaboration with other institutions, could serve as a platform for bringing together asset owners, managers and other stakeholders to further exchange experiences and disseminate the benefits of SDG investing with the financial community and other stakeholders. The Task Force can develop analytical work to support and contextualize these discussions into the broader SDG implementation and Addis Agenda follow-up.*

Incentivizing the private sector to adopt global standards on responsible business conduct can promote better alignment of social and private goals. *The Task Force also recognizes the need to improve definitions, standards, measurement and disclosure of ESG impact and of new instruments, such as green bonds. Given the proliferation of competing reporting guidelines for businesses, there is a need to introduce greater standardization in sustainability metrics, and to ensure that metrics are aligned to global standards so as not to duplicate efforts.*

Ultimately, to fully mainstream SDG investing, new products need to be developed. The financial sector excels at innovation when demand is there. This raises questions about the level of demand for ESG investing and whether investment professionals

necessarily know their clients' preferences. As there is no systematic review of investor preferences, *one simple solution would be for advisors, consultants, brokers and others financial professionals to ask investors and beneficiaries for their sustainability preferences, similar to other know-your-customer requirements.[5]*

The Task Force recognizes that even with long-term horizons, and the incorporation of material long-term ESG drivers of value, markets may provide insufficient financing for sustainable development across countries and sectors. This is the case when the risk-adjusted returns are not competitive with other opportunities, due to high risks or externalities that are not priced into private investment decisions (see chapter II). Risk-sharing tools, such as blended finance, can be used to attract greater private investment (see chapter III.C).

Greater efforts to reduce domestic risks along with partnerships between foreign and domestic investors—and multilateral, regional and domestic development banks, and development finance institutions (DFIs) that understand local context—can help address the difference in risk perceptions.

The achievement of the SDGs is also dependent on finance being channelled to LDCs and other vulnerable countries, such as LLDCs and SIDS, in an inclusive manner, as well as to micro and smaller enterprises, women and poor and underserved segments of society. *Governments can examine the use of blended finance and similar mechanisms to spur investment, including by broadening the range of financing instruments accessible to small and medium-sized enterprises (SMEs); however, more analysis is required to design financial instruments that respond to the unique situation of countries with special needs, such as LDCs.*

The digitalization of finance offers new possibilities towards advancing inclusive finance and its alignment with the 2030 Agenda for Sustainable Development. Fintech should be included as an integral part of national development plans on the

---

4   For example, see the European Union's attempt to do this via a "High-level Expert Group on Sustainable Finance", (2016). Available from https://ec.europa.eu/info/business-economy-euro/banking-and-finance/sustainable-finance_en#high-level-expert-group-on-sustainable-finance.

5   For example, in the United States of America, the Financial Industry Regulatory Authority (FINRA) suitability rule includes asking about investment objectives, including "generating income, funding retirement, buying a home, preserving wealth or market speculation". See http://www.finra.org/investors/suitability-what-investors-need-know.

financial system. At the same time, ***effective regulation is necessary to monitor any systemic or consumer risks that may arise from digitalization of finance.***

Collaboration between international institutions, regulators and fintech entrepreneurs could help to develop international norms for effective use of fintech. ***The application of financial technology also has the potential to lower the cost of remittances.*** Innovative applications can help address the loss of correspondent banking and provide a boost to developing countries that receive significant remittances from overseas.

2.   Trends in investment and cross-border capital flows

Global investment growth hit a low in 2016, having contracted significantly since the global economic and financial crisis, with weak investment in part reflecting the fact that companies were channelling profits to shareholders in the form of dividend distribution or share buybacks, rather than to productive investment. Investment weakness shifted from advanced economies to developing countries over this period.[6] In developed countries, investment increased in 2017, although from a low base. In developing countries, investment dynamics differed across countries, in large part reflecting commodity-sector developments.

Following broader trends, total FDI to developing countries, which tends to be a more stable form of capital flow, amounted to approximately $653 billion in gross terms in 2017, with FDI to LDCs estimated to be around $32.6 billion (or around 2 per cent of total global FDI flows). However, it remains heavily concentrated in a few countries and in the extractive industries, often providing few forward and backward productive linkages within the economy.[7]

Portfolio flows, primarily from institutional investors, remain volatile. Net inflows to most regions were positive in 2017. Overall, however, there was a net outflow from developing countries of $124 billion in 2017, mainly driven by large outflows from East and South Asia.[8] Risks of monetary tightening in some developed economies, after several years of near-zero or negative interest rates, could lead to further volatility and outflows of portfolio capital, which could derail SDG investment. Indeed, an analysis of high-frequency data of capital flows in select developing countries has shown that cross-border portfolio and bank flows, in particular, are subject to periodic episodes of high volatility.[9]

Figure 1

Private flows to low- and middle-income countries 2012–2016
(Percentage of total external flows, 2015 prices)

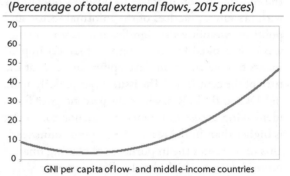

Source: UN/DESA, based on OECD (forthcoming).

Overall, as shown in figure 1, private capital inflows represent up to 50 per cent of cross-border capital flows in upper-middle-income countries, but only 5 to 10 per cent of capital inflows in LDCs and other countries with lower per capita incomes. Thus, challenges for implementation of the agenda include how to incentivize greater investment, and how to ensure that it is long-term, aligned with sustainable development, and reaches those most in need.

6   *World Economic Situation and Prospects 2018* (United Nations publication, Sales No. E.18.II.C.2); World Bank, "Global Economic Prospects" (January 2018).

7   United Nations Conference on Trade and Development (UNCTAD), "Global FDI Flows Slipped Further in 2017", Investment Trends Monitor, Issue 28 (January 2018). Available from http://unctad.org/en/PublicationsLibrary/diaeia2018d1_en.pdf.

8   United Nations Department of Economic and Social Affairs, based on the International Monetary Fund World Economic Outlook (October 2017).

9   *World Economic Situation and Prospects 2017* (United Nations publication, Sales No. E.17.II.C.2).

3   The investment climate and the domestic enabling environment

The 2002 Monterrey Consensus, 2009 Doha Declaration and 2015 Addis Agenda[10] include a range of commitments on strengthening the enabling environment for private sector business and investment in developing countries. Many countries have made important strides in this area, including reforms to the legal framework, promoting transparency, and reducing red tape. These improvements are reflected in the cost of starting a business, which has fallen by more than 80 per cent on average in LDCs since 2002.[11]

However, the gap between developed and many developing countries remains significant. Recent surveys show that access to finance is now the most common obstacle to business operations, with tax rates, practices of the informal sector, and political instability also significant (access to finance was only ranked fourth in terms of largest impediments to investment in developing countries at the turn of the century).[12] The issue is particularly acute in LDCs and LLDCs, where the percentage of firms identifying access to finance as a major constraint is higher than in the rest of developing countries.[13] This underscores the importance of making finance more inclusive, which should allow domestic SMEs to develop (see section 5 on inclusive finance.)

The Organization for Economic Cooperation and Development (OECD) *Policy Framework for Investment* (PFI), which was updated in 2015, aims to support governments in creating an enabling environment for investment. The PFI encourages policymakers to ask appropriate questions about their economy, their institutions and their policy settings on twelve different policy areas affecting the investment climate. The PFI has been used worldwide, including within regional economic communities (such as the Association of Southeast Asian Nations and the Southern African Development Community).[14]

Other issues often highlighted by investors include the lack of investible projects, particularly in infrastructure. This calls for the development of infrastructure plans, efforts to translate plans into pipelines and pipelines into concrete projects. (This year's Task Force report considers these issues in more detail in chapter II). Again, this is particularly relevant in LDCs and LLDCs where inadequate physical infrastructure and remoteness from world markets is a major obstacle to private investment. Improved infrastructure, combined with sound investment promotion and facilitation policies, should attract more foreign investments into these countries. Continued support to LDCs and LLDCs in these areas is therefore crucial.

Foreign investors tend to highlight domestic risks more than local investors. This has led to a discussion of risk perception vs. actual risks, with some analysts arguing that foreign investors overstate domestic risks. An alternative explanation, however, is that foreign investors lack the ability to analyse intricate political and other risks, such as currency risks, across developing countries. The two notions are thus difficult to untangle since risk

10   *Report of the International Conference on Financing for Development, Monterrey, Mexico, 18-22 March 2002* (United Nations publication, Sales No. E.02. II.A.7), para. 21; United Nations, "Doha Declaration on Financing for Development: outcome document of the Follow-up International Conference on Financing for Development to Review the Implementation of the Monterrey Consensus" (New York, 2009), para. 25; *Addis Ababa Action Agenda of the Third International Conference on Financing for Development (Addis Ababa Action Agenda)* (United Nations publication, Sales. E.16.I.7), para. 36.

11   World Bank, Doing Business database. Available from https://tcdata360.worldbank.org/indicators/cost.start.biz?indicator=460&viz=line_chart&years=2003,2016.

12   Guy P. Pfeffermann and Gregory Kisunko, "Perceived Obstacles to Doing Business: Worldwide Survey Results" (July 1999). Available from http://documents.worldbank.org/curated/en/316911468762620790/pdf/302400Precei ve1IFC0discussion0paper.pdf.

13   The percentage is about 35 per cent in LDCs and 29 per cent in LLDCs, while it is 24 per cent in other developing countries. See http://www.enterprisesurveys.org.

14   For further information, see http://www.oecd.org/investment/pfi.htm and http://www.oecd.org/investment/countryreviews.htm.

and uncertainty are integrally linked. In addition to greater efforts to reduce domestic risks, partnerships between foreign and domestic investors—along with multilateral, regional and domestic development banks and DFIs knowledgeable about the local context—can help address the difference in risk perceptions.

In this regard, national, regional and global development banks can play an instrumental role in mobilizing private capital for specific projects through co-financing, providing risk guarantees and other instruments. They can also use their experience to improve the quality of projects through technical assistance while ensuring that investments are aligned with sustainable development. However, when project risks are too high, the cost of bringing the private sector might become prohibitive. This may explain why the current level of blending instruments in LDCs remains limited (see chapter III. C). More analysis is therefore required to design financial instruments that respond to the unique situation of countries with special needs.

Multilateral development banks can also play a role in advancing the development of domestic capital markets, especially local currency bond markets. Well-developed bond markets can increase access to long-term finance and reduce excessive reliance on foreign debt in both middle-income countries and LDCs. In 2017, the World Bank Group established its Joint Capital Markets Program (J-CAP) initiative, which seeks to further capital market development through advisory and analytical work, structuring and delivering of key financial transactions, and knowledge dissemination.

4. Aligning the global financial system with long-term investment for sustainable development

Aligning investment with long-term sustainable development will require actions, by both private and public actors. This will necessitate reorienting global financial markets through better aligning incentives along the investment chain (as shown in box 1) with long-term sustainable investment.

4.1 Incentivizing greater long-term investment by financial intermediaries

Institutional investors with long-term liabilities, such as pension funds, life insurance, endowments and sovereign wealth funds, have been looked to as a potential source of SDG financing. Infrastructure investment should be particularly attractive to these investors because of its low risk and stable real-return profile, which matches their real liabilities (e.g., many pension funds pay beneficiaries a return over inflation).[15]

Long-term institutional investors are estimated to hold around $80 trillion in assets.[16] However, the potential size of their portfolios that are well-suited for illiquid investments, such as infrastructure, is significantly less than the headline number. For example, in the case of pension funds, around 40 per cent of liabilities are distributed within 10 years, and 60 per cent within 20 years.[17] In addition, the shift over the last two decades from defined benefits to defined contributions has allowed individuals to more easily draw down their pensions and switch between providers, making it more difficult for pension funds to

15   Since short-term investors that need liquidity are often willing to pay a higher price for liquid assets, long-term investments generally earn a "liquidity premium".

16   Willis Towers Watson, "The Global Pension Assets Study 2017" (2017). Available from https://www.willistowerswatson.com/en/insights/2017/01/global-pensions-asset-study-2017; PwC, "The Rising Attractiveness of Alternative Asset Classes for Sovereign Wealth Funds" (2018). Available from https://www.pwc.lu/en/alternative-investments/docs/pwc-sovereign-wealth-funds.pdf; PwC, "Asset & Wealth Management Insights: Asset Management 2020 Taking Stock" (2017). Available from https://www.pwc.com/gx/en/asset-management/asset-management-insights/assets/am-insights-june-2017.pdf.

17   United Nations Task Team (UNTT), "Challenges in Raising Private Sector Resources for Financing Sustainable Development", *UNTT Working Group on Sustainable Development Financing* (2014). Available from https://sustainabledevelopment.un.org/content/documents/2106UNTT%20Chapter%20III.pdf.

Box 1

A flow-of-funds analysis

An integrated assessment of the possibilities and impediments to mobilizing long-term investment for sustainable development can be undertaken through a flow-of-funds framework from sources of funds to uses and outcome (see figure 1.1).

The journey from one end to the other end is, however, far from straightforward. Funds can flow through different routes (e.g., directly to companies or through financial intermediaries, such as institutional investors of financial institutions) and investment outcomes create new savings, leading to another round of what is, in effect, a cycle. There is also the possibility for money to circulate in both directions, creating churning in the system. Some asset owners also invest through secondary financial intermediaries (such as a pension fund investing through a money manager). The result is a chain of intermediaries; while the ultimate beneficiaries (e.g., pensioners) may have a long-term outlook, the intermediaries often have progressively shorter-term incentives that are ultimately not aligned with the owners of capital.

Finally, there is a range of other actors, such as investment consultants, rating agencies, brokers, and regulators that help guide investment decisions and set incentives within the system. The incentives and impediments faced by all the actors in the financial chain will determine the magnitude, time horizon and quality of investment, with implications for incomes, employment, and social and environmental outcomes.

Source: UN/DESA.

Figure 1.1

A flow-of-funds framework

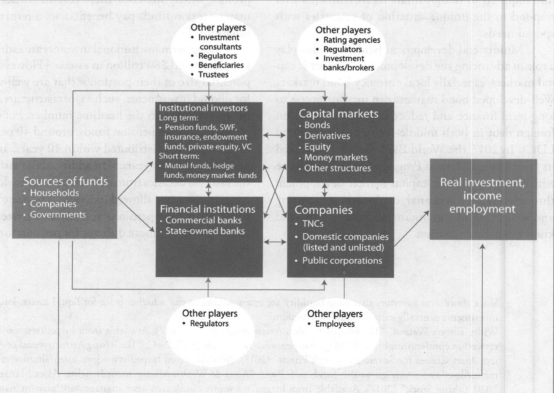

Source: UN/DESA.

Note: TNCs stands for transnational corporations, SWF for sovereign wealth fund, and VC for venture capital.

undertake long-term illiquid investments. Overall, in this context, total long-term liabilities are closer to $40 trillion than $80 trillion. Nonetheless, a reallocation of a small percentage of assets, say 3 to 5 per cent, towards long-term investment in sustainable development could have an enormous impact. Yet, even this relatively small shift will be extremely challenging as the incentives of asset managers and other financial intermediaries are not sufficiently aligned with long-term investment in sustainable development.

To date, much of the investment by institutional investors has been short-term oriented, as reflected in the volatility of capital flows as well as the short holding period of stocks in some developed markets, which has fallen from an average of eight years in the 1960s to eight months today.[18] In addition, as shown in figure 2, the majority of pension and insurance assets are primarily invested in liquid assets, such as listed equities and bonds in developed

countries. While investment in "other" assets (generally, illiquid investments, such as real estate, hedge funds and private equity) increased somewhat over the past decade, investment in infrastructure still represents less than 3 per cent of pension fund assets, with the majority in advanced economies.

Commercial banks have traditionally been an important source of infrastructure project finance, including in developing countries where long-term bond markets tend to be less developed. However, commercial banks have been scaling back infrastructure finance since the global financial and economic crisis. In addition to regulatory requirements, banks tend to have shorter- to medium-term liabilities, and there is evidence that the decline in infrastructure finance represents a shift in the banks' business model towards strengthening risk management.[19]

There are a range of factors that constrain the ability and willingness of investors with longer-term liabilities to invest in illiquid assets:

Figure 2
Pension fund asset allocation as an aggregate of the seven largest pension markets, 2009–2016
(Percentage)

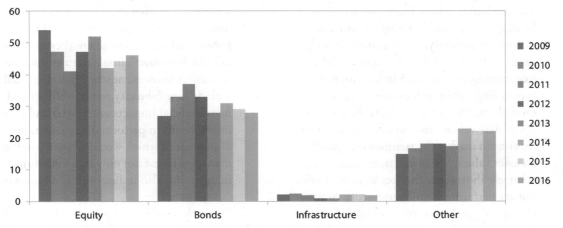

Source: Willis Towers Watson Global Pension Assets Study, Willis Towers Watson Global Alternatives Survey and UN/DESA calculations.
Note: "Other" includes investment in private equity fund of funds, direct hedge funds, direct private equity funds, funds of hedge funds, and illiquid credit. The seven largest pension markets are Australia, Canada, Japan, Netherlands, Switzerland, the United Kingdom of Great Britain and Northern Ireland and the United States of America.

18   Ned Davis Research, White paper series (July 2017). Available from https://www.mfs.com/content/en_us/mfs-insights/lengthening-the-investment-time-horizon.html.

19   Inter-agency Task Force Expert Meeting on Financial and Corporate Incentives for Long-Term Investment (United Nations Headquarters, New York, 15 December 2017). See https://developmentfinance.un.org/expert-meeting-financial-and-corporate-incentives-long-term-investment.

- **Prudential regulations and capital requirements**. Solvency II for European Union insurance companies and Basel III for commercial banks impose higher costs for riskier holdings based on maturity and credit ratings, which may have the unintended consequence of impacting investment incentives (see chapter III.F). Institutional investors also often have regulatory limits based on the asset class characteristics (e.g., unlisted securities) or credit rating of their investments. For example, these limits may inhibit their activities in developing countries regarding sub-investment grade assets or their investments in illiquid assets, such as unlisted infrastructure companies.

- **Insufficient capacity.** Another impediment is that many institutional investors do not have the capacity to do the necessary due diligence to invest directly in infrastructure and other illiquid assets. Other than possibly for the largest asset owners it is generally not cost effective for diversified investors to build this expertise in-house. Instead, they make investments through secondary financial intermediaries, whose incentives tend to be shorter-term and less aligned with the ultimate beneficiary, such as through hedge funds, real estate or private equity funds.

- **Accounting measures.** Mark-to-market accounting, which values assets based on daily market prices, reflects the most up-to-date valuations, but also incorporates short-term market fluctuations into portfolio asset values. These practices mean that relatively short-term changes in market prices impact performance measurements. Since managers' compensation is often tied to performance, these standards can institutionalize a short-term bias.

- **Benchmarks.** Many external investment managers are judged on their performance against benchmarks, which are calculated using mark-to-market pricing. This has been shown to lead to a short-term bias and increased herding behaviour.[20] In response, efforts have been made to develop long-term indexes, like the S&P Long-Term Value Creation Global Index, which is designed to measure stocks that rank high in global equity markets, using both proprietary sustainability and financial quality criteria. How effectively this can substitute for existing shorter-term benchmarks is not yet clear.

- **Compensation.** Compensation tied to short-term performance measures and benchmarks can incentivize short-term investment outlooks. The fee structure of some managers (a 2 per cent management fee and 20 per cent performance fee, which is typical in private equity and hedge fund investment) is characterized by asymmetric returns—meaning that managers have a potential upside monetary gain but no downside penalty when losses are realized. This asymmetry provides managers with incentives to increase risk and leverage to boost short-term returns.

- **Institutional issues and firm culture**. Other factors include high mobility of portfolio managers between firms, which may represent a further disincentive to long-term investing, as managers can earn a high bonus, and then move to another firm before tail risk has materialized. Firm culture can also affect investment strategies. This could include how fiduciary responsibilities and non-financial impacts are viewed and taken into account in performance evaluations of managers, which would impact whether managers invest not only in a long-term manner, but also in line with ESG impacts.

One way to address the issue of limits on illiquid investments is to try to repackage investment in a liquid form for investors, such as through green bonds or SDG bonds (see box 2). This is behind the call to develop infrastructure as an "asset class." The expectation is that standardizing infrastructure as an asset class and creating a benchmark of performance would create liquidity and attract greater investment,

20   International Monetary Fund, *Global Financial Stability Report: Market Developments and Issues* (2005). Available from http://www.imf.org/External/Pubs/FT/GFSR/2005/02/.

Box 2
Innovative bonds instruments

Green bonds, and other innovative bond instruments, such as Sustainable Development Goals (SDG)-linked bonds,[a] have increased substantially since the first green bonds were issued by the European Investment Bank and World Bank in 2007 and 2008, respectively. More recently, the World Bank issued an SDG-bond in 2017, with returns linked to the stock market performance of companies considered to be sustainability leaders,[b] while the Seychelles are planning to issue a blue bond to support the transition to sustainable fishing, with guarantees from the World Bank and the Global Environment Facility. Credit-rating agencies are in the process of developing green bond evaluations tools.[c]

From 2007 to 2013, multinational development banks issued the bulk of green bonds (above 70 per cent); however corporate bonds have made up the bulk of the market since 2015. Global green bond issuance was $155.5 billion in 2017,[d] at about 3 per cent of the global bond market,[e] with Chinese renminbi the third-most important currency of green bond issuance.

Although data is limited, to date, green bonds do not appear to lower the cost of finance for issuers[e] compared to conventional bonds.[f] One issue that impedes growth of the market is the lack of a clear definition of what type of projects would qualify as green bonds. There are several existing principles and standards to determine whether a bond qualifies as green,[g] although these do not have a legal basis and often do not clearly distinguish between conventional bonds and green bonds, or their level of greenness. Proceeds that are currently classified as green include renewable energy, energy efficiency, sustainable waste management, sustainable land use (forestry and agriculture), biodiversity, clean transportation, and clean water. More controversially, green can also include nuclear energy or fossil fuel power plants with decreased carbon intensity. This fragmentation of standards creates uncertainty for investors; there is thus a need to harmonize standards to further develop the market, bringing together multilateral development banks,[h] as well as other stakeholders and and the private sector. Carbon pricing and other efforts to value externalities would also support the market by creating demand and lowering the cost of financing through green bonds.

Source: UN/DESA.

a United Nations Development Programme (UNDP), "The Pros and Cons of Ethical Debt Instruments", 12 September 2017. Available from http://www.undp.org/content/undp/en/home/blog/2017/9/12/The-pros-and-cons-of-ethical-debt-instruments.html.

b Returns are linked to the "Solactive SDG World Index," which includes 50 companies considered leaders on sustainability, or that dedicate at least 20 per cent of their activities to sustainable products.

c S&P Global, "Updated Proposal for a Green Bond Evaluation" (2016). Available from https://www.spglobal.com/our-insights/Proposal-For-A-Green-Bond-Evaluation-Tool.html.

d See https://www.climatebonds.net/.

e Climate Bonds Initiative, Global Green Bonds Mid-Year Summary 2017. Available from https://www.climatebonds.net/files/files/Global_Green_Bonds_S1_Summary-2017.pdf.

f International Finance Corporation (IFC). *Green Bond Pricing in the Primary Market*, January 2016 - March 2017 (2017). Available from https://www.climatebonds.net/files/files/CBI-Green%20Bond%20Pricing%20Report_Jan16-Mar17_040817.pdf.

g The fact that prices of green bonds tend to rise in the first days after they are issued has been pointed to as evidence of outperformance. However, the same patterns emerge with conventional bonds.

h See https://www.icmagroup.org/green-social-and-sustainability-bonds/.;See https://www.climatebonds.net/standards.; High-Level Expert Group on Sustainable Finance, Financing A Sustainable European Economy (Belgium, 2018). Available from https://ec.europa.eu/info/publications/180131-sustainable-finance-report_en.; EIB and China Society for Finance and Banking "The Need for a Common Language in Green Finance", (2018). Available from http://www.eib.org/attachments/press/white-paper-green-finance-common-language-eib-and-green-finance-committee.pdf.

particularly by investors who are constrained from buying illiquid assets. Developing this asset class has to be done with care, as it is creating liquid instruments on illiquid assets. This could attract investors with short-term investment horizons, with the potential of creating short-term bubbles that could impede rather than help long-term sustainable development. Indeed, many of the financial market crises over the past 25 years involved some form of mis-pricing of liquidity.

4.2   Aligning investment by financial intermediaries with the SDGs

Aligning investments with the SDGs includes several facets. To the extent that private investment creates decent jobs, it already contributes to the SDGs. To the extent that it includes investment in sustainable productive capacity and sustainable and resilient infrastructure it also contributes to the SDGs. However, while the investment industry has traditionally focused on creating economic value, a short-term investment horizon implies that investors may not be giving adequate attention to long-term risks, and may overlook the long-term value of ESG practices. SDG investing implies a shift to long-term investment horizons, with sustainability at its core.

One approach to promoting alignment of investment with SDGs is through encouraging investors to carry our environmental and social due diligence with respect to their investment portfolios as is recommended under the United Nations Guiding Principles for Business and Human Rights and the OECD Guidelines for Multinational Enterprises. Strong due diligence processes can help ensure that negative impacts of investments on society and the environment are avoided, and furthermore that investments are channelled towards projects and companies that behave responsibly and ultimately help achieve the objectives of the SDGs.[21]

Growing interest in sustainable investments

There has also been growing interest in sustainable investing. A recent survey of 22,000 investors in 30 countries, found that sustainability investing is more important to 78 per cent of respondents than it was five years ago.[22] Other surveys have found that nearly two thirds of respondents between the ages of 18 and 34 said they would like their money to support companies that are making a positive contribution to society,[23] with more than 80 per cent of millennials and more than 75 per cent of women interested in ESG investing.[24]

An increasing number of asset managers and owners have also committed to integrating ESG criteria in their capital allocation process. In a recent survey of institutional investors globally, 67 per cent use ESG principles as part of their investment approach.[25] This is reflected in the increasing number of asset owners who are signatories to the Principles for Responsible Investing (PRI)—principles that include incorporating ESG into investment analysis, decision-making and practices, as well as disclosure and reporting—and who hold a total of $16.3 trillion in assets under management as of 2017.[26]

For most PRI signatories, ESG criteria are generally incorporated as additional factors in the investment evaluation to the extent that they have a material impact on financial returns, or as an overlay to investment decisions when all else is equal, along with some ESG screens by some investors. In other words, the objective of most PRI signatories is to maximize commercial returns.

21   Organization for Economic Cooperation and Development (OECD), "Responsible Business Conduct for Institutional Investors" (2017). Available from http://mneguidelines.oecd.org/RBC-for-Institutional-Investors.pdf.

22   Schroders, "Global Investor Study 2017: Sustainable investing on the rise" (28 September 2017). Available from http://schroders.com/en/media-relations/newsroom/all_news_releases/schroders-global-investor-study-2017-sustainable-investing-on-the-rise/.

23   Legg Mason, "Decoding Investor Behaviour: Bridging the disconnect between hope and reality", Global Investment Survey" (2017). Available from http://www.leggmason.com.hk/en/gis/.

24   Morningstar, "Sustainable Investing Takes Off: A new generation of investors wants strategies that deliver performance and peace of mind" (2016). Available from Morningstar-Mag_ESG_decjan16_.pdf.

25   Royal Bank of Canada (31 October 2017). Available from http://www.rbc.com/newsroom/news/2017/20171031-gam-esg.html.

26   The data presented is for asset owners (i.e., pension funds, etc.) Assets under management for managers and other financial service providers who are signatories to PRI reached $68.4 trillion.

Figure 3

Asset owner signatories to the Principles for Responsible Investing, 2006–2017
(Trillions of United States dollars, number of asset owners)

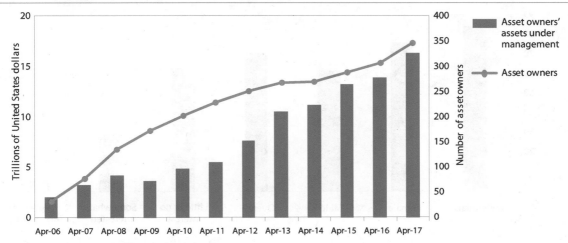

Source: Principles for Responsible Investment (2018).

A smaller but growing class of investors—so-called impact investors,[27] who hold assets under management of around $22 billion[28]—have the intention to generate ESG impacts alongside financial returns in their decision-making process. Impact investing includes a range of investors, from philanthropists—whose financial return objective might be to earn only sufficient economic return to conserve their capital base—to investors who expect market-risk-adjusted returns alongside ESG impact.[29]

At the same time, a growing community of financiers and investors are embedding impact analysis (positive and negative) into mainstream financial products and services. This impact-based approach is seen as a way to build new profitable markets while also addressing the SDGs financing gap. In January 2017, a group of bankers and investors under the United Nations Environment Programme Finance Initiative's launched the "Principles for Positive Impact Finance," a framework to help banks, investors and their stakeholders transition to impact-based approaches and become significant players in the delivery of the SDGs.[30]

Trade-off between financial returns and other impacts?

The fact that many investors who consider ESG criteria do continue to pursue competitive financial returns raises the question of whether there are trade-offs between financial return and other impacts, or whether they are mutually supportive. While studies that test the relationship between returns and ESG factors have a range of results, the bulk of analyses indicates that many ESG strategies may boost returns and reduce risk or, at worst, do not have a negative impact.[31]

Yet, in a recent survey of investor managers, around three quarters of those interviewed either doubted or were unsure of how well ESG investing

27 Organization for Economic Cooperation and Development, *Social Impact Investment: Building the Evidence Base* (2015). Available from http://www.oecd.org/publications/social-impact-investment-9789264233430-en.htm.

28 *Global Intermediary Identification Number* (GIIN), "Annual Impact Investor Survey" (2017). Available from https://thegiin.org/assets/GIIN_AnnualImpactInvestorSurvey_2017_Web_Final.pdf.

29 *Global Intermediary Identification Number* (GIIN) (2018). Available from https://thegiin.org/impact-investing/need-to-know/#what-is-impact-investing.

30 See http://www.unepfi.org/positive-impact/positive-impact/.

31 Gunnar Friede, Timo Busch and Alexander Bassen, "ESG and Financial Performance: aggregated evidence from more than 2000 empirical studies", *Journal of Sustainable Finance & Investment* (2015). Available from http://www.tandfonline.com/doi/pdf/10.1080/20430795.2015.1118917.e.

Figure 4

People interested in environmental, social and governance investing, 2016
(Percentage of survey participants)

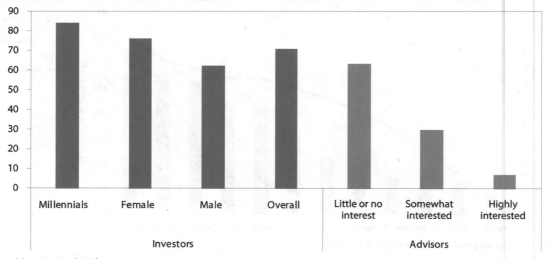

Source: Morningstar (2016).

performs.[32] Similarly, according to surveys, investment brokers and advisors are also more skeptical of the benefits of ESG than their clients.

This raises a second question: if the relationship between ESG investing and returns is positive, why do so few financial professionals have a high interest in ESG investing? (See, for example, figure 4). If such a relationship was confirmed, portfolio managers should in theory be the first ones to be interested in ESG investing. On the other hand, traditional portfolio theory also argues that by investing only in socially responsible opportunities, managers are limiting the opportunity set, and thus unlikely to earn a competitive market return. Indeed, earlier ESG strategies based on excluding "sin" stocks tended to underperform against purely profit-oriented investments.[33]

There is therefore a need to evaluate existing studies to better understand this relationship. A recent study isolated those ESG factors with material impacts on profits from those without material impacts, and found that incorporating investments with material impacts led to significant portfolio outperformance.[34] In essence, the study found that—not surprisingly—incorporating long-term non-financial risks in decision-making (such as climate risks), leads to long-term financial outperformance.

Clarifying definitions

Another impediment to mainstreaming SDG investing is the lack of clear definitions on investment criteria as well as the lack of adequate measurement and reporting mechanisms. It is unclear how officially defined SDG targets translate into private investment criteria, and there is no clear set of rules for ESG disclosures (see box 3), which makes reporting, benchmarking, and comparing studies on the impact of such investing on returns difficult. Improving ESG standards and clarifying factors behind long-term outperformance should drive more investors towards sustainable investments.

32   Royal Bank of Canada, *Responsible investing grows even as opinions remain divided, RBC Global Asset Management Survey*, 31 October 2017. Available from http://www.rbc.com/newsroom/news/2017/20171031-gam-esg.html.

33   CNBC, "How to win in Socially Responsible Investing don't exclude bad stocks", 16 June 2017. Available from https://www.cnbc.com/2017/06/16/how-to-win-in-socially-responsible-investing-dont-exclude-bad-stocks.html.

34   Mozaffar Khan, George Serafeim & Aaron Yoon, "Corporate Sustainability: First Evidence on Materiality", (9 November 2016), The Accounting Review, Vol. 91, No. 6, pp. 1697–1724.

Fiduciary duties

Long-term institutional investors, such as pension funds, are bound by fiduciary duty to focus on benefits to their participants and beneficiaries. There is no clear agreement on what "benefits" entails, although in most cases it is interpreted to mean purely financial impacts. Some countries, such as South Africa, have introduced regulation that incorporates ESG impacts that affect material long-term financial performance into fiduciary duty. The United States of America updated their regulations in 2015, after the adoption of the Addis Agenda, to state that material ESG considerations should be a component of a fiduciary's analysis. ESG factors can also be "tiebreakers" between investments with similar risk-return characteristics, although fiduciaries are not allowed to accept a lower expected return for ESG impact.[35]

Nonetheless, to the extent that fiduciary duty is to focus on benefits, and to the extent that ESG factors are material, one could argue that failing to consider long-term ESG value drivers in portfolio decision-making would be a failure of fiduciary duty. A further step would be to at least allow benefits to be defined more broadly, if so desired by the plan beneficiaries, although this would require managers to have a greater understanding of beneficiary preferences.

4.3   Other actors' role in the investment chain

Additional actors across the investment chain play a role in streamlining sustainability in investment strategies. These actors include investment consultants, advisors, brokers and credit-rating agencies (CRAs) among others. Investment consultants provide advisory services to asset owners, and often shape investment decisions. To date, consultants do not systematically include ESG considerations in their investment recommendations, even when such factors are material to financial performance.[36] CRAs also provide information that guides investments. However, the time horizon for ratings is relatively short—between 2 and 5 years for corporate debt[37]—and often tend to be procyclical. This means that they also help institutionalize a shorter-term outlook. CRAs are increasingly factoring material ESG risks into their analysis, although this is not done systematically. A longer-term outlook should complement their assessment as sustainability considerations impact long-term performance. Sustainability-rating agencies could also play a complementary role as they give ratings on company ESG performance, although scope and coverage vary widely.[38]

Sell-side analysts, brokers and advisors of high net worth individuals also consider impact investments. As noted above, investment advisors are sceptical of ESG performance. Similarly, a recent study by Aviva Investors finds that sell-side analysts are not encouraged to produce long-term and ESG-oriented research, due in part to the perception that investors do not require such research and to fears of jeopardizing the commercial relationship between investment banks and the corporates they are analysing.[39]

Stock exchanges also increasingly include ESG considerations as part of their listing requirements,

35   Employee Benefits Security Administration, "Interpretive Bulletin Relating to the Fiduciary Standard Under ERISA in Considering Economically Targeted Investments", Department of Labor (2015). Available from https://www.federalregister.gov/documents/2015/10/26/2015-27146/interpretive-bulletin-relating-to-the-fiduciary-standard-under-erisa-in-considering-economically.

36   European Union High-Level Expert Group on Sustainable Finance, *Financing a Sustainable European Economy* (2018). Available from https://ec.europa.eu/info/sites/info/files/180131-sustainable-finance-final-report_en.pdf.

37   *United Nations Environment Programme*, "Shifting Perceptions: ESG, Credit Risk and Ratings – Part 1: The State of Play" (2017). Available from http://unepinquiry.org/publication/shifting-perceptions-esg-credit-risk-and-ratings-part-1-the-state-of-play/.

38   Harvard Law School Forum on Corporate Governance and Financial Regulation, "ESG Reports and Ratings: What They Are, Why They Matter" (2017). Available from https://corpgov.law.harvard.edu/2017/07/27/esg-reports-and-ratings-what-they-are-why-they-matter/.

39   Aviva Investors, *Aviva Investors Investment Research: Time for a Brave New World?* (2017). Available from https://www.avivainvestors.com/content/dam/aviva-investors/united-kingdom/documents/institutional/research-brave-new-world.pdf.

usually on a "comply-or-explain" basis. Sixty-eight exchanges have signed up to the Sustainable Stock Exchanges Initiative and the stock exchanges that provide sustainability information and do well in terms of disclosure tend to be found in jurisdictions that have regulatory guidance on sustainability disclosure.[40]

The Addis Agenda called for mainstreaming sustainable development considerations across regulatory and norm-setting bodies. SDG incentives can also be incorporated into regulatory frameworks on a national level. For example, the Central Bank of Brazil focuses on socio-environmental risk management flows as part of its core functions as a prudential bank regulator; the Bangladesh Bank supports rural enterprises and green finance; and the Bank of England has a prudential review of climate risks for the insurance sector of the United Kingdom of Great Britain and Northern Ireland, based on a connection between its core prudential duties and the United Kingdom Climate Change Act.[41]

Climate risk assessment

Policymakers have an interest in ensuring that the financial system is resilient to all forms of risk. Disclosure of material climate-related financial information is a prerequisite for financial firms to manage and price climate risks appropriately. The Financial Stability Board's (FSB) Task Force on Climate-related Financial Disclosures (TCFD) published recommendations for voluntary climate-related financial disclosures in June 2017. To date, more than 240 companies holding a combined market capitalization of over €5.1 trillion have indicated support

for the recommendations.[42] In addition, the International Monetary Fund (IMF) also analyses the financial stability implications of climate change (see chapter III.F).

4.4 The impact of financial sector incentives on the real economy

Institutional investors also play an important role as shareholders and investors in companies. They have enormous influence in shaping corporate strategy and investment decisions of companies in which they hold equity. There is evidence that short-term pressures from investors are at least partly responsible for inhibiting long-term investment and value-creating behavior by companies. In 2016, S&P 500 companies spent over 100 per cent of their earnings on dividends and share buybacks—which boost stock prices in the short run—rather than raising long-run company value through investments.[43] A *McKinsey Quarterly* survey found that 87 per cent of corporate executives and directors feel pressured to demonstrate strong financial performance within two years or less; 65 per cent say short-term pressure has increased over the past five years;[44] and 55 per cent would delay investments in projects with positive returns to hit quarterly earnings targets.[45]

This short-term focus is due to a combination of factors, including

- Corporate boards, which are often not equipped to evaluate company performance on anything other than short-term results;
- Growing importance of institutional shareholders (see box 4) and pressures from

---

40   See http://www.sseinitiative.org/sse-partner-exchanges/list-of-partner-exchanges/.

41   Business Commission on Sustainable Development, *Ideas for a Long-Term and Sustainable Financial System* (January 2017). Available from http://s3.amazonaws.com/aws-bsdc/BSDC_SustainableFinanceSystem.pdf.

42   See https://www.fsb-tcfd.org/tcfd-supporters-february-2018/.

43   McKinsey, *Elevating the Customer Experience",* Quarterly Survey (2016). Available from https://www.mckinsey.com/~/media/mckinsey/business%20functions/operations/our%20insights/mckinsey%20quarterly%202016%20number%203%20overview%20and%20full%20issue/q3_2016_mckquarterly_full%20issue.ashx.

44   Dominic Barton, Jonathan Bailey, and Joshua Zoffer, "Rising to the Challenge of Short-Termism" (Boston, FCLT Global, 2016). Available from https://www.fcltglobal.org/docs/default-source/default-document-library/fclt-global-rising-to-the-challenge.pdf.; Dominic Barton and others, "Measuring the Economic Impact of Short-Termism", McKinsey Global Institute Discussion Paper (McKinsey & Company, February 2017). Available from https://www.mckinsey.com/~/media/McKinsey/Global%20Themes/Long%20term%20Capitalism/Where%20companies%20with%20a%20long%20term%20view%20outperform%20their%20peers/MGI-Measuring-the-economic-impact-of-short-termism.ashx.

45   McKinsey Quarterly Survey (2016); McKinsey analysis; S&P.

Box 3
Sustainability reporting and benchmarking

Sustainability reporting by companies has grown significantly over the last decade, but has not been even across all regions (see figure 4.1). According to a recent survey of more than 5000 companies, 3 in 4 companies now publish corporate responsibility reports, with 60 per cent of them including some of that information in their financial reports.[a] However, the effectiveness of sustainable reporting is dependent on the quality and clarity of information. In the above study, the majority of institutional investors who employ environmental, social and governance (ESG) criteria across all regions are not satisfied with the disclosure of ESG metrics provided by corporations. Indeed, there is widespread investor confusion—and in some instances frustration—over the wide variety of quality in ESG data.[b]

To institutionalize and facilitate SDG investing, it is important to report on ESG indicators in an open, transparent and comprehensible manner. Both Governments and the private sector can help to address this challenge. In France, for instance, article 173 of the energy transition law (the Act of 17 August 2015) now requires listed companies to disclose their climate-related financial risks along with the measures adopted to reduce them.[c] Similarly, private-led efforts, such as the Financial Stability Board Task Force on Climate-related Financial Disclosures, as well as efforts led by the United Nations Global Compact and the Global Reporting Initiative, are helping set the ground for a new wave of standardized sustainability disclosure. This is particularly important and welcome given the large number (more than 400) of sustainability reporting policy instruments currently in place globally.[d]

Corporate sustainability benchmarks can help investors and other stakeholders use disclosures by translating individual reporting into comparable assessments of the degree to which corporate performance is aligned with the SDGs. This would also help address the proliferation of competing reporting guidelines for businesses and the lack of standardization of sustainability metrics. In this regard, the World Benchmarking Alliance, which would develop, fund, house and safeguard free, publicly available, corporate sustainability benchmarks,[e] is being established to rank companies on their performance across a range of SDG-related indicators such as climate change, gender, access to health care. Such indicators and benchmarks would provide investors, including institutional investors and their beneficiaries and trustees, with transparent information that justifies investments in companies that operate in a sustainable manner. If large institutional investors use these in their investment decision-making, it could put pressure on more companies to improve their standing in the benchmarks by better aligning their business activity with sustainable development. The league tables will also help individuals make more sustainable investment choices as they are provided with transparency that usually sits behind a pay wall.

Figure 4.1
Regional distribution of Global Reporting Initiative Sustainability Reports (G4), 2013–2017
(Percentage of reports)

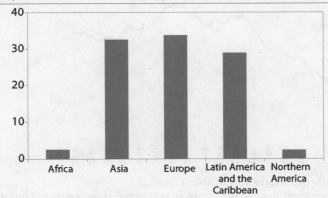

Source: GRI Sustainability Disclosure database (2018).
Note: Data reported according to G4 Sustainability Reporting Guidelines. Available from https://www.globalreporting.org/information/g4/Pages/default.aspx.

Source: UN/DESA.

a KPMG, "KPMG Survey of Corporate Responsibility reporting" (2017).

b KPMG, "Carrots & Sticks: Global Trends in Sustainability Reporting Regulation and Policy" (2016). Available from https://
home.kpmg.com/xx/en/home/insights/2016/05/carrots-and-sticks-global-trends-in-sustainability-reporting-regulation-
and-policy.html.

c United Nations Principles for Responsible Investment and others, French Energy Transition Law: Global Investor Briefing
(2016). Available from https://www.unpri.org/download?ac=1421.

d KPMG, "Carrots & Sticks: Global Trends in Sustainability Reporting Regulation and Policy" (2016). Available from https://
home.kpmg.com/xx/en/home/insights/2016/05/carrots-and-sticks-global-trends-in-sustainability-reporting-regulation-
and-policy.html.

e See https://developmentfinance.un.org/private-sector-efforts-and-initiatives-environmental-social-and-governance-fac-
tors.

Box 4
Shift in stock ownership

Increasing pressure from investors corresponds to a shift in stock ownership from household and small investors to institutional investors. In the United States of America, for example, the majority of stocks were held by households in the 1960s, with a minority of equities held by financial market players (including institutional investors); by 2000, this relationship had reversed, with up to 70 per cent of stocks held by institutional investors, either directly or through intermediaries.

Figure 2.1
United States holdings of equities by household and financial institutions, 1965–2016
(*Percentage of total holdings*)

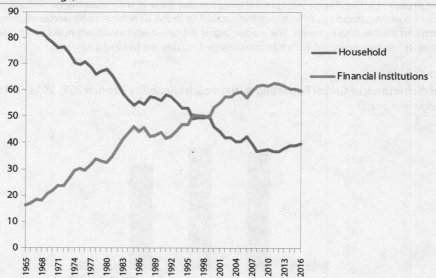

Source: *Financial Accounts of the United States*, Federal Reserve (2018).
Note: "Households" includes non-profit organizations. "Financial institutions" excludes monetary authority.

capital markets, including through quarterly reporting;[46] and

- Management incentives, such as stock options.[47]

Two thirds of respondents in a *McKinsey Quarterly* survey cited corporate boards and executives and one third cited institutional shareholders as the primary source of short-term pressure. Incentivizing institutional investors to have a longer-term horizon that is aligned with sustainable development, and to engage with companies on their long-term and transition agenda, could have the benefit of encouraging longer-term corporate time horizons, and greater long-term corporate investment. In addition, reforms to corporate boards could reduce short-term pressures.

5. Financial inclusion

There is a growing body of evidence that more inclusive financial markets support economic growth and employment and reduce inequalities.[48] In the Addis Agenda, Governments committed to "work to ensure that our policy and regulatory environment supports financial market stability and promotes financial inclusion in a balanced manner, and with appropriate consumer protection".[49] In essence, much of financial inclusion is outside of the regulatory perimeter. The challenge for regulators is to design rules that control risks while still allowing inclusive finance to flourish.

While there has been enormous progress in increasing access to financial services since the start of the millennium, large gaps remain between countries, regions and genders. According to the World Bank's Findex database, 62 per cent of the world's adult population had a bank account in 2014, up from 53 per cent in 2011. While more than 80 per cent of adults in developed countries have accounts, this percentage drops below 50 per cent in developing countries and below 27 per cent in LDCs. In addition, a gender gap in access to finance persists; account ownership among women is about 58 per cent, versus 65 per cent for men.

The reach of financial inclusion is much greater when innovative measures of financial intermediation are included, such as mobile money agents. These instruments are especially prevalent in economies where traditional financial access is relatively scarce.[50] Innovative digital services tools helped 700 million adults worldwide gain access to formal financial services between 2011 and 2014,[51] with the number expected to grow. In sub-Saharan Africa, for example, the number of mobile money accounts has almost reached the level of bank accounts as of 2015 (see figure 5).[52]

Coverage of commercial bank loans, an additional traditional indicator of financial inclusion (figure 6), has also increased over the past decade, although regional differences remain, with coverage in Africa and Oceania particularly low. At the same time, as shown in figure 7, the ease of getting credit has worsened in LDCs, SIDS and LLDCs.

The unmet financing needs of micro, small and medium-sized enterprises (MSMEs), estimated to be $5.2 trillion in developing countries, or 1.4 times the current level of MSME-lending, is a major constraint to private sector development in many countries. Women-owned businesses comprise 28

---

46 FCLT Global, *A Roadmap for Focusing Capital on the Long Term* (Boston, 2015). Available from https://www.fclt-global.org/docs/default-source/default-document-library/a-roadmap-for-fclt.pdf?sfvrsn=0.

47 National Commission on the Causes of the Financial and Economic Crisis in the United States, *The Financial Crisis Inquiry Report* (2011). Available from http://fcic-static.law.stanford.edu/cdn_media/fcic-reports/fcic_final_report_full.pdf.

48 The *Consultative Group to Assist the Poor* (CGAP), "What is the Impact of Financial Inclusion Efforts" (Washington, D.C., 2018). Available from http://www.cgap.org/about/faq/what-impact-financial-inclusion-efforts.

49 Addis Ababa Action Agenda, para. 38. Available from http://www.un.org/esa/ffd/wp-content/uploads/2015/08/AAAA_Outcome.pdf.

50 International Monetary Fund, "Financial Access Survey", 2 October 2017. Available from https://www.imf.org/en/News/Articles/2017/10/02/pr17383-imf-releases-2017-financial-access-survey.

51 World Bank, Global Findex database. Available from http://www.worldbank.org/en/programs/globalfindex.

52 GSMA, *2016 State of Mobile Money in Sub-Saharan Africa* (2017). Available from https://www.gsma.com/mobilefordevelopment/wp-content/uploads/2017/07/2016-The-State-of-Mobile-Money-in-Sub-Saharan-Africa.pdf.

Figure 5
Growth of registered mobile money accounts and deposit bank accounts in sub-Saharan Africa, 2007–2015
(Number of accounts in millions)

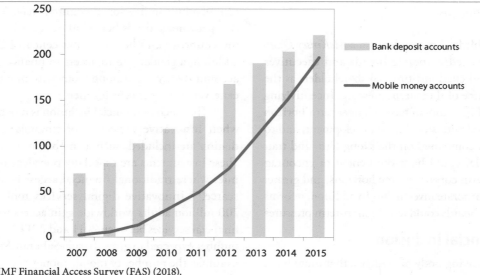

Source: IMF Financial Access Survey (FAS) (2018).

Figure 6
Loan accounts with commercial banks, 2004–2016
(Number of accounts per 1000 adults)

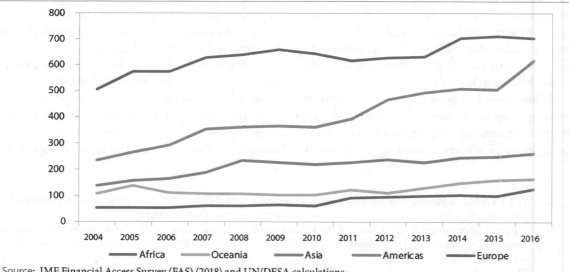

Source: IMF Financial Access Survey (FAS) (2018) and UN/DESA calculations.

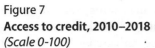

Figure 7
Access to credit, 2010–2018
(Scale 0-100)

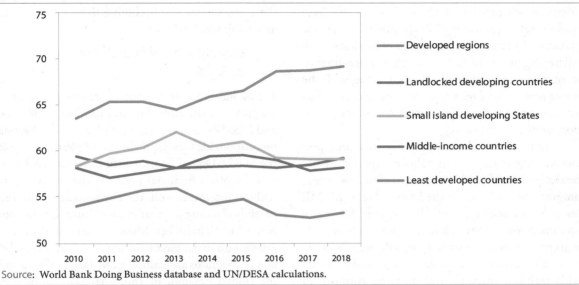

Source: World Bank Doing Business database and UN/DESA calculations.

per cent of MSMEs and account for 32 per cent of the MSME finance gap.[53]

While bank loans represent the main source of finance for MSMEs, commercial banks have traditionally found lending to some MSMEs challenging because of information asymmetry, lack of collateral, and the higher cost of serving smaller transactions.[54] Obtaining credit thus poses particular challenges for MSMEs with high-risk profiles, limited credit history and few pledgeable assets in developing countries, as well as for innovative and high-growth MSMEs in developed countries.[55] Regulation can also impact incentives, and may have unintended consequences on MSME lending. To ease the capital cost associated with SME lending, the Basel Committee on

Banking Supervision revised the risk weighting on loans to SMEs from 100 to 85 per cent in December 2017[56] (see chapter III. F).

Access to diversified financial instruments can increase MSME resilience to changing conditions in credit markets.[57] For instance, leasing, which can enable firms without a credit record or eligible collateral to fund equipment investment, can be of particular interest in developing countries where credit infrastructure is not yet fully established or eligible collateral is still largely restricted to land or real estate. The provision of guarantees has been one of the most widespread government policies to lower costs and improve MSME access to credit.[58] In this regard, blended finance facilities, and national,

53   See http://www.smefinanceforum.org/data-sites/msme-finance-gap.

54   International Finance Corporation, *The SME Banking Knowledge Guide* (Washington, D.C., 2010). Available from https://www.ifc.org/wps/wcm/connect/b4f9be0049585ff9a192b519583b6d16/SMEE.pdf?MOD=AJPERES.

55   International Finance Corporation, *Closing the Credit Gap for Formal and Informal Micro, Small, and Medium Enterprises* (Washington, D.C., 2013). Available from https://www.ifc.org/wps/wcm/connect/4d6e6400416896c0 9494b79e78015671/Closing+the+Credit+Gap+Report-FinalLatest.pdf?MOD=AJPERES.

56   See https://www.bis.org/bcbs/basel3.htm.

57   Organization for Economic Cooperation and Development, "New Approaches to SME and Entrepreneurship Financing: Broadening the Range of Instruments" (Paris, 2015). Available from https://www.oecd.org/cfe/smes/ New-Approaches-SME-full-report.pdf.

58   Organization for Economic Cooperation and Development, *Financing SMEs and Entrepreneurs 2018: An OECD Scoreboard* (Paris, 2018). Available from http://www.oecd.org/cfe/smes/financing-smes-and-entrepreneurs-23065265.htm.

international and multilateral development banks have an important role to play, such as through the World Bank Group's $2.5 billion Private Sector Window[59] (see chapter III.C). Other elements that have worked well in promoting MSME financing in some countries include utilizing a range of institutions in enhancing access to finance (such as microfinance institutions and cooperative banks), along with the use of new technologies (such as mobile money and agent networks) with appropriate consumer protection, as discussed below.

In parallel to these supply-side measures, policies aiming at improving MSME capacity to successfully seek affordable finance include awareness programmes to increase the knowledge of MSME owners and managers of all available financing options. Some countries have put initiatives in place to improve investor readiness, including accelerators or incubators, which provide startups and MSMEs with training (finance and pitching training in particular), as well as mentoring, coaching and networking opportunities.[60] With the increasing digitalization of finance, enhancing financial and digital literacy is also becoming more important to achieving financial inclusion.

5.1 Digitalization of finance and financial inclusion

The digitalization of finance offers new possibilities for greater financial inclusion, including for women and MSMEs, and alignment with the 2030 Agenda for Sustainable Development and implementation of the SDGs. Digital finance or fintech (financial technology) offers financial products directly to users without intermediation, thereby reducing costs and possibly reaching populations without access to commercial bank branches. Mobile money services have grown into major payments services, with over 6 billion transactions annually (e.g., M-Pesa in Kenya and the United Republic of Tanzania, Ecocash in Zim-

---

Box 5
Trends in global private philanthropy for development

The 2030 Agenda for Sustainable Development emphasised private philanthropy's role in advancing the SDGs. The modalities and magnitude of foundations' giving has long been subject to various interpretations, due to limited availability of statistical evidence. Recently, the Organization for Economic Development and Cooperation (OECD) Development Co-operation Directorate (DCD), in collaboration with the OECD Global Network of Foundations Working for Development (NetFWD), carried out a large-scale survey on global private philanthropy for development that collected comparable, activity-level information on developmental activities of over 140 foundations from all over the world for 2013–2015.[a] The survey analyses the sectoral and geographic focus of philanthropic giving and its modalities.

The preliminary survey results show that during 2013–2015, philanthropic giving amounted to $23.8 billion, with an upward trend over the survey period. India was the largest recipient country, resulting particularly from significant giving by the Bill and Melinda Gates Foundation, Tata Trusts and the IKEA Foundation. Whereas Africa was by far the most targeted region, at 28 per cent, the largest share of giving (45 per cent) was global or multi-continental in scope. In terms of sectoral allocation, philanthropic giving predominantly targeted health and reproductive health, which together accounted for 53 per cent of the three-year total, followed by education (9 per cent), agriculture (9 per cent) and government and civil society (8 per cent, including human rights, gender, civil society development and transparency and accountability). The OECD-DCD will continue efforts in 2018 to reach out to the most influential philanthropic foundations for more regular reporting.

  a See http://www.oecd.org/dac/financing-sustainable-development/development-finance-standards/beyond-oda-foundations.htm.

---

59   See http://ida.worldbank.org/financing/ida18-private-sector-window.

60   Organization for Economic Cooperation and Development (OECD), *Towards Effective Approaches to Support Implementation of the G20/OECD High-Level Principles on SME Financing*, OECD Working Party on SMEs and Entrepreneurship" (Paris, 2017); OECD, "Fostering markets for SME finance: Matching business and investor needs", in *Financing SMEs and Entrepreneurs 2017: An OECD Scoreboard* (Paris, 2017). Available from http://www.oecd-ilibrary.org/industry-and-services/financing-smes-and-entrepreneurs-2017/fostering-markets-for-sme-finance-matching-business-and-investor-needs_fin_sme_ent-2017-6-en.

babwe). In Kenya, the expansion of mobile money lifted two per cent of households in the country above the poverty line; the effect of access to mobile banking on consumption has been more significant for female-headed households than for male-headed households, with the use of mobile money helping 185,000 women move from subsistence farming to higher-return business occupations.[61]

In many developing countries, inadequate financial infrastructure, such as private credit bureau and public credit registries, has hampered the expansion of financial inclusion. The increased availability of digital data—whether from digital records of financial transactions, digital records from mobile phone use, or non-individualized big data—can enable providers to lower costs and reach more clients while saving clients time and money.[62] Fintech firms can use data to predict creditworthiness and borrower performance using algorithms based on big data,[63] thus bypassing credit bureaus and other intermediaries and increasing lending.

However, there are risks associated with the rapid advance of digital finance. Consumers who may have relatively lower financial literacy may also have relatively lower digital literacy, and therefore are less able to make sound decisions regarding appropriate financial services. There are a number of new players, particularly fintech providers, and many new products and services and delivery channels that are not currently covered by regulatory frameworks and authorities. If not appropriately regulated, they can pose risks to customers, as well as potentially broader systemic risks. Effective financial regulation has several roles, including (i) monitoring institutional as well as systemic risks, including providing incentives for institutions to take systemic risk into account; (ii) providing consumer protection; and (iii) supporting competition and impeding monopolistic and oligopolistic behaviour.[64]

Through better data and speed, technologies can make risk management more effective, but they also raise new risks or change the nature of risks, such as in data protection and privacy, keeping client funds safe, responsibility of providers across the value chain, and client recourse, among others.[65] Digital channels can change the nature of fraud, with providers and agents also exposed to different risks: throughout several countries in Africa, 10 to 50 per cent of agents have suffered from fraud, which can lead to a loss of consumer confidence.[66] As a result, there is increasing attention to "regtech," that is, using technology for better regulation. In a number of cases, regulators are using "regulatory sandboxes" so as not to hamper innovation while not exposing the broader market to unknown risks. Regulators from around the world—particularly in developing and emerging markets—are collaborating through the Alliance for Financial Inclusion[67] and other mechanisms to share lessons learned, and are continuing to engage with

---

61 Tavneet Suri and William Jack, "The Long-Run Poverty and Gender Impacts of Mobile Money", *Science* Vol. 354, Issue 6317, pp. 1288-1292 (9 December 2016). Available from http://science.sciencemag.org/content/354/6317/1288.full.

62 Gregory Chen and Xavier Faz, "The Potential of Digital Data: How Far Can It Advance Financial Inclusion?", *Focus Note 100* (CGAP, Washington, D.C., 2015). Available from http://www.cgap.org/sites/default/files/Focus-Note-The-Potential-of-Digital-Data-Jan-2015.pdf.

63 International Monetary Fund, "Banking on Change", *Financing & Development*, Vol. 54, No. 3 (September 2017). Available from http://www.imf.org/external/pubs/ft/fandd/2017/09/griffoli.htm; Bank for International Settlements and Financial Stability Board, *Fintech Credit: Market Structure, Business Models and Financial Stability Implications* (Basel, 2017). Available from http://www.fsb.org/wp-content/uploads/CGFS-FSB-Report-on-FinTech-Credit.pdf.

64 International Monetary Fund (2017); Financial Stability Board, *Financial Stability Implications from Fintech: Supervisory and Regulatory Issues that Merit Authorities' Attention* (Basel, 2017). Available from http://www.fsb.org/2017/06/financial-stability-implications-from-fintech/.

65 Better Than Cash Alliance, "Responsible Digital Payments Guidelines", 15 July 2016. Available from https://www.betterthancash.org/tools-research/case-studies/responsible-digital-payments-guidelines.

66 The *Consultative Group to Assist the Poor*, "Fraud in Mobile Financial Services: Protecting Consumers, Providers, and the System" (Washington, D.C., 2017). Available from http://www.cgap.org/sites/default/files/Brief-Fraud-in-Mobile-Financial-Services-April-2017.pdf.

67 See https://www.afi-global.org/.

the global financial standard-setting bodies to ensure that global standards take different country contexts into consideration.

The FSB, IMF and others have reported on financial sector guidance, regulatory policies and supervisory practices to support the stability and integrity of the financial system with the emerging digitalization of finance.[68] Financial system regulation needs to take fintech into consideration. Given its cross-border nature, it is important to ensure that discussions are happening between different national regulatory authorities. Such dialogue is already underway as part of the Financial Inclusion Global Initiative (FIGI), led by International Telecommunications Union, the World Bank Group and the Committee on Payments and Market Infrastructures.[69] Among other objectives, FIGI aims to enable national authorities in developing and emerging markets to better harness the potential of digital technologies for financial inclusion, and to manage associated risks.

5.2   Supporting women entrepreneurship

According to available estimates, approximately one fourth to one third of the world's formal sector enterprises are owned and operated by women. Women entrepreneurs tend to experience far more difficulties than men in starting and expanding their businesses, which can be linked to laws that have a differential impact on men and women—those related to land ownership and inheritance, for example—as well as cultural norms and social attitudes. Data show that women are less likely than men to start businesses and grow their small firms into larger enterprises.[70] Lack of access to finance and financial services is repeatedly identified as the major constraint for women business owners.[71]

In light of this, Governments in both developed and developing countries have introduced policies and programmes to develop women entrepreneurs. For example, in Africa, technical and financial support have been provided to Burkina Faso, Burundi, Liberia, Kenya, Sudan and Swaziland as part of a project to develop business incubators that empower women entrepreneurs. The project will impact more than 50,000 women and youth, according to the New Partnership for Africa's Development (NEPAD). In 2017, the World Bank Group created a new facility, Women Entrepreneurs Finance Initiative (We-Fi), with more than $1 billion to help women in developing countries gain increased access to the finance, markets and networks necessary to start and grow a business. In addition, programmes for women's empowerment that increase cultural acceptance, highlighting female entrepreneurs as role models and raising public awareness, have proved successful.

Another initiative, established by the Women's Empowerment Principles (WEPs), a partnership initiative of UN Women and the United Nations Global Compact, provides a set of considerations for the private sector to focus on to promote gender equality in the workplace, marketplace and community. The WEPS include a range of considerations relating to the establishment of high-level corporate leadership to advance gender equality: fair treatment of all women and men at work; ensuring the health, safety and well-being of all women and men workers; promotion of education, training and professional development for women; and the implementation of enterprise development, supply chain and marketing practices that empower women, among other principles. More than 1,775 business leaders around the world have demonstrated leadership on

68   Financial Stability Board, *Summary Report on Financial Sector Cybersecurity Regulations, Guidance and Supervisory Practices* (Basel, 2017). Available from http://www.fsb.org/wp-content/uploads/P131017-1.pdf.; International Monetary Fund, "International Monetary Fund and Fintech" (Washington, D.C., 2018). Available from http://www.imf.org/en/About/Key-Issues/Fintech.

69   FIGI is a three-year programme initiated in 2017 with support from the Bill and Melinda Gates Foundation.

70   Andre Sammartino and Sarah Gundlach, "Women, Global Trade and What It Takes to Succeed", (Women in Global Business, 2015). Available from https://minervaaccess.unimelb.edu.au/bitstream/handle/11343/145370/FINAL%20WIGB_MLB_Uni_Report_2015.pdf?sequence=5&isAllowed=y.

71   International Finance Corporation, "Solutions to Increase Access to Finance for Women-Owned Businesses in the Middle East and North Africa" (Washington, D.C., 2012). Available from http://www.ifc.org/wps/wcm/connect/156534804f860a72be27fe0098cb14b9/12316-vv-sme-report.pdf?MOD=AJPERES.

gender equality through the WEPs. The work of the United Nations Secretary-General's High-level Panel on Women's Economic Empowerment (WEE) led to the establishment of the Group of Champions for WEE, comprised of 20 Member States that have come together to advance WEE.

5.3 Connecting remittances to fintech and financial inclusion

In 2017, remittance flows to developing countries are projected to have totalled $596 billion,[72] up from $573.6 billion in 2016,[73] following a decline in 2015 and 2016 generally following global growth trends. According to the African Development Bank, remittances have been the largest source of cross-border flows to Africa since 2010, accounting for about a third of total external inflows to Africa. At the same time, the levels of remittances are likely to be higher than reported, as underreporting and flawed estima-

tion methods (particularly around informal flows) prevent an accurate measure.[74]

Remittances have an important impact on growth in recipient economies. Similar to domestic wages, remittances increase the disposable income of households, stimulating consumption with a multiplier effect on the economy. Their impact on savings and investment, and hence on growth, will depend, to a large extent, on financial inclusion.[75] Linking remittance financial flows to beneficiary accounts with financial service providers translates into more formally sent remittances,[76] and enables recipients to store and save their remittances and to leverage them for building entrepreneurial capital.

In 2017, the average cost of sending remittances was around 7.2 per cent.[77] Although there has been a sustained downward trend in the average cost of sending remittances in the last decade, it is still far from the 3 per cent committed to in the Addis

Figure 8

Women-owned and managed companies, by region, 2010–2014

(Percentage of total)

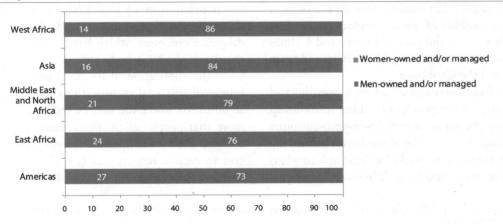

Source: ITC, Unlocking Markets for Women to Trade (2015).

72   World Bank, "Migration and Remittances" Brief No.28 (Washington, D.C., 2017).

73   World Bank, "Migration and Remittances Data" (Washington, D.C., October 2017). Available from http://www. worldbank.org/en/topic/migrationremittancesdiasporaissues/brief/migration-remittances-data.

74   *International Fund for Agricultural Development, Global Forum on Remittances, Investment and Development 2017 Official Report.* Available from https://www.ifad.org/documents/38714170/39135645/GFRID2017_official_report. pdf/a9e52e66-7c93-4217-9896-86099e73afa5.

75   *World Economic Situation and Prospects 2018* (United Nations publication, Sales No E.16.II.C.2)

76   Organization for Economic Cooperation and Development, *Interrelations between Public Policies, Migration and Development* (OECD Publishing, Paris, 17 February 2017). Available from http://dx.doi.org/10.1787/9789264265615-en.

77   World Bank, "Migration and Remittances" Brief No. 28, (Washington, D.C., October 2017).

Agenda and in the means-of-implementation target under SDG 10c. Policymakers can introduce measures to stimulate competition to lower costs and expand access to regulated service providers. Collaboration between sending and recipient countries can be fostered to create cross-border partnerships that influence the market structure and reduce costs. In general, the establishment of operational partnerships among policymakers and regulators, financial industry representatives and technology entrepreneurs, both at national and global levels, would be important in increasing transparency and competition in the remittance market and, subsequently, in bringing down high remittance costs and enhancing financial inclusion.[78]

Correspondent banking is an important means of facilitating cross-border movements of funds, and enables financial institutions to access financial services in different currencies and foreign jurisdictions, thereby supporting remittances flows. The number of worldwide correspondent banking relationships continues to decline, active correspondent relationships declined by 8 per cent across all currencies from 2011 to mid-2017. Regionally, there are increases in the average number of active corridors per country for North America and Eastern Europe and declines in all other regions, including Africa, Asia, and Latin America and the Caribbean.[79]

The fixed costs associated with opening and maintaining a correspondent banking relationship, particularly the application of know-your-customer (KYC) requirements, is one of the drivers behind the decline in the number of relationships, at least when there is not sufficient volume of business to compensate for these costs.[80] Relationships are most affected in smaller countries and jurisdictions for which the compliance with standards for anti-money laundering and combating the financing of terrorism (AML/CFT) is insufficient or unknown. The decline in relationships appears to lead to a greater concentration, where countries and banks rely on fewer correspondent banks, and longer payment chains, which means that an increasing number of intermediaries are involved in processing the same payment.

The FSB has coordinated an action plan to assess and address the decline in correspondent banking, including through domestic capacity-building and strengthening tools for due diligence in correspondent banks.[81] Improving the regulatory alignment across countries — including consistent implementation of AML/CFT and KYC regulations, and encouraging greater collaboration and sharing of information among financial institutions, as called for in the Addis Agenda — could reduce the unintended consequences of regulation on correspondent banking.[82] There are ongoing private sector efforts in this regard. As an example, the Wolfsberg Group (an association of 13 global banks) has created a questionnaire that aims to standardize KYC due diligence processes, which has been welcomed by the standard-setting bodies.[83]

The application of financial technology and improved financial inclusion has the potential to significantly lower the cost of remittances, as the more that people adopt digital channels to transact with the formal financial system, the lower the cost to receive remittances is for them.[84] In particular, Fintech can be used to lower the cost of

78   *International Fund for Agricultural Development, Global Forum on Remittances, Investment and Development 2017 Official Report.*

79   Financial Stability Board, *FSB correspondent banking data report*, updated (Basel, 6 March 2018). Available from http://www.fsb.org/wp-content/uploads/P060318.pdf.

80   Financial Stability Board, *FSB correspondent banking data report* (Basel, 4 July 2017). Available from http://www.fsb.org/2017/07/fsb-correspondent-banking-data-report/.

81   Financial Stability Board, "FSB action plan to assess and address the decline in correspondent banking. Progress report to G20 summit" (Basel, July 2017). Available from http://www.fsb.org/wp-content/uploads/P040717-3.pdf.

82   Financial Action Task Force, *Guidance. Private sector information sharing* (Paris, 2017). Available from http://www.fatf-gafi.org/media/fatf/documents/recommendations/Private-Sector-Information-Sharing.pdf.

83   Financial Stability Board, "BCBS, CPMI, FATF and FSB welcome industry initiative facilitating correspondent banking", 6 March 2018. Available from http://www.fsb.org/2018/03/bcbs-cpmi-fatf-and-fsb-welcome-industry-initiative-facilitating-correspondent-banking/.

84   GSMA, "Mobile money is driving a price revolution in international remittances", 31 October 2016. Available from https://www.gsma.com/mobilefordevelopment/programme/mobile-money/new-gsma-research-shows-that-mobile-money-is-driving-a-price-revolution-in-international-remittances.

cross-border transfers, thereby helping to address the loss of correspondent banking relationships that many developing countries have seen in recent years (see chapter III.D). This could provide a significant boost to developing countries that receive significant remittances from overseas.[85] Innovative solutions as described in box 6, could potentially be replicated on a large scale. [86] Finally, technologies and financial instruments can be used to attract diaspora investments.[87]

Box 6
A remittance mobile wallet in Nepal

Nepal has a high dependence on remittances. As a percentage of gross domestic product, remittances have the broadest reach of any financial flow, especially to the rural areas. In Nepal, the United Nations Capital Development Fund provided technical assistance to the largest remittance service provider in the country, IME Ltd., to launch a remittance mobile wallet, IME Pay. Through IME Pay, IME partnered with its subsidiary IME LIFE Insurance to provide general and life insurance to all remittance recipients at a nominal premium. The insurance is provided as a default opt-in along with the mobile wallet and has led to insurance penetration in an otherwise highly fragmented informal insurance market. Within a month of launch in March 2017, IME Pay was adopted by over 25,000 customers.

Source: UN/DESA.

---

85   International Monetary Fund, "Leveraging Financial Technology for the Underbanked", 19 September 2016. Available from https://www.imf.org/en/News/Articles/2016/09/17/NA091916-Leveraging-financial-Technology-for-the-Underbanked.

86   See http://imeremit.com.np.

87   International Fund for Agricultural Development, *Global Forum on Remittances, Investment and Development 2017 Official Report.*

Chapter III.C
International development cooperation

1. Key messages and recommendations

In response to the vast investment needs associated with the Sustainable Development Goals (SDGs), international public finance has increased since 2015, and efforts continue to increase its quality and effectiveness. Development cooperation is increasingly focused on strengthening developing countries' capacities to mobilize additional public and private resources for sustainable development, in particular by exploring the catalytic role of official development assistance (ODA) and other flows. The challenging geopolitical environment and increasing intensity and frequency of environmental crises is also contributing to a shift towards linking development cooperation more closely to addressing challenges such as climate change and mitigation of conflict. These priorities are aligned with the 2030 Agenda for Sustainable Development and the SDGs, but there is a risk that changing aid allocation patterns creates funding gaps in countries most in need of support and in investment areas critical to leaving no one behind.

In 2016, ODA increased by 10.7 per cent in real terms, continuing a long-standing trend in rising ODA. The previous decline in ODA to the least developed countries (LDCs) has been reversed, but overall disbursements to countries most in need of concessional resources and most vulnerable to external shocks have stagnated in recent years. *ODA providers should continue efforts to fulfil the commitments they have made and to further increase their ODA allocations to LDCs and other vulnerable countries.*

Multilateral development banks (MDBs) and development finance institutions have continued to step up efforts to provide financial support, technical assistance and policy advice in support of the 2030 Agenda for Sustainable Development. Together, they have an indispensable role to play in financing the SDGs, including infrastructure in particular, and in ensuring that social and environmental sustainability considerations are embedded in investments that will lock in development paths until 2030 and beyond. *To this end, MDBs should continue to strengthen their collaboration — including in their diagnostic work, support for project preparation and technical assistance — and to strengthen country capacities.*

Bilateral and multilateral South-South development cooperation is expanding in scope and magnitude, including through intraregional and interregional collaboration. *Raising the visibility of South-South cooperation and further documenting its added value and impact on sustainable development, would support SDG implementation.*

An increasing share of development finance is dedicated to or aligned with climate purposes. Climate finance is channelled through many multilateral and bilateral mechanisms and funds. This provides recipient countries with a range of options, but also contributes to a complex landscape that makes monitoring and reporting, access, and effective use a challenging endeavour. *Efforts by the Green Climate Fund (GCF) to enhance access to its funding are critical in this regard and other providers should also work towards simplifying access, particularly for vulnerable countries.*

While humanitarian funding is increasing, it is outpaced by the growth in financing needs. *Donors should continue efforts to deliver on their Grand Bargain commitments to better humanitarian financing. They should further increase multi-year and flexible humanitarian financing, and increase investment in development assistance in crisis contexts, with a view to reducing risk and vulnerability and to building resilience.*

As many developing countries have recently graduated or will graduate from concessional financing windows thanks to strong per capita income growth, they are at risk of losing access to sufficient and affordable long-term financing for SDG investments. Many of these are small and climate vulnerable countries. *To address these concerns, additional support should be provided to countries to manage the transition to new sources of financing as part of their integrated national financing frameworks. A wider use of existing exceptions to eligibility based mainly on per capita income, such as the International Development Association (IDA) small-state exception, should be explored.* Exceptions have also recently been introduced to make non-concessional financing available to low-income countries for projects with potential for strong returns through the IDA18 Scale-Up Facility. *Building on this experience, development banks should consider introducing additional flexibilities to access appropriate sources of financing, depending on project characteristics.*

Providers are increasingly focusing on the ability of development finance to mobilize additional private or commercial financing, often referred to as "blended finance," with a view to maximizing the impact of scarce public concessional resources and mobilize funding that would otherwise not have been available for SDG investments. *Providers should also engage with host countries at the strategic level, to ensure that priorities in their project portfolios align with national priorities and that blending arrangements are in the public interest.* To increase the effectiveness of blended finance, relevant actors have worked on the defining principles for blending. *The international community should consider how these principles relate to respective commitments in the Addis Ababa Action Agenda (hereafter, Addis Agenda) and the overarching principles of development effectiveness, and discuss this relationship in a universal forum such as the Financing for Development (FfD) Forum or the Development Cooperation Forum.*

Use of blended finance instruments is growing rapidly, but has so far largely bypassed LDCs. *As blended finance becomes an increasingly important modality, providers will need to take steps to ensure that vulnerable countries, where blending has so far proved to be much more challenging, do not see a fall in their overall share of international development finance, both by increasing complementary public investments and by exploring how to more effectively deploy blending in challenging contexts.*

The 2030 Agenda for Sustainable Development focus on results has made the effectiveness of development cooperation relevant across the agenda and its various means of implementation. In response, many actors are working to improve the quality, impact and effectiveness of development cooperation, including by ensuring that interventions support country ownership. Yet, further efforts are needed—in the area of tied aid, for instance. While the share of tied aid has fallen in 2016, reducing transaction costs and strengthening local economies, *donors should redouble efforts to fully untie aid, particularly as private sector development becomes a bigger priority.*

2. Trends in international development cooperation

2.1 Official development assistance

In 2016, ODA provided by members of the Organization for Economic Cooperation and Development (OECD) Development Assistance Committee (DAC) amounted to $145.7 billion. This represented an increase of 10.7 per cent in real terms over 2015, and continues a long-standing trend in rising ODA.[1] The increase is partly due to increases in funds for hosting and processing refugees within donor countries; but even without them, ODA still has risen by 8.6 per cent in real terms since 2015. Six DAC mem-

---

[1] Preliminary 2017 ODA figures were published by the Organization for Economic Cooperation and Development (OECD) in April 2018, after this report went to print. An update to this analysis is published in the online annex. Available from https://developmentfinance.un.org/international-development-cooperation.

bers (Denmark, Germany, Luxembourg, Norway, Sweden and the United Kingdom of Great Britain and Northern Ireland) met or exceeded the United Nations target of 0.7 per cent of gross national income (GNI). However, on aggregate, DAC donors combined fell short of that target, providing 0.32 per cent of GNI on average. The aggregate increase is marred, however, by (i) the failure to increase concessional finance to countries most in need and (ii) the decline in the share of ODA over which recipient countries have a significant say.

Disbursements of ODA to countries most in need of concessional resources and most vulnerable to external shocks have stagnated in recent years. Despite an increase in ODA to LDCs in 2016 of less than 1 per cent in real terms to $43.1 billion, the medium-term trend is one of stagnation (see figure 1). Moreover, ODA flows to LDCs are very unevenly allocated, with almost half directed to seven countries in 2014 and 2015.[2] In the Addis Agenda, donors had committed to reversing the decline in ODA to LDCs. While this was achieved on aggregate, nine DAC members saw their aid to LDCs decrease between 2015 and 2016. On the other hand, six donors provided 0.15 per cent or more of their GNI as ODA to LDCs, with five of them exceeding 0.20 per cent of GNI.

Aid to small island developing States (SIDS) did increase significantly, from $5.1 billion in 2015 to $7.1 billion in 2016. This increase was driven by Spain's restructuring of Cuba's debt, which accounted for $2 billion in aid. Short of this exceptional measure and the 2010 spike in ODA inflows to Haiti due to the earthquake, ODA to SIDS has not kept pace with the overall increase in aid flows since 2000, and remains very concentrated in a few SIDS, despite the increasing frequency, volatility, and intensity of weather-related hazards many of them are exposed to. ODA trends to landlocked developing countries (LLDCs) and African countries broadly mirror the patterns for LDCs and SIDS.[3]

This is of concern because vulnerable countries are most reliant on ODA to complement scarce domestic public resources and have only limited access to other forms of external financing. While gross ODA disbursements amount to only 1.3 per cent of government revenue in all developing countries on average, this figure is much higher in LDCs, where ODA represents about 15 per cent of government revenue on average. In 16 LDCs, gross ODA disbursements amount to a fifth of total domestic revenue or more, and in four of them it exceeds 50 per cent.[4] ODA also represents the largest external financial flow for 22 SIDS, accounting for over 40 per cent of all external financing.[5]

The share of aid that providers can programme for individual countries and regions, and over which partner countries could have a significant say— so-called country programmable aid (CPA)—has fallen in recent years. CPA excludes items such as humanitarian aid, in-donor refugee costs and administrative costs. In 2015, CPA amounted to 49 per cent of total gross bilateral ODA, or $52 billion, as compared to 53 to 55 per cent in the five previous years.[6] Budget support, an aid modality particularly well aligned with development effectiveness principles such as country ownership, declined in parallel. In 2016, general and sector budget support amounted to 1.9 per cent of total bilateral aid commitments of DAC donors. ODA spent within donor countries—such as refugee costs, scholarships and administrative costs—accounts for a growing share, increasing from 12 per cent of bilateral aid in 2010 to 20 per cent in 2016 (see figure 2).

2   Organization for Economic Cooperation and Development, *Development Co-operation Report 2017: Data for Development* (Paris, OECD Publishing, 2017). Available from http://www.oecd.org/dac/development-co-operation-report-20747721.htm.

3   For additional details on regional trends and regional distribution of official development assistance (ODA), please refer to the online annex to this Report. Available from https://developmentfinance.un.org/international-development-cooperation.

4   United Nations Department of Economic and Social Affairs (UN/DESA) staff calculations, based on OECD/Development Assistance Committee (DAC) and International Monetary Fund (IMF) data.

5   Organization for Economic Cooperation and Development, *Making Development Co-operation Work for Small Island Developing States* (Paris, OECD Publishing, forthcoming).

6   Organization for Economic Cooperation and Development, *Development Co-operation Report 2017.*

Figure 1
Net ODA, 2000–2016
(Billions of United States dollars, 2015 constant prices)

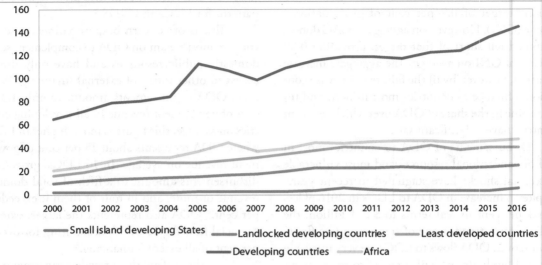

Source: OECD/DAC data.

Figure 2
Net bilateral ODA commitments by DAC countries by type of aid
(Share of total)

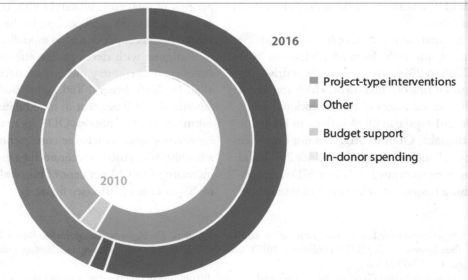

Source: OECD/DAC data.
Notes: In-donor spending includes scholarships and student costs in donor countries, development awareness, refugees in donor countries, administrative costs not included elsewhere; other aid includes experts and other TA, debt relief, core contributions and pooled programmes and funds.

Aid to social sectors such as health and education had grown rapidly in the first decade of the millennium during the era of the Millennium Development Goals, but since its peak in 2009 has decreased slightly in real terms. Donors' focus has shifted to economic aid and support for production sectors, including investments in transport and storage, energy, and other economic sectors (see figure 3), in line with the broader focus of the SDGs.

Gender equality and women's empowerment are key cross-cutting priorities in the Addis Agenda. In 2015-2016, DAC countries committed a total of $41.4 billion of ODA targeting gender equality and women's empowerment on average per year. The DAC country average for the share of development assistance that had a gender equality and women's empowerment objective was 40 per cent in 2015-2016. While DAC peer reviews find that DAC countries' political commitment to gender equality and women's empowerment is strong, implementation remains difficult. This is partly a result of difficulties of mainstreaming gender equality and

women's empowerment across development cooperation programmes. Recommendations by the DAC focus on operationalizing the political commitment, noting that DAC members need leadership, guidance, resources, capacity and a stronger focus on the results of investment in gender equality.

2.2 Lending by multilateral development banks

In the Addis Agenda, development banks were requested to update and develop their policies in support of the 2030 Agenda for Sustainable Development, and to better leverage their balance sheets to increase lending in support of sustainable development.[7] In response, the MDBs have stepped up their efforts: in 2016, annual disbursements of non-grant subsidized finance from the seven MDBs reached $65.8 billion, an increase of 15 per cent over 2015 (see figure 4). Two new multilateral institutions were founded that provide additional financing. Efforts have also focused on further increasing the volume of finance directly provided by MDBs, including

Figure 3

Net bilateral ODA commitments by DAC countries by sector, 2000–2016
(Billions of United States dollars, 2015 constant prices)

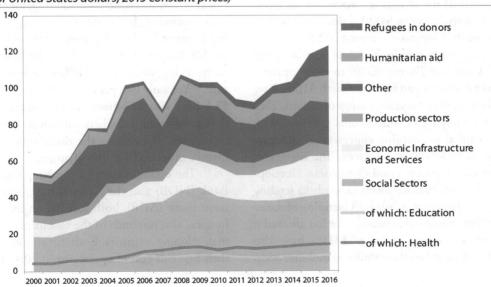

Source: OECD/DAC data.

Notes: Other includes multi-sector and cross-cutting aid, commodity aid and general programme assistance, debt relief, administrative costs donors, and unallocated aid.

---

7   *Addis Ababa Action Agenda of the Third International Conference on Financing for Development (Addis Ababa Action Agenda)* (United Nations publication, Sales. E.16.I.7), para.7.

Figure 4
Multilateral development bank financing, 2000–2016
(Billions of United States dollars)

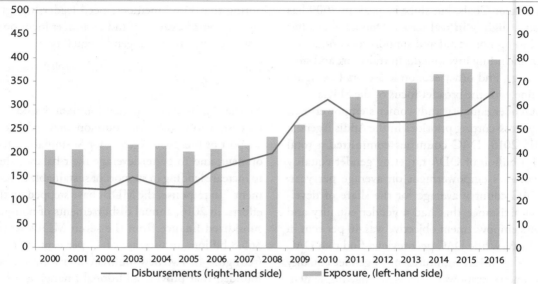

Source: UN/DESA calculations, based on annual reports from MDBs.
Notes: Concessional lending classified as ODA is excluded. Includes combined non-grant subsidized finance from Asian Development Bank, African Development Bank, European Bank for Reconstruction and Development, Inter-American Development Bank, Inter-American Investment Corporation, International Bank for Reconstruction and Development, and International Finance Corporation.

making optimal use of balance sheets, on strengthening the catalytic role of MDB actions, and on further enhancing cooperation among MDBs.

In response to calls in the Addis Agenda as well as at the Group of Twenty (G20) to make optimal use of their resources and balance sheets, MDBs have undertaken or are considering a range of actions. They include the merging of concessional windows with ordinary capital or enabling concessional windows to access capital-market resources. The merger of the Asian Development Fund's and Asian Development Bank's core balance sheets expands its lending capacity by 50 per cent[8] while IDA blending of donor contributions with market-issued debt has allowed it to increase its lending capacity.[9] MDBs have also increasingly focused on their ability to mobilize addi-

tional private investment—including, for example, in the adoption of the World Bank Group's "Maximizing Finance for Development" approach. In 2016, the MDBs directly mobilized $49.9 billion in private co-financing, of which $7.1 billion went to infrastructure.[10] Yet, only two per cent of this co-financing, or $1 billion was mobilized for low-income and least developed countries where infrastructure gaps tend to be greatest (see also the discussion on blended finance in section 4 of this chapter).

The establishment of the New Development Bank (NDB) and the Asian Infrastructure Investment Bank (AIIB), both focused on infrastructure finance, also responds to the vast infrastructure gap in developing countries. Both institutions completed their first full year of operations in 2016, with com-

8   See https://www.adb.org/news/adf-ocr-merger-boost-support-region-s-poor.
9   Multilateral Development Banks, "Second Report to the G20 on the MDB Action Plan to optimize balance sheets". Available from http://www.bundesfinanzministerium.de/Content/DE/Downloads/G20-Dokumente/Hamburg_Genannte_Berichte/Second-Report-on-MDB-Action-Plan.pdf?__blob=publicationFile&v=2.
10   Multilateral Development Banks, "Mobilization of private finance by Multilateral Development Banks. 2016 Joint Report (Report published April 2017, Annex published July 2017). Available from http://documents.worldbank.org/curated/en/860721492635844277/pdf/114433-REVISED-11p-MDB-Joint-Report-Mobilization-Jul-21.pdf.

bined commitments of infrastructure financing of $3.2 billion.[11] The NDB, which was established in 2014, expected to commit between $2.5 billion to $3 billion in new lending in 2017. The AIIB approved financing of about $1.8 billion for 12 projects between January and November 2017, but its investment capacity is much larger: the paid-in capital pledge in its articles of agreement amounts to $20 billion, exceeding the 2017 amount of paid-in capital of the World Bank Group's International Bank for Reconstruction and Development of $16 billion.

To achieve the SDGs, MDBs will need to both achieve greater scale and ensure that social and environmental sustainability considerations are embedded in their lending, in particular for infrastructure investments that will lock-in development paths until 2030 and beyond. This could include further aligning internal staff incentives with metrics relevant to achieving the 2030 Agenda for Sustainable Development and the SDGs, rather than focusing them primarily on lending volumes. In the context of optimizing balance sheets, the Addis Agenda also included a call on development banks to use all tools to manage their risks, including through diversification, which warrants further study.

Shareholders of the MDBs should continue to work towards a shared vision of the MDB system. In this context, the G20 Eminent Persons Group on Global Financial Governance will make recommendations to achieve greater coherence of shareholder objectives, policies and compliance standards across international financial institutions, including the MDBs, later this year (see also chapter III.F).

Cooperation among MDBs has increased significantly since the adoption of the Addis Agenda, including through the Global Infrastructure Forum, which was called for in the Addis Agenda, and the Infrastructure Data Initiative, which brings together all the MDBs to jointly set standards for reporting on infrastructure investment. MDBs could further strengthen collaboration in their diagnostic work, support for project preparation and technical assistance. Greater cooperation should serve to support the ultimate objective of strengthening country systems and country capacities.[12] Cooperation could also be enhanced on financing structures — for example, by the establishment of scalable platforms that can be used to leverage resources across MDBs. Such platforms can support actors that have limited capacities, while allowing the MDBs to pool their resources and expertise. One example of such efforts is SOURCE, a new platform to develop sustainable infrastructure across the MDBs.[13] Another example is the Global Emerging Markets Risk Database,[14] a comprehensive database of credit risk information that provides MDBs and development finance institutions with pooled data on credit default rates.

2.3   South-South cooperation

South-South cooperation is undergoing expansion in its scope and magnitude. An increasing diversity of Southern actors, governmental and nongovernmental, is engaged in development cooperation in the South-South space, including MDBs. The United Nations Department for Economic and Social Affairs (UN/DESA) tracks development cooperation trends in South-South cooperation by considering official concessional resources (concessional loans and grants, debt relief and technical cooperation) provided by developing countries for development purposes.[15] Estimates from partial data suggest the financial component of such South-South development cooperation may have grown to reach $26 billion in 2015.

11   New Development Bank, "Towards a greener tomorrow: annual report 2016" (Shanghai, 2017). Available from https://www.ndb.int/wp-content/uploads/2017/10/NDB-ANNUAL-REPORT-2016.pdf; Asian Infrastructure Investment Bank, "Connecting Asia for the future: annual report and accounts 2016" (Beijing, 2017). Available from https://www.aiib.org/en/news-events/news/2016/annual-report/.content/download/Annual_Report_2016.pdf.

12   Amar Bhattacharya and others, "The new global agenda and the future of the multilateral development bank system" (Washington, D.C., Brookings Institute and the Center for Global Development, February 2018). Available from https://www.brookings.edu/wp-content/uploads/2018/02/epg_paper_on_future_of_mdb_system_jan30.pdf.

13   See https://public.sif-source.org/about/about-source/.

14   See http://www.gems-riskdatabase.org.

15   Some Southern partners also consider non-concessional loans and commercial transactions in trade and investment as another distinct feature of their cooperation.

However, definitions and categories used for reporting South-South cooperation are often not comparable. For example, country practices differ in reporting indirect as well as direct costs of their projects. Methodologies to calculate the grant element in official loans may also vary. Estimates of development cooperation from academic institutions or international organizations can differ from those of official sources, especially as they apply common frameworks ex post to data originally collected for other purposes. The non-financial modalities significant to South-South development cooperation—capacity-building, technology development and transfer, joint action for policy change and partnerships—are not easily valorized.[16]

Southern contributions to multilateral institutions may be more visible, as in the case of South-ern partners' support to operational activities of the United Nations development system, which rose by nearly 10 per cent between 2015 and 2016 to $3.062 billion (see figure 5).[17]

South-South cooperation often focuses on promoting regional integration. An example is the Mesoamerican Integration and Development Project (addressing cross-border energy, transport and telecommunication infrastructure), which received loans, grants, guarantees and public-private partnership support from the Inter-American Development Bank and the Central American Bank for Economic Integration.[18] Overall, the number of bilateral South-South cooperation projects within Latin America increased by almost a third between 2010 and 2015. Most projects focused on economic issues, such as strengthening of productive sec-

Figure 5

Southern partners' contributions to the United Nations operational activities for development by funding type, 2011–2016

(Billions of United States dollars)

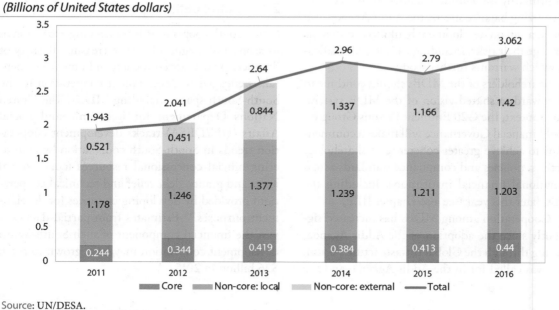

Source: UN/DESA.

16   United Nations, Report of the Secretary-General on trends and progress in international development cooperation (forthcoming); United Nations Development Cooperation Forum. Summary document of the DCF Argentina High-level Symposium, 6 to 8 September 2017. Available from https://www.un.org/ecosoc/sites/www.un.org.ecosoc/files/files/en/dcf/dcf-argentina-summary.pdf.

17   Funding data from the Report of the Secretary-General on implementation of General Assembly resolution 71/243 on the quadrennial comprehensive policy review of operational activities for development of the United Nations system, 2018 (A/73/63-E/2018/8); Southern partners refers in this example to the G77 + China.

18   For more information, see Mesoamerican Integration and Development Project (MIDP). Available from http://www.proyectomesoamerica.org/joomla/index.php?option=com_content&view=article&id=229&Itemid=57".

tors, or infrastructure, with social welfare another major priority.[19] China's Belt and Road Initiative is another example of enhanced regional cooperation. The Initiative aims to promote the connectivity of African, Asian and European continents through better policy coordination, infrastructure connectivity, closer trade relations, financial integration, and cultural, academic and other exchanges. At the Belt and Road Forum in May 2017, China pledged approximately $124 billion in new financial support for activities under Belt and Road, including through the Silk and Road Fund and lending by the China Development Bank and the Export-Import Bank of China.[20]

Triangular cooperation is also gaining importance, with both numbers of projects and budgets allocated to this modality increasing.[21] Cooperation between countries in the same region is the most common arrangement, including, for example, South Africa's cooperation with 15 traditional donor countries to support countries in the Southern African region. In order to provide a global platform for exchanges on triangular cooperation, the Global Partnership Initiative (GPI) on effective triangular cooperation[22] aims to analyse, monitor and systematize experiences and best practices; elaborate a set of voluntary principles; and consolidate frameworks of triangular cooperation that ensure country-led ownership, as well as inclusive partnerships for sustainable development.

2.4   Climate finance

Available evidence suggests that international public climate finance is increasing, both through dedicated channels and by aligning existing development finance with climate goals. The United Nations Framework Convention on Climate Change Standing Committee on Finance estimated bilateral total public climate specific finance from developed to developing countries at $26.6 billion in 2014.[23]

Climate finance is channelled through many multilateral and bilateral mechanisms and funds, which provides recipient countries with a range of options, but also contributes to a complex landscape that makes monitoring and reporting, access and effective use a challenging endeavour. The Green Climate Fund (GCF), expected to become the primary channel of climate finance, and fully operational since 2015, has taken steps to address some of these concerns. To enhance access to its funding, it has simplified approval processes for small projects, and accredited a rising number of direct national access entities. To ensure that its projects follow a country-driven approach, the GCF also works with designated national authorities that need to approve all projects. Finally, the GCF provides support for "readiness activities," particularly for vulnerable countries.[24] Overall, the GCF has approved projects with $2.7 billion in funding commitments by November 2017.[25]

19   Ibero-American General Secretariat, *Report on South-South Cooperation in Ibero-America 2017* (Madrid, Ibero-American program for the strengthening of South-South Cooperation, 2017). Available from http://www.informesursur.org/?lang=en#informe.

20   See http://www.xinhuanet.com/english/2017-05/14/c_136282982.htm.

21   Development Assistance Committee, "Building the knowledge base on triangular co-operation – Findings from the 2015 OECD survey on triangular co-operation. Interim report" (OECD, May 2016). Available from http://www.oecd.org/dac/dac-global-relations/Interim%20Report%20Triangular%20Co-operation%202015%20Survey%20-%20May%202016.pdf.

22   This initiative is led by a core group that includes Canada, Japan, Mexico, the Islamic Development Bank, the OECD and the United Nations Office for South-South Cooperation.

23   The Standing Committee carries out a comprehensive global assessment of all public climate finance flows biennially, with the next biennial assessment of climate finance flows to be published later in 2018.

24   Climate Funds Update, "The Green Climate Fund", Climate Finance Fundamentals 11 (Washington, D.C., Heinrich Böll Stiftung North America, November 2017). Available from https://www.odi.org/sites/odi.org.uk/files/resource-documents/11851.pdf.

25   Green Climate Fund, "GCF in numbers. A snapshot of key figures, facts and results of the Fund to date" (Incheon, Republic of Korea, 2017). Available from http://www.greenclimate.fund/documents/20182/24871/GCF_in_Numbers.pdf/226fc825-3c56-4d71-9a4c-60fd83e5fb03.

An increasing share of overall development finance is dedicated to or aligned with climate purposes. In 2015, aid activities targeting climate change mitigation amounted to $19.6 billion, with activities for adaption at $15.1 billion. ODA for adaptation purposes in particular has grown quickly, almost doubling since 2010.[26] Recent analysis from the OECD found that bilateral climate-related development finance continued this upward trend in 2016.[27] The World Bank Group aims to dedicate 28 per cent of its lending to climate action by 2020, and announced at the One Planet Summit in Paris, France, in December 2017 that it would cease to fund any upstream oil and gas activities after 2019. In this context, it is also critical that disaster risk reduction measures are incorporated into all development assistance programmes and infrastructure financing, in line with the Sendai Framework for Disaster Risk Reduction.

The MDBs are also major issuers of green bonds (see chapter III.B). The 23 national and regional development banks (from both developed and developing countries) that are members of the International Development Finance Club made $159 billion of climate finance commitments in 2016, an increase of $25 billion over 2015.[28] The overwhelming share of these commitments was for mitigation—in particular, non-concessional lending for green energy. Adaption finance amounted to $5 billion.

Climate change has differentiated impacts on women and men, with women and girls typi-cally more adversely affected by climate-related impacts and disasters.[29] To address these concerns, the Twenty-third Conference of the Parties recently adopted a Gender Action Plan to promote gender-responsive climate policy and mainstream gender equality considerations in climate action and programming. This includes efforts to strengthen the capacity of parliaments, funding ministries, and non-governmental organizations (NGOs) to integrate gender-responsive budgeting into climate finance, access and delivery. One proposal to pursue co-benefits of climate action and gender equality is to include a requirement to disclose the gender-differentiated impact of the proceeds of bonds certified as green.[30]

2.5   Humanitarian finance

The prevalence of humanitarian crises undermines development progress. An estimated 87 per cent of people in extreme poverty reside in countries affected by fragility, environmental vulnerability or both.[31] Financial requirements for response plans and appeals coordinated by the United Nations rose from $5.1 billion in 2007 for humanitarian responses in 29 countries to $24.7 billion in 2017 for responses in 38 countries. While funding of the appeals also increased over this period from $3.4 billion to $13.8 billion, it was outpaced by growing requirements, resulting in a widening gap between humanitarian needs and available resources.[32]

The steep rise in total funding requirements is mainly driven by a set of large-scale protracted crises.

26   OECD.Stat Creditor Reporting System and UN/DESA calculations.

27   Development Assistance Committee, "Climate-related development finance in 2016" (OECD, December 2017). Available from http://www.oecd.org/dac/financing-sustainable-development/development-finance-topics/Climate-related-development-finance-in-2016.pdf.

28   International Development Finance Club, "IDFC green finance mapping report 2016" (Paris, December 2017). Available from http://www.idfc.org/Downloads/Publications/01_green_finance_mappings/IDFC_Green_Finance_Mapping_Report_2017_12_11.pdf.

29   Mariama Williams, "Climate Finance: Why does it matter for women?" in *Financing Gender Equality – Realising Women's Rights through Gender Responsive Budgeting*, Zohra Khan and Nalini Burn, eds. (London, Palgrave Macmillan, 2017).

30   Yannick Glemarec, Seemin Qayum and Marina Olshanskaya, "Leveraging co-benefits between gender equality and climate action for sustainable development: mainstreaming gender considerations in climate change projects" (New York, UN Women, October 2016).

31   Development Initiatives, "Global Humanitarian Assistance Report 2017" (Bristol, United Kingdom, Development Initiatives, Ltd., 2017). Available from http://devinit.org/post/global-humanitarian-assistance-2017/.

32   Assessment by the Global Humanitarian Overview, which encompasses all appeals and response plans coordinated by the United Nations. Funding data for 2017 as reported by donors and recipient organizations to the Financial

Nineteen of the 21 humanitarian response plans for humanitarian crises have been ongoing for 5 or more years, with 3 crises having had plans and appeals each year for at least 18 years. Recognizing that development is the most effective way to build resilience, a longer-term approach to addressing humanitarian needs must include development investments. This includes investments targeting gender equality to help overcome the lack of funding for the needs and representation of crisis-affected women and girls. The World Humanitarian Summit has argued for a shift from funding short-term activities towards collective financing outcomes that reduce needs, risk and vulnerability. Some donors and international financing institutions are increasing multi-year humanitarian funding and longer-term programming approaches in protracted crises.

Nonetheless, challenges remain in accelerating this change. Donors should deliver on their Grand Bargain commitments. They should further increase humanitarian multi-year and flexible financing. Humanitarian, development, peacebuilding and climate change financing should be better sequenced, layered, aligned and risk-informed. The Agenda for Humanity called for innovation in financing for disaster response and in ensuring that an early warning triggers timely action and the release of funds. Progress in this area and the expanding role of the Central Emergency Response Fund (CERF) are discussed in the section on shocks financing in chapter III.F.

The use of local and national actors remains low, at an estimated 2 per cent (the Grand Bargain called for channelling at least 25 per cent of humanitarian funding through local actors by 2020). Greater efforts in this regard would also contribute to strengthening national capacities.[33] Expanding the investment in pooled-funding mechanisms constitutes one opportunity to do so. The country-based pooled funds, managed by the United Nations Office for the Coordination of Humanitarian Affairs, have grown significantly in recent years and allocate a growing share of their funding directly to national NGOs.

The increasing focus of international public financing flows on climate challenges and humanitarian crises discussed in sections 2.4 and 2.5 above is a direct response to risks and shocks affecting progress and gains in sustainable development. At the same time, the challenging geopolitical environment and increasing intensity and frequency of extreme weather events and resulting crises is heralding a shift towards linking development cooperation more closely to addressing regional and global challenges such as mitigation of conflict and other drivers of migration and climate change. These priorities are fully aligned with the 2030 Agenda for Sustainable Development and the SDGs, but changing aid-allocation patterns may create funding gaps in countries most in need of support, such as LDCs and SIDS, and in areas critical to leaving no one behind. Section 3 below on graduation explores this allocation challenge from the perspective of countries that lose access to specific financing windows or types of support.

3. Graduation and access to concessional finance

As many developing countries have recently graduated or will graduate from concessional financing windows thanks to strong per capita income growth, concerns have been raised over their access to sufficient and affordable long-term financing for SDG investments. As per capita income increases above low-income thresholds, access to external (concessional and non-concessional) public finance often decreases faster than can be compensated by increasing tax revenues in per capita terms—the so-called "missing-middle" challenge.[34] Extreme weather events and other external shocks have exacerbated these concerns: countries vulnerable to external shocks often exceed per capita income thresholds but

Tracking Service as of 23 January 2018. See Office for the Coordination of Humanitarian Affairs, "Humanitarian funding update" (December 2017). Available from https://reliefweb.int/sites/reliefweb.int/files/resources/Humanitarian%20Funding%20Update_GHO_31DEC2017.pdf.

33 Development Initiatives, "Global Humanitarian Assistance Report 2017".

34 Homi Kharas, Annalisa Prizzon and Andrew Rogerson, "Financing the post-2015 Sustainable Development Goals: a rough roadmap" (London, Overseas Development Institute, 2014). Available from https://www.odi.org/sites/odi.org.uk/files/odi-assets/publications-opinion-files/9374.pdf.

have limited capacity to mobilize public resources domestically due to their small size, remoteness, and/or vulnerability.

Graduation is relevant in several contexts, including (i) graduation from access to the concessional windows at MDBs; (ii) graduation from LDC status; and (iii) graduation from ODA eligibility. In all cases, per capita income is an important criterion. For LDC graduation, it is one of three components, complemented by the Human Asset Index and an Economic Vulnerability Index composed of indicators of structural vulnerability to economic and environmental shocks. For graduation from soft windows of MDBs, per capita income is complemented by an assessment of creditworthiness. ODA eligibility relies on income alone.

A country's categorization as a low-, middle- or high-income country is not directly related to graduation; it is instead an analytical classification by the World Bank, updated annually. However, the classification is an input to decisions on lending eligibility from MDBs. At about $1,200 per capita income, the point at which countries are re-classified as middle-income countries, consideration for a graduation process from soft windows of MDBs is triggered. Incidentally, the income threshold for LDC graduation is set at a similar level. The move from middle-income to high-income on the other hand, at per capita incomes of about $12,200, triggers graduation from ODA eligibility (see figure 6).

3.1   LDC graduation

Because development partners generally do not use LDC status per se to allocate resources, LDC graduation usually has only limited impact on concessional financing flows. Information provided by major donors shows that in most cases, graduation has limited impact on bilateral development cooperation programmes. In some cases, graduation may trigger a shift towards concessional loans rather than grants, or towards loans with less favorable terms.[35]

Graduation affects a country's eligibility for specific multilateral instruments, including for climate finance (the Least Developed Countries Fund), trade capacity-building (the Enhanced Integrated Framework in Aid for Trade), and financial inclusion (the United Nations Capital Development Fund). However, to date these have corresponded to relatively small shares of total funding available.

A country may be recommended for graduation from LDC status by the Committee for Development Policy (CDP), an independent advisory body of the United Nations Economic and Social Council (ECOSOC), if it meets the graduation threshold in two of the three criteria in two consecutive triennial reviews.[36] If endorsed, graduation becomes effective three years after the General Assembly takes note of the ECOSOC endorsement of the recommendation of the CDP. Hence, the graduation process takes at least six years. There are also safeguards in place to ensure smooth transition, including by extending and gradually phasing out LDC-specific support measures related to ODA volumes and modalities, market access and World Trade Organization agreements.[37]

3.2   Graduation from concessional windows of MDBs

Graduation from the soft windows of the MDBs—the World Bank Group's IDA, the Asian Development Bank's Asian Development Fund, and the African Development Bank's (AfDB) African Development Fund—has a more direct impact on financing volumes and terms. Consideration for graduation is triggered when per capita income exceeds the operational cut-off, for example $1,215 for IDA in 2016. If accompanied by a positive creditworthiness assessment (based on political risk, debt burdens, growth prospects and other factors), a country receives time-bound transitional terms from IDA, and International Bank for Reconstruction and Development financing is phased in while IDA financing is gradually phased out. The full process

---

35   Based on background research and consultations with development partners carried out in the context of impact assessments of graduation from least developed country status for the Committee for Development Policy.

36   Gross national income per capita of $1,230 or above, human assets index of 66 or above, and economic vulnerability index of 32 or below. See https://www.un.org/development/desa/dpad/least-developed-country-category/ldc-graduation.html.

37   See the Support Measures Portal for LDCs. Available from https://www.un.org/ldcportal/.

Figure 6

Distribution of countries by per capita income levels and graduation thresholds, 2016

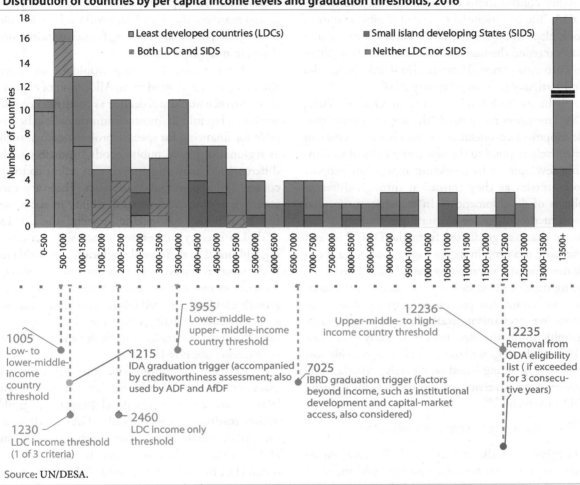

Source: UN/DESA.

typically takes multiple years, and is accompanied by a graduation task force that aims to ensure a smooth path of transition.[38] Exceptions exist for small States, which remain eligible to access IDA funding even if they exceed income thresholds. More recently, funds from the concessional financing facility are available to middle-income countries that host large numbers of refugees.

Graduating countries are faced with "harder" terms of regular assistance by MDBs, even though maturities and interest rates are still more favourable than market terms. Relatedly, the shift in financing sources tends to impact the sectoral allocation of international public finance, with less focus on social sectors such as health, which are often financed in grant form. Other sources of concessional finance, such as bilateral ODA, also remain available; and under IDA, transition support is granted to countries that have recently graduated—most recently for Bolivia (Plurinational State of), India, Sri Lanka and Viet Nam.

3.3 Graduation from ODA eligibility

The OECD/DAC reviews the list of countries eligible for ODA every three years. If a country exceeds the high-income threshold for three consecutive

---

38   Graduation from the soft windows of the Asian Development Bank and the African Development Bank follows a similar process.

years, it is removed from the list and development finance contributions can no longer be counted as ODA. The last triennial review of eligible countries took place in November 2017. Three countries that had exceeded the high-income threshold from 2014 to 2016 were removed from the list (Chile, Seychelles and Uruguay as from 1 January 2018).

In its high-level meeting in October 2017, DAC members recognized "the need to ensure that development co-operation approaches and tools can effectively respond to the new complexity of sustainable development by providing appropriate support to countries as they transition through different phases of development".[39] In response, a proposal for a methodology for reinstating a country or territory that has graduated from the DAC List and later suffers a drop in its per capita income has been drafted for consideration by the DAC. A plan is also being developed on how to take forward the decision to "establish a process to examine short-term financing mechanisms available to respond to catastrophic humanitarian crises in recently graduated HICs, including, without prejudice, a possible role for ODA spending based on objective criteria while ensuring no diversion of resources from existing ODA recipients".[40]

3.4   Improving the overall landscape

The missing-middle challenge underlines the importance of a smooth transition process, and the need to strengthen the support provided to countries as they undergo graduation. United Nations agencies already provide support to LDCs as they graduate, including through an LDC graduation task force. The United Nations Resident Coordinator and the United Nations Country Team also provide support for smooth transition. This type of engagement could be a model for more systematic engagement of United Nations country teams in helping countries plan transitions in financing mixes. Changes in the terms and volumes of the available external financing mix also call for a more strategic approach to

manage the overall resource envelope available for sustainable development investments, in an integrated manner. The Task Force will explore the role of integrated national financing frameworks in more depth in next year's report.

A more ambitious step would be to move towards a system of gradation. Allocation of concessional finance would still decline as countries become wealthier, but middle-income countries would be eligible for financing for specific projects/sectors, such as regional or global public goods,[41] possibly with differentiated financing options that reflect country contexts and project characteristics. There are also attempts to create additional flexibility in accessing regular windows for specific projects. The IDA18 Scale-Up Facility makes non-concessional financing additional to their regular allocation available to IDA countries for projects with potential for strong returns on investment, development impact and growth dividends. The AfDB is considering moderately concessional loans, which have higher interest rates but long maturities suitable for infrastructure investments (see box 1).

Existing exceptions and multidimensional assessments already address limitations of an income-only assessment of development and 'graduation readiness'. They include IDA's small-state exception, which allows states with a population of 1.5 million or less to access the most concessional IDA financing terms even if their per capita income exceeds the IDA operational cut-off. Similarly, use of the creditworthiness criteria by MDBs allows them to take into account the broader macroeconomic situation, debt risks and other factors, so that graduation is a process, rather than a sudden event.

There is room for different agencies to learn from each other's attempts to address diverse circumstances of countries. The replenishment cycles of the concessional windows of the MDBs are one entry point for achieving greater harmonization. A wider-reaching proposal is to use broader assess-

---

Box 1

Moderately concessional loans: an innovative mechanism to better leverage existing official development assistance (ODA)

African Development Bank

Similar to other regions, an acute tension exists in African Development Fund (ADF) countries between the vast public investment requirements for the Sustainable Development Goals (SDGs) and public debt sustainability. Countries need to frontload infrastructure investments as a foundation for long-run growth and development. Such investments will pay off only over the longer run, but will have an immediate and sizable impact on public and external debt.

The progressive hardening of terms on graduation typically involve both higher financing costs and shortening grace periods and loan maturities. Long maturities are particularly valuable in the light of exceptionally long payback periods of investments in infrastructure and human capital. To address this, the African Development Bank (AfDB) is considering moderately concessional loans (MCLs) with longer maturities. These could carry a concessional interest rate of, say, 3-4 per cent on US dollar loans with a maturity of 40 years and grace period of 10 years, terms that are far superior to the terms ADF country governments have been obtaining on their Eurobond issues or other commercial loans.[a]

Two criteria have been proposed to determine eligibility for MCLs: (i) gross national income (GNI) per capita or (ii) the Africa Human and Infrastructure Development Index (AHIDI), which is a composite of the non-income (health and education) elements of the United Nations Development Programme's Human Development Index (HDI) and the AfDB Africa Infrastructure Development Index, and thus a broad indicator for economic capacity. For illustrative purposes, using 2012 ADF country allocations, applying AHIDI, 14 countries would be eligible for MCLs, while applying GNI per capita, 8 countries would be eligible for MCLs.[b]

While there is very likely to be demand for MCLs, the question remains of how to mobilize additional capital to be able to issue them without jeopardizing the Bank's AAA credit rating. One solution put forward would be a "big bond," which would frontload official development assistance (ODA) while simultaneously lowering the fiscal burden on donors, building on the structure of the International Financing Facility for Immunization. With interest rates in donor countries still near historical lows, a window of opportunity exists to raise up to $100 billion by securitizing annual ODA flows of about $5 billion over a 30-year period.[c] Another solution could be a Group of Twenty or other fund for project preparation. If countries would allocate about $1 billion per year to solid project preparation in Africa (in order to finance preparation of ten big infrastructure projects per year), the MDBs could crowd in private finance for project implementation.

a   Luisa Teixeira Felino and Brian Pinto, "Debt sustainability and development implications of moderately concessional lending terms for ADF countries", ADF Policy Innovation Lab Working Paper Series, No. 3 (African Development Fund, June 2017). Available from https://frmb.afdb.org/documents/78/Debt Sustainability and Development Implications of MCL Terms for ADF Countries_ADF Lab Working Paper No.3.pdf.

b   African Development Fund, "Long-Term Financial Capacity of the ADF", Discussion Paper, ADF-13 First Replenishment Meeting (Tunis, Tunisia, February 2013). Available from https://www.afdb.org/fileadmin/uploads/afdb/Documents/Boards-Documents/First_ADF-13_Replenishment_Meeting_-_Long-Term_Financial_Capacity_of_the_ADF.pdf.

c   African Development Bank "Reinvigorating African concessional finance: Report of the High Level Panel on Transforming Trust in the AfDB Group into Influence", Report of the High-level Panel on Transforming Trust in the AfDB Group into Influence (Tunis, Tunisia, African Development Bank Group's Policy Innovation Lab, 2017). Available from https://frmb.afdb.org/documents/78/Reinvigorating African Concessional Finance - Report of the High Level Panel on Transforming Trust in the AfDB Group into Influence.pdf.

---

ments of progress more systematically. For example, the LDC category could be used in a wider range of processes. New measures have also been put forward in this context, such as the structural gap approach used by the Economic Commission for Latin America and the Caribbean (see box 2) or the United Nations Development Programme's SIDS-specific criteria.[42]

---

42   Gail Hurley, "Financing for development and small island developing States: a snapshot and ways forward" (New York, United Nations Development Programme and United Nations Office of High Representative for Least Devel-

---

Box 2
Structural gap analysis

Economic Commission for Latin America and the Caribbean (ECLAC)

Recognizing the heterogeneity of middle-income countries, the Economic Commission for Latin America and the Caribbean (ECLAC) has proposed structural gap analysis as an alternative to using income levels to classify countries. Middle-income countries are characterized by disparate social conditions, significant and persistent levels of poverty and inequality, and differing environmental vulnerabilities. They also remain economically and socially vulnerable, due to undiversified production and export structures, shallow financial markets, dependence on external financial flows, and other factors. Their capacity to mobilize domestic and external resources also varies greatly, and depends on factors beyond per capita income, including external conditions beyond their control. This makes per capita income an incomplete criterion for allocating international resources.

The structural gaps approach identifies key structural obstacles that are holding back sustained, equitable and inclusive growth in middle-income countries, such as regressive tax systems and low tax collection, limited redistributive effects of social spending, high inequality, low labour productivity, and lagging infrastructure spending. The ECLAC approach uses a comprehensive set of indicators that reflects country-specific obstacles and allows them to prioritize development needs in a particular country and a given time.

This approach would also allow countries and regions to identify and order development priorities, needs and challenges, and to decide which areas and gaps to prioritize and confront. It could thus contribute to broadening the policy dialogue, including on sources of financing and allocation criteria at the global level.

---

4.   Catalytic aid and blended finance

The impact of development cooperation is greatest when it is catalytic—when it accelerates economic growth and sustainable development, and helps mobilize additional resources for development. The catalytic effect of development cooperation can be varied; it can come through capacity-building and the strengthening of enabling environments and investment climates, or the financing of public investments and services that are often a precondition for markets and private business to thrive. These development impacts are sometimes referred to as "transformative" or supporting the domestic growth context. The catalytic effect of ODA can also be more direct, by directly mobilizing additional public and private financing for development.

To support the mobilization of additional domestic public resources, donors have increased their engagement in tax capacity-building, even though the share of ODA for this purpose remains low (see chapter III.A). There is also renewed interest in phasing out tax exemptions for ODA, which run counter to efforts to strengthen national tax systems (see box 3).

The biggest focus to date, however, has been placed on development finance's ability to crowd in, leverage, or catalyse additional private or commercial financing, often referred to as "blended finance". The use of blending instruments is increasing, putting a spotlight on their allocation across country groups, their development impact, and their alignment with key development effectiveness principles such as country ownership and transparency. Existing experience suggests that there would be benefit for all stakeholders to further consider how blending modalities can support and be aligned with relevant principles in the Addis Agenda and the overarching principles of development effectiveness.

4.1   The blended finance landscape

Blended finance uses financial instruments such as grants, loans, guarantees and equity to improve the risk-return profile of investments, to mobilize additional commercial financing that would not have been available without public intervention. While there is no universally agreed definition of blended finance, in its broadest sense it includes all development finance that mobilizes commercial finance

---

oped Countries, Landlocked Developing Countries and Small Island Developing States, 2015). Available from http://www.undp.org/content/undp/en/home/librarypage/poverty-reduction/FfD-SIDS-UNDP-OHRLLS.html.

for sustainable development.[43] Based on this broad interpretation, the use of such instruments has been growing. Seventeen out of 23 DAC members responding to a recent survey reported that they are engaging in blended finance, often through intermediaries such as development finance institutions and development banks.[44] While there is no comprehensive estimate of blended finance globally, a 2016 OECD survey found that between 2012-2015, $81.1 billion was mobilized from the private sector by five instruments surveyed (guarantees, syndicated loans, credit lines, direct investments in companies, and shares in collective investment vehicles), with the amounts mobilized increasing over the period.[45]

Donors often use pooled vehicles such as facilities and funds to channel their resources towards blended finance. Such vehicles either pool public and private resources at the capital structure level or provide finance to intermediaries to do so. Between 2000 and 2016, 167 new blended finance facilities, with approximately $31 billion in combined commitments, and 189 blended finance funds were launched.[46] The European Union, which is the single largest contributor to blended finance facilities, has made the European Fund for Sustainable Development a key pillar of its External Investment Plan to address investment gaps in the European Neighbourhood and Africa, with a budget of €2.6 billion and a guarantee of €1.5 billion.

In line with blended finance's focus on mobilizing commercial or private finance, blending facilities and funds tend to target SDG investment areas where the business case is clearer—such as energy, growth, infrastructure and climate action, and, to a lesser extent, water and sanitation—as well as cross-cutting priorities such as poverty and gender (see figure 7). Blending currently plays a much smaller role in areas such as ecosystems, reflecting the strong public good character of these investments, where public finance is often the most effective financing option (see chapter II).

Perhaps most importantly, blended finance so far largely eschews the poorest countries. The OECD survey found that only 7 per cent of private finance was mobilized for projects in LDCs, mirroring the similarly skewed distribution of MDB mobilization of private finance noted above. As blended finance becomes an increasingly important modality of development cooperation, providers will need to take steps to ensure that LDCs and other vulnerable countries do not see a fall in their overall share of development finance. This includes increasing complementary investments in their public infrastructure, institutions and capacities. It also calls for exploring how to more effectively deploy blending in challenging contexts. The United Nations Capital Development Fund is currently carrying out analytical work to understand challenges and risks in applying blended finance in LDCs. The newly established IDA18 Private Sector Window, which has a clear target of mobilizing private investment to the poorest IDA countries, is another such step.

4.2 Effectiveness of blended finance

A number of lessons can be learned from existing experiences with blended finance instruments. For blended finance to achieve its stated goals, it should achieve both financial additionality (mobilize addi-

---

43   The Addis Agenda noted that blended finance "combines concessional public finance with non-concessional private finance and expertise from the public and private sector" (see Addis Ababa Action Agenda, para. 48). In October 2017, 20 development finance institutions (DFIs) have adopted a common definition on blended concessional finance in the context of private sector operations: *Combining concessional finance from donors or third parties alongside DFIs' normal own account finance and/or commercial finance from other investors, to develop private sector markets, address the Sustainable Development Goals (SDGs), and mobilize private resources.* The OECD provides a list of how actors define blended finance in Organization for Economic Cooperation and Development, *Making Blended Finance Work for the Sustainable Development Goals* (Paris, OECD Publishing, 2018), p. 49f. Available from http://dx.doi.org/10.1787/9789264288768-en.

44   Organization for Economic Cooperation and Development, ibid.

45   Julia Benn, Cécile Sangaré and Tomáš Hos, "Amounts mobilised from the private sector by official development finance interventions, OECD Development Co-operation Working Paper (Paris, OECD Publishing, 30 August 2017). Available from http://dx.doi.org/10.1787/8135abde-en.

46   Organization for Economic Cooperation and Development, *Making Blended Finance Work for the Sustainable Development Goals.*

Figure 7
SDG targeting by blended finance funds and facilities
(Percentage)

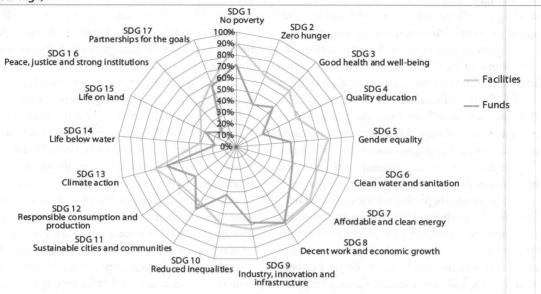

Source: OECD 2017 Survey on blended finance funds and facilities, as published in OECD, *Making Blended Finance Work for the Sustainable Development Goals* (Paris, OECD Publishing, 2018).

tional commercial financing) and development additionality (ensure that the investment has development impact and is aligned with the SDGs). Development additionality in particular has proven to be a source of concern in existing projects, due to limited availability of reliable evidence on the sustainable development impact of blending. Many blending projects have not monitored development impacts, and evaluations are not routinely made publicly available.[47] Those that are public have shown mixed results. An evaluation of blending facilities found that blending projects have often been of high quality and have mobilized additional finance, but that they generally had a modest impact on poverty.[48] Donor Governments should work towards ensuring that blended finance facilities they support enhance the quality of their monitoring, evaluation and, ultimately, sustainable development impact.

This is particularly important for intermediary institutions. Intermediaries are important conduits and facilitators for blended finance, due to their capacity to manage financial risks and their experience in engaging with the private sector. On the other hand, they are often less well equipped to monitor and evaluate sustainable development impact. Their monitoring and evaluation systems need to be strengthened to ensure effective use of blending instruments.

Sustainable and long-lasting development impact also relies on national ownership. Projects that are aligned with national priorities and plans and that involve local and national actors are much more likely to have long-lasting impacts. One lesson from recent experiences is that commitment and leadership by national Governments is critical to achieving scale — to moving from individual projects towards building an enabling environment, regulatory frameworks and pipelines of suitable projects. Local ownership also entails working towards local value retention, ensuring that linkages are built

---

47   Ibid.

48   Analysis for Economic Decisions (ADE), "Evaluation of blending. Final report vol. 1 – main report" (Louvain-la-Neuve, Belgium, European Commission, 2016). Available from https://ec.europa.eu/europeaid/sites/devco/files/evaluation-blending-volume1_en.pdf.

with local suppliers or downstream users. Currently, recipient-country involvement in decision-making is relatively low in blended finance, due to the project form of many blending operations.[49] However, blended finance providers can engage with host countries at the strategic level, to ensure that priorities in their project portfolios align with national priorities, and with a view to strengthening host-country capacities and enabling environments. They can also work with host Governments to identify and exploit opportunities to work with local actors.

Recipient countries on the other hand should select projects carefully and diligently assess the structure and use of blending instruments, to ensure that projects share risks and rewards fairly. This includes putting in place sound fiscal risk management frameworks that account for contingent liabilities and clear accountability mechanisms.[50] Additional data and transparency are also needed, particularly as the use of such instruments grows, and efforts are underway. To provide for reliable and comparable data on blending, the OECD/DAC statistical system has started collecting data on financing mobilized from private sector instruments in 2017 (see box 4). The forthcoming OECD *Global Outlook on Financing for Development* will also examine catalytic uses of ODA through its statistical collection and analytical work.

Relevant actors have also worked on defining principles for blending. In the Addis Agenda, Member States had agreed on a set of overarching principles for blended finance and public-private partnerships.[51] The OECD/DAC Blended Finance principles,[52] approved at the DAC High-level Meet-

ing held in Paris from 30 to 31 October 2017, are targeted at the policy level and aim to ensure that blended finance is deployed in the most effective way. The G20 released "Principles for the MDBs' strategy for crowding-in Private Sector Finance for growth and sustainable development,"[53] which provide a common framework among MDBs to increase levels of private investment in support of their development objectives. A working group of development finance institutions and multilateral development banks in 2017 updated principles and guidance for providing blended concessional finance.[54] There is a case for the international community to explore how these various sets of principles developed by "implementers" relate to respective commitments made in the Addis Agenda and the overarching principles of development effectiveness, and to discuss this relationship in a universal forum such as the FfD Forum or the Development Cooperation Forum (DCF).

5. Development effectiveness

The 2030 Agenda for Sustainable Development has brought a strong focus on results; this has further underlined effectiveness as an issue of broad relevance across the agenda and its various means of implementation. In response, efforts continue at all levels and by all actors to improve the quality, impact and effectiveness of development cooperation.

The primary entry point for increasing effectiveness is strengthening country ownership and action, guided by coherent national development cooperation policies, which in turn should be anchored in cohesive and nationally owned sustainable development strategies and integrated financing

49   Cordelia Lonsdale, "Aligning blended finance with the Busan principles of development effectiveness", Development Initiatives Discussion Paper (Bristol, United Kingdom, Development Initiatives, Ltd., October 2016). Available from http://devinit.org/wp-content/uploads/2016/10/Aligning-blended-finance-with-the-Busan-principles-of-development-effectiveness_DI_discussion-paper.pdf.

50   See also Agreed Policy Recommendations of the first session of the UNCTAD Intergovernmental Expert Group on Financing for Development. Available from http://unctad.org/en/pages/MeetingDetails.aspx?meetingid=1442.

51   See *Financing for Development: Progress and Prospects. Report of the Inter-agency Task Force on Financing for Development 2017* (United Nations publication, Sales No. E.17.I.5), p. 19. Available from https://developmentfinance.un.org/sites/developmentfinance.un.org/files/Report_IATF-2017.pdf.

52   Available from http://www.oecd.org/dac/financing-sustainable-development/development-finance-topics/OECD-Blended-Finance-Principles.pdf.

53   Available from http://www.bundesfinanzministerium.de/Content/DE/Downloads/G20-Dokumente/principles-on-crowding-in-private-sector-finance-april-20.pdf?__blob=publicationFile&v=2.

54   Available from http://www.ifc.org/wps/wcm/connect/30635fde-1c38-42af-97b9-2304e962fc85/DFI+Blended+Concessional+Finance+for+Private+Sector+Operations_Summary+R....pdf?MOD=AJPERES.

Box 3

Tax exemptions for official development assistance (ODA)

Aid-funded projects are often exempt from taxation, through tariffs on imported goods, value-added tax, or income taxes for personnel and enterprises, with a view to ensuring that a greater (or the full) share of aid is allocated towards the targeted project or programme. However, such exemptions run counter to broader efforts to reduce exemptions in tax systems, and to the overall aim of strengthening the mobilization of domestic resources. In response, Members States committed in the Addis Agenda to "consider not requesting tax exemptions on goods and services delivered as government-to-government aid, beginning with renouncing repayments of value-added taxes and import levies."[a]

This issue has been on the agenda of the United Nations Committee of Experts on International Cooperation in Tax Matters since its first session in 2005. Draft guidelines were produced in 2007. The International Monetary Fund (IMF), Organization for Economic Cooperation and Development (OECD), United Nations and World Bank Group have since continued to raise the issue. While progress was initially slow, it has recently gathered momentum. Following the early example of France, the World Bank, the Inter-American Development Bank and the Asian Development ment Bank, the Netherlands and Norway started to refrain from asking for tax exemptions. In 2015, Denmark, the Netherlands, Poland and Sweden submitted a joint letter to the European Commission, calling on the European Union to phase out the practice. In 2017, the Addis Tax Initiative decided to examine the issue. The United Nations Tax Committee will also continue its work on this topic in its current session. In February 2018, at the first Global Conference of the Platform for Collaboration on Tax, the Platform's partners (i.e., the IMF, OECD, United Nations and World Bank Group) noted that they intended to "review current practice, and provide guidance and recommendations, on the tax treatment of ODA funded goods and services".

a   *Addis Ababa Action Agenda of the Third International Conference on Financing for Development (Addis Ababa Action Agenda)* (United Nations publication, Sales. E.16.I.7), para. 58.

---

frameworks.[55] The DCF Survey probes best practice and capacity development needs in the design, implementation and monitoring of national development cooperation policies, including their alignment with national development strategies, links to the full range of means of implementation, and the roles of different actors in design and oversight. The UN/DESA DCF survey examines how such policies are adjusting to the demands of the 2030 Agenda for Sustainable Development, with 2018 findings forthcoming.[56]

Country ownership is strengthened by untying aid, which removes barriers to open competition for ODA-funded procurement and allows local procurement and strengthening of local economies.

The share of tied ODA has continued to decline, from 22 per cent in 2015 to 19 per cent in 2016. Progress is uneven, however (see figure 8). Effectiveness also hinges on untying aid not only formally, but also de facto — for example, by transparently notifying the public of aid offers ex ante. However, such transparency provisions are met inconsistently.[57] Greater efforts should be made to provide relevant information about tenders to potential bidders, in particular domestic bidders. The growing role of blended finance, which often aims to leverage private investment, increases the importance of ensuring that aid is fully untied and thus also effective in supporting private sector development in developing countries.[58]

---

55   Addis Ababa Action Agenda, para. 9.

56   The 2017/2018 DCF Survey exercise is currently underway. Its findings will be presented to the upcoming 2018 High-level Meeting of the Development Cooperation Forum, to be held at United Nations Headquarters in New York on 21-22 May 2018.

57   Development Co-operation Directorate Development Assistance Committee, "2017 Report on the DAC Untying Recommendation" (Paris, Organization for Economic Cooperation and Development, 3 April 2017). Available from https://www.oecd.org/dac/financing-sustainable-development/development-finance-standards/2017-Report-DAC-Untying.pdf.

58   Further guidance on the OECD/DAC Blended Finance Principles, especially on Principle 5 (monitor blended finance for transparency and results), is closely coordinated with the foreseen update of the Global Partnership Monitoring Framework.

Box 4

Modernization of official development assistance (ODA) and the Development Assistance Committee (DAC) statistical system

The statistical system of the Organization for Economic Cooperation and Development (OECD) Development Assistance Committee (DAC) is being modernized to better reflect the new global development landscape.[a] This process includes official development assistance (ODA) modernization. Changes include recording ODA in grant equivalents (agreed in 2014, only grants and the "grant portion" of concessional loans would be counted as ODA, encouraging the use of grants and highly concessional loans); clarifications to the eligibility of activities in the field of peace and security (agreed in 2016, ensuring consistent statistical reporting, and approving the ODA eligibility of development-related training for military staff in limited topics); and clarifications to the reporting rules for in-donor refugee costs (agreed in 2017, improving consistency, comparability, and transparency of reporting).

The DAC also adopted principles to encourage the use of private sector instruments (loans, equity, mezzanine finance and guarantees to private sector entities in developing countries). However, a detailed methodology of how to count donor effort in deploying such instruments has not yet been finalized, even as donors have started reporting private sector instruments as ODA. The DAC is committed to reaching a conclusion by consensus on this topic.

Work is also ongoing in relation to the rules for updating the DAC List of ODA Recipients. Methods for measuring the SDG focus of development cooperation are also being developed (adjustments to purpose codes and policy markers, such as a marker for tracking donor spending on disaster risk reduction across sectors, and possible new SDG fields) to keep the statistical classifications relevant and fit for purpose for monitoring the SDG agenda, including purpose codes to directly measure donors' support for the enabling environment for development financing[b] From 2017, the OECD will also measure donors' support for remittances facilitation, promotion and optimization.

Total official support for sustainable development

A new statistical measure, total official support for sustainable development (TOSSD), is being developed with a view to measuring a broader range of resources deployed to finance, including "all officially-supported resource flows to promote sustainable development in developing countries, to support development enablers and to address global challenges at regional or global levels".[c]

In response to the call of the Addis Ababa Action Agenda to "hold open, inclusive and transparent discussions"[d] on TOSSD, the OECD organized multi-stakeholder consultations in 2016 and 2017, and established an international TOSSD Task Force composed of a diverse set of stakeholders in the second quarter of 2017 to further clarify its scope and statistical features.[e]

The TOSSD Task Force has concluded its discussions on a number of key features of the TOSSD framework. The framework is comprised of two pillars: cross-border flows and development enablers and global challenges. The cross-border flow pillar will aim to capture all resources provided by government and official agencies, including state-owned enterprises and possibly other enterprises under significant government influence, to ODA recipients or countries that opt to be TOSSD recipients. Private resources mobilized by official development interventions will also be included, but presented separately. The Task Force has also discussed a number of "satellite indicators" to reflect flows that are important for development, but are not officially supported (e.g., remittances).

The TOSSD Task Force has advanced work in the first pillar, while some issues remain to be clarified. For example, two methods have been suggested for measuring in-kind technical cooperation (purchasing power parities or a standard salary table). Work on the development enablers and global challenges pillar aims to start in the second quarter of 2018. Governance questions will be subject to further discussion.

a   For more details, see http://www.oecd.org/dac/financing-sustainable-development/modernisation-dac-statistical-system.htm.

b   Codes for Public Financial Management, Banking and Financial Sector Development and Domestic Resource Mobilization were introduced in 2015.

c   See https://www.oecd.org/dac/TOSSD%20flyer%20DAC%20HLM%202017.pdf.

d   *Addis Ababa Action Agenda of the Third International Conference on Financing for Development (Addis Ababa Action Agenda)* (United Nations publication, Sales. E.16.I.7), para. 55.

e   All documentation and information is available from http://www.oecd.org/dac/financing-sustainable-development/development-finance-standards/tossd-task-force.htm.

Progress has also been made in increasing transparency of development cooperation, even if access to information relevant for development planning, budgeting, execution and monitoring and evaluation remains insufficient. Since 2014, more development cooperation has been recorded on national budgets submitted for parliamentary oversight, and tracking budget allocations for gender equality and women's empowerment has also increased. Development partners have improved their reporting to the OECD/DAC Creditor Reporting System, the OECD/DAC Forward Spending Survey, and the International Aid Transparency Initiative (IATI). Progress was most notable on the timeliness and comprehensiveness of publicly available development cooperation data, while the publication of forward-looking information continues to be a challenge.[59] Concerted efforts are being made to increase the use of available data, particularly at country level, and several countries announced plans to integrate IATI data into their Aid Information Management Systems.

Southern partners are also enhancing efforts to monitor the quality and effectiveness of their development cooperation. They are designing assessment systems and processes for their projects and programmes, in line with the Nairobi outcome.[60] For many Governments, this coincides with the institutionalization of coordination mechanisms and legal frameworks, as is the case, for example, with Brazil, China, India, Mexico, Thailand and others. Many of these initiatives correspond with the principles defined in the Nairobi outcome docu-

Figure 8

Tying Status of ODA by Individual DAC countries, 2014–2016
(Percentage)

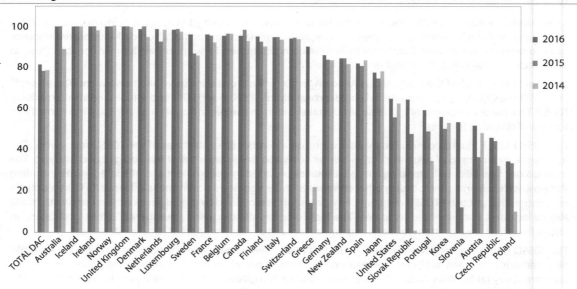

Source: OECD.Stat; OECD Development finance data, Statistics on resource flows to developing countries. Available from http:// www.oecd.org/dac/financing-sustainable-development/development-finance-data/statisticsonresourceflowstodevelopingcountries. htm.

59   Organization for Economic Cooperation and Development/United Nations Development Programme, *Making Development Co-operation More Effective. 2016 Progress Report* (Paris, OECD Publishing, 2016). Available from http://www. undp.org/content/undp/en/home/librarypage/development-impact/making-development-co-operation-more-effective--2016-progress-re.html.

60   P. Esteves, "How Governments of the South assess the results of South-South cooperation: case studies of South-led approaches", Development Cooperation Forum Policy Brief No. 20 (New York, Development Cooperation Forum, forthcoming).

ment of the High-level United Nations Conference on South-South Cooperation. Contributions by regional institutions include the Ibero-American General Secretariat's technical support for quantification and assessment through the Ibero-American Program to Strengthen South-South Cooperation. Various intraregional development cooperation mechanisms and frameworks have also emerged to enhance policy coordination; examples include the Forum on China-Africa Cooperation, the India-Africa Forum Summit, the BRICS Summit, and the IBSA Summit.

The United Nations development system is seeking ways to improve the effectiveness of its development cooperation through the Quadrennial Comprehensive Policy Review (QCPR). Restricted aid earmarked for specific projects contributes to fragmentation, competition and overlap among entities, and discourages United Nations system-wide focus,

strategic positioning and coherence. Mobilizing of core funding is one of several issues addressed in the Secretary-General's proposed Funding Compact, an agreement by Member States and the United Nations development system that aims to reverse highly fragmented funding and improve transparency and accountability.[61]

In presenting his proposals on repositioning of the United Nations development system to better respond to the 2030 Agenda for Sustainable Development, the Secretary-General has placed the effectiveness of the system's development cooperation front and center, emphasizing three key principles: reinforcing national ownership; developing country-contextual responses; and ensuring the effective delivery of development results on the ground (see chapter III.F for an update on the repositioning process).

Box 5
Development cooperation and development finance assessments

Costa Rica is working on a national strategy for effective development cooperation, which aims to put in place a mechanism to manage and coordinate official development assistance (ODA), South-South cooperation, and other funding modalities and partnerships for the 2030 Agenda for Sustainable Development. The strategy, which will be agreed through a participatory and inclusive approach, applies a strong gender equality and human rights focus, and emphasizes reducing inequalities and poverty, environmental sustainability and resilient infrastructure.

Malawi's third Growth and Development Strategy (2017-2020) recognizes the importance of increased development finance and its effective utilization to maximize impact. Currently, 75 per cent of development cooperation projects use government results indictors, 55 per cent rely on government monitoring data, and the use of country systems has decreased. The Government plans to review its Development Cooperation Strategy to address issues of effectiveness, enhancing ownership, alignment, harmonization and mutual accountability. In 2017, the Government began a Development Finance Assessment to examine how development cooperation can be used to leverage private finance and other sources of financing.

Honduras and the Dominican Republic organized national multi-stakeholder follow-up forums to reflect on the Global Partnership for Effective Development Cooperation monitoring results and explore how to implement effectiveness commitments. The forum in Honduras led to a road map to operationalize effectiveness commitments at the national level, complementing and informing ongoing efforts to develop a new development cooperation policy and its currently ongoing Development Finance Assessment. The forum in the Dominican Republic focussed on consensus building around the new development cooperation policy, which applies to the country's dual role as recipient and provider, aligns development cooperation with the Sustainable Development Goals and aims for a whole-of-government-approach while also engaging non-state actors.

---

61 United Nations, Report of the Secretary-General on Repositioning the United Nations development system to deliver on the 2030 Agenda: our promise for prosperity and peace on a healthy planet (A/72/684 – E/2018/7). Available from https://documents-dds-ny.un.org/doc/UNDOC/GEN/N17/460/52/pdf/N1746052.pdf?OpenElement.

Chapter III.D
International trade as an engine for development

1. Key messages and recommendations

The Addis Ababa Action Agenda (hereafter, Addis Agenda) acknowledges that international trade is an engine for inclusive economic growth and poverty reduction. At the same time, if the right mix of policies is not implemented, trade may leave some individuals and communities behind. Political leaders have therefore called for policies that ensure the gains from trade are shared more widely.[1] Having in place overall economic policies and systems that promote job growth, decent work, social mobility and social protection can create a conducive framework within which specific policies of trade adjustment can be more successful. Well-designed and gender-responsive policies tailored to country circumstances—such as job search assistance, training programmes, and lifelong education—can augment workers' skills and facilitate employment. Complementary policies in areas across the 2030 Agenda for Sustainable Development, such as housing, financial inclusion and infrastructure, also play a role in easing adjustment. *Collectively, World Trade Organization (WTO) members can show leadership by reiterating their commitment to open, fair and mutually beneficial trade as a key driver of economic growth and a major engine for prosperity.*

Developing countries, especially commodity-dependent countries, appreciate that increasing the economic and social benefits of trade requires diversifying their production. Appropriate investment and access to markets is necessary. The international community has committed to supporting them through Aid for Trade, support for trade facilitation, and continued preferential market access for the exports of the least developed countries (LDCs). Targeted technical assistance and trade-related capacity-building are essential to integrating vulnerable countries into the trading system—particularly LDCs, landlocked developing countries (LLDCs) and small island developing States (SIDS)—and ensuring they are not left behind.

Emerging trends, such as global expansion of internet connectivity, have increasingly influenced international trade and enhanced trade's contribution to the Sustainable Development Goals (SDGs) in recent years. For instance, e-commerce is transforming global business, and opening international markets, including for micro, small and medium-sized enterprises (MSMEs). E-commerce may provide untapped potential for enhancing inclusive trade growth in developing countries. *Policymakers should explore opportunities for encouraging further growth in cross-border e-commerce to harness relevant opportunities for development and create conditions, procedures and resources in the best interest of inclusive development.*

Global consumers and businesses are paying greater attention to the impact of trade upon social and environmental sustainability.[2] This is reflected in the inclusion of provisions that address labour conditions, empowerment of women and/or environmental sustainability in bilateral and regional free trade agreements (FTAs). At the same

---

1   G20 Leaders' Communique Hangzhou Summit (2016).
2   United Nations Conference on Trade and Development, *Trade and Environment Review 2016,* UNCTAD/DITC/TED/2016/3. Available from http://unctad.org/en/PublicationsLibrary/ditcted2016d3_en.pdf.

time, these measures should not inadvertently act as non-tariff barriers to exports from developing countries. *Open dialogue is warranted on aligning new trade agreements with the SDGs, including through inclusion of gender equality and core labour standards.*

Trade finance plays a key role in enabling global trade flows, creating economic value, and driving inclusion by helping developing countries participate in global trade. Easing constraints on the supply of trade finance and supply chain finance, including credit and risk mitigation in regions where trade potential is the greatest, could help MSMEs grow and support the development of the poorest countries. *Export credit agencies and multilateral development banks (MDBs) could explore further developing trade and supply chain finance programmes. Trade finance can be enhanced by promoting standardization of trade finance instruments and consistent implementation of anti-money laundering (AML), countering the financing of terrorism (CFT) and know your client (KYC) regulations across jurisdictions.*

2. Developments in international trade

2.1 World trade flows

The volume of world trade grew by 3.7 per cent in 2017 and appears set to continue at a similar pace through 2019 (see figure 1). While marking a recovery from the slowdown in 2015 and 2016, global trade growth has returned to the slow-growth trend that characterized the period of the recovery from the 2008 world financial and economic crisis.

The dollar value of world trade recovered in 2017 from the two previous years of absolute decline, owing to a strengthening in commodity prices, and it appears set to accelerate in 2019. Many commodity exporters experienced a drastic fall in their export earnings in dollar terms in 2015-2016, while maintaining their export volumes. Sub-Saharan Africa's export earnings in 2015 and 2016, for example, declined by an average of about 20 per cent per year.[3]

Within the overall developments in international trade, there are a number of notable trends. The Addis Agenda and SDG target 17.11 pledge to

Figure 1
Value and volume of world exports, 2009–2019
(*Percentage change*)

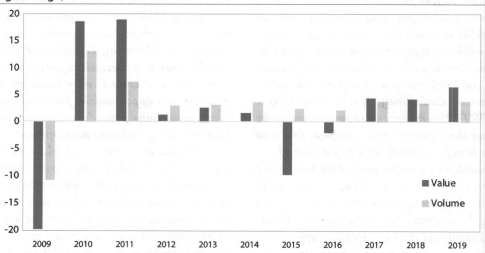

Source: United Nations (2017), World Economic Situation and Prospects 2018: Annex table A.13.
Note: 2017 is based on partial estimates; 2018–2019 is based on forecasts.

---

3   United Nations Conference on Trade and Development, "Key Statistics and Trends in International Trade 2017" (Geneva, forthcoming).

double the LDC share in global exports by 2020. Yet, exports of LDCs as a share of the global total declined in recent years, as shown in figure 2. Much of this change may be explained by the recent fall in commodity prices, and thus some recovery should be visible when data become available for 2017 and 2018. Nevertheless, it will be difficult to achieve this SDG target by 2020.

One reason for the disappointing trend in the LDC share of global trade is the high dependence of many of these countries on commodity exports, including both agricultural commodities and natural resources. As shown in figure 3, more than 40 per cent of LDCs count on commodities for over 30 per cent of their exports, and more than 20 per cent rely on them for over 50 per cent of their exports. For LLDCs, the corresponding indicators of commodity dependence are even starker. African countries, in particular, suffer from a lack of export diversification.[4]

Nonetheless, LDCs and other countries have been working to diversify their exports and some results are now visible. For example, the number of international tourist arrivals in Africa has continued to grow, with an average annual increase of 6 per cent over the last two decades.[5] Tourism in Africa today contributes on average 8.5 per cent of gross domestic product (GDP) and supports 1 out of every 14 jobs in the region. Intraregional sustainable tourism strategies can support economic diversification, sustainable growth and development.

2.2 Digitalization and trade

At the same time, e-commerce, or the buying or selling of goods or services online, is transforming the global business and trade landscape at an unprecedented speed, opening international trade opportunities that most developing countries have yet to fully grasp. Cross-border e-commerce today accounts for 12 per cent of globally traded goods.[6]

Figure 2

Least developed countries' share of global merchandise exports and imports, 2000–2016
(*Percentage*)

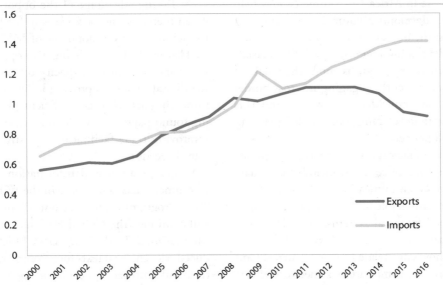

Source: UNCTADStats (2018).

4   Economic development in Africa report 2017, (United Nations publications, Sales No: E.17.II.D.2).
5   Ibid.
6   McKinsey Global Institute, "Digital globalization: The new era of global flows", February 2016. Available from https://www.mckinsey.com/business-functions/digital-mckinsey/our-insights/digital-globalization-the-new-era-of-global-flows.

Figure 3
Commodity dependency index, 2016
(Percentage of countries)

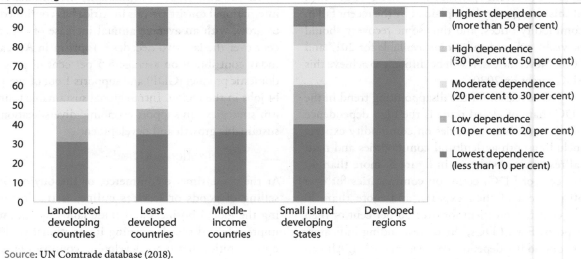

Source: UN Comtrade database (2018).

However, there is still a gap between developed and developing countries. Companies in developed countries export to twice as many markets on average as those in developing countries, and three times as many as those in Africa.[7] E-commerce may help companies in developing countries to export to more markets; the highest growth of e-commerce is observed in developing regions, especially in Asia.[8] Future growth is expected, as more than half of companies not currently engaging in cross-border e-commerce have considered doing so, and this share is higher in developing countries (65 per cent) and Africa (68 per cent).[9]

A number of factors act as potential constraints on the use of e-commerce. These include inadequate information and communications technology (ICT) infrastructure; unreliable and costly power supply; underdeveloped financial systems; weak legal and regulatory frameworks; low levels of ICT literacy; and lack of knowledge related to e-commerce. Concerns also exist over competition, as network effects may lead to monopolies or oligopolies in some parts of the e-commerce value chain, leading to greater value capture outside of developing countries. The handling of data is also a concern, both in terms of privacy and in relation to how to attribute value addition for the purposes of taxation (see chapter III.A).

Taking advantage of the opportunities from e-commerce is one possible way for policymakers to facilitate the development of MSMEs (see box 1). However, fully utilizing the opportunities of e-commerce requires capacity-building, reducing the digital divide, improving knowledge and skills, improving access to cost-efficient platforms, assuring sound payment and delivery services, as well as improving trade facilitation and streamlining customs procedures.

Cooperation and information exchange on e-commerce has taken place in the WTO under the Work Programme on Electronic Commerce, which will continue. The United Nations Commission on International Trade Law (UNCITRAL) has produced relevant legal texts for e-commerce law reform that could further support cross-border digital transactions, particularly by increasing the uniformity of countries' legal rules governing e-transactions,

---

7   International Trade Centre, "New Pathways to E-commerce: A Global MSME Competitiveness Survey", (Geneva, September 2017). Available from http://www.intracen.org/publication/New-Pathways-to-E-commerce/.

8   *Information Economy Report 2017*, (United Nations publications, Sales No: E.17.II.D.8).

9   International Trade Centre, "New Pathways to E-commerce: A Global MSME Competitiveness Survey".

Box 1

E-commerce: Does it contribute to inclusive growth?

Information communications and technology (ICT) can bring down transaction costs and enable the remote delivery of more goods and services, facilitating the scaling up of micro, small and medium-sized enterprises (MSMEs). ICT use can enhance the productivity of enterprises, which remains far from being fully exploited in most developing countries.

The digital economy can offer opportunities for entrepreneurship, innovation and new job creation. New payment solutions or innovative logistics associated with e-commerce can help MSMEs overcome infrastructural barriers to their market expansion. It can also enable them to engage in peer-to-peer collaboration in innovation and to use alternative funding mechanisms such as crowdfunding.

Being online can also level the playing field for women-owned firms. The share of women-owned firms doubles when moving from traditional offline trade to cross-border e-commerce. For Africa, three out of four firms trading exclusively through e-commerce identified themselves as women-owned.

However, the digital economy also poses challenges for developing-country MSMEs, including lack of technical skills and business knowledge, expensive membership fees in e-commerce platforms, and difficulty in registering or complying with platform requirements. MSMEs, with their small consignment, face a limited choice in logistics and delivery service providers as well as challenges in finding warehouses in the destination market. The share of logistics cost over final price in developing countries is nearly double of that in developed countries.[a]

a ITC , "New pathways to e-commerce: a global MSME competitiveness survey", 25 September 2017. Available from http://www.intracen.org/publication/New-Pathways-to-E-commerce/.

---

e-signatures and digital authentication, and thus their interoperability to support cross-border e-commerce.

3.   The multilateral trading system

3.1   Progress on multilateral trade negotiations

The Addis Agenda recognizes the importance of multilateral trade negotiations at the WTO, yet significant challenges exist to reach consensus at the WTO as members' views on many issues diverge substantially. The Eleventh WTO Ministerial Conference (MC11), held in Buenos Aires from 10 to 13 December 2017, adopted five ministerial decisions, although substantive outcomes were not possible in most areas. Most progress was made in reducing fisheries subsidies that harm sustainable development prospects, with a commitment from members to secure a deal which delivers on SDG target 14.6 by the end of 2019.[10] The next two years will be critical in defining the technical ground for common disciplines on which agreement may be reached and

finding the political will needed for a final multilateral outcome.

Other MC11 decisions included extending the practice of not imposing customs duties on electronic transmissions for another two years, and continuing the moratorium on bringing non-violation and situation complaints under the Agreement on Trade-Related Aspects of Intellectual Property Rights (TRIPS). There were also decisions on the continuation of the work programme on small economies and on the creation of a working party on the accession of South Sudan.

However, despite serious efforts from all members, no agreement was possible on a number of the substantive issues under discussion, including public stockholding for food security purposes and other issues under the agricultural negotiations pillar. At the conclusion of MC11, Ministers expressed their disappointment over the lack of progress, and committed to continuing the negotiations related to all remaining relevant issues, including advancing work on the three pillars of agriculture (domestic support, market access and export competition)

---

10   SDG 14.6 sets a target for eliminating illegal, unreported, and unregulated (IUU) fishing subsidies and for prohibiting certain forms of fisheries subsidies that contribute to overcapacity and overfishing, with special and differential treatment for developing countries and least developed countries.

as well as non-agricultural market access, services, development, TRIPS, WTO rules, and trade and environment.

Three proponent groups announced new initiatives to advance talks at the WTO on the issues of e-commerce, investment facilitation and MSMEs. Each group includes developed countries, LDCs, and other developing countries, with participation open to all WTO members. Seventy-one members, accounting for 77 per cent of global trade, initiated the exploratory work towards future WTO negotiations on trade-related aspects of e-commerce. On investment facilitation, 70 WTO members, who account for about 73 per cent of trade and 66 per cent of inward foreign direct investment (FDI), agreed to structured discussions with the aim of developing a multilateral framework. Eighty-seven WTO members, accounting for 78 per cent of world exports, issued a joint statement declaring their intention to create an informal multilateral working group on MSMEs that would address obstacles to participation of these firms in international trade. Additionally, 118 WTO members and observers agreed to support the Buenos Aires Declaration on Women and Trade, which seeks to remove barriers to, and foster, women's economic empowerment.

3.2   Trade restricting and facilitating measures

During the period from mid-October 2016 to mid-October 2017, WTO members applied 108 new trade-restrictive measures, including new or increased tariffs, customs procedures, quantitative restrictions and local content measures. This equates to an average of 9 measures per month compared to 15 in the previous period. However, WTO members also implemented 128 measures aimed at facilitating trade, including eliminated or reduced tariffs and simplified customs procedures. At almost 11 tradefacilitating measures per month, this remains significantly lower than the monthly average of 18 recorded in the previous annual overview report. WTO members continue to implement more trade-facilitating than trade-restrictive measures, a trend observed over the past four years. The estimated trade coverage of import-facilitating measures ($169 billion) is more than two times larger than

that of import-restricting measures ($79 billion), although regional differences exist.

In addition, the import-facilitating measures implemented during the review period in the context of the expansion of the Information Technology Agreement are estimated at about $385 billion, or 2.4 per cent of the value of world merchandise imports. In the area of trade remedy measures, the review period saw a slight deceleration, both in initiations of investigations and in terminations of measures, compared to the previous annual overview and to the whole of 2016. Anti-dumping measures continue to make up the bulk of all trade remedy initiations.

3.3   Implementation of the Bali and Nairobi outcomes

The implementation of the agreements in the WTO Ministerial Meetings in Bali (2013) and Nairobi (2015) continues. As regards the elimination of agricultural export subsidies, three WTO members provided implementation updates on the reduction of agricultural export subsidies. On Preferential Rules of Origin for LDCs, all elements in the Ministerial Decision that required follow-up action by the Committee on Rules of Origin have been implemented. The Committee has intensified its technical work to examine members' existing practices with respect to preferential origin requirements for LDCs in order to better understand these requirements, to analyse their possible impact on the ability of LDCs to fully utilize preferences, and to encourage the adoption of best practices. It is encouraging that some preference-granting members have already informed the Committee about positive modifications to their preferential rules of origin as a result of discussions related to the Ministerial Decision.

Regarding the LDCs Services Waiver, which would provide services exports with preferential treatment, the number of notifications of preferences in favour of LDC services and service suppliers stands at 24 (on the part of 51 members). In welcoming the preferences, the LDC Group at WTO called on members to help LDC suppliers avail themselves of those preferences. Members were urged to develop projects in LDCs that built supply capacity on the ground and to raise awareness of the Waiver among their respective domestic constituencies.

The WTO Committee on Trade and Development (CTD) undertook its annual review of the steps taken to provide duty-free, quota-free (DFQF) market access to LDCs. However, due to divergent views among some members on the scope and coverage of DFQF access on offer, the WTO secretariat could not issue the report as mandated in the Bali Ministerial Decision on the issue. Regarding the Monitoring Mechanism for Special and Differential Treatment provisions, members continued their discussion on this matter at the CTD and shared their thoughts on why the Monitoring Mechanism had not yet been tested and whether or not to review the Mechanism at this stage as contemplated in the Bali Ministerial Decision.

4. Promoting international trade that is consistent with the SDGs

In order to spread the benefits of international trade more widely, it is important that more individuals and firms are able to participate. This can be done by ensuring market access for LDCs by lowering tariffs; reducing the costs of trade through trade facilitation; building trade capacity through Aid for Trade; easing the supply of credit to exporters and importers through trade finance; and including women in international trade. Voluntary sustainability standards can help align international trade with the 2030 Agenda for Sustainable Development.

4.1 Market access for LDCs

Overall, zero tariffs apply to more products exported by developing countries and LDCs. In 2016, the product coverage of duty-free treatment for LDCs increased by 10 percentage points from the level in 2010, and by 16 percentage points from 2005. For developing countries as a whole, duty-free market access was granted to 50 per cent of products that they exported in 2016. The biggest expansion of zero tariffs between 2015 and 2016 was observed in the textile and clothing sectors, although the clothing sector remains the most protected.

While average tariffs facing key exports of LDCs to developed-country markets have not shown much reduction in the past several years, the graduation of some middle-income countries from the European Union (EU) Generalised Scheme of Preferences (GSP), as of January 2015, has caused a slight increase in the tariffs applied to textile exports from developing countries in 2015 and 2016.

4.2 Trade facilitation

The WTO Trade Facilitation Agreement (TFA), a key outcome of the WTO Ninth Ministerial Con-

Figure 4

Duty-free access of least developed countries' exports, 2005–2016

(Percentage)

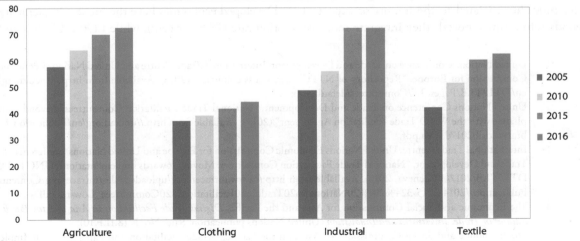

Source: Elaborations from ITC Market Access Map database (2018).

ference, held in Bali from 3 to 7 December 2013, entered into force on 22 February 2017, after more than 15 years of negotiations. The agreement aims to expedite cross-border trade, improve transparency, increase possibilities for participation in global value chains, and reduce the scope for corruption. At the end of 2017, 126 out of 164 WTO members have ratified the TFA. Members also made strides on the notification front, especially regarding the submission of implementation schedules. To date, 102 developing-country and least developed country members have given notice of the provisions they considered themselves able to implement at the time the TFA entered into force and that have since taken effect. Thirty-six also indicated which provisions require additional time to be implemented (the so-called category B commitments). Twenty-seven members further notified provisions on which they consider that they need capacity-building support for implementation (category C commitments).

The agreement contains a provision (article 23.2) requiring members to "establish and/or maintain a national committee on trade facilitation or designate an existing mechanism to facilitate both domestic coordination and implementation of provisions of this Agreement". National Trade Facilitation Committees enable the planning and implementation of successful trade facilitation reforms.[11, 12, 13]

Cross-border trade can also be facilitated by single-window facilities. Compressing administrative procedures related to the import or export of goods into a single portal, they integrate multiple government agencies into a common platform. As of 2017, twelve African countries use single-window facilities. Asia-Pacific countries have continued to develop their single-window facilities, including through a United Nations treaty that was formally signed by several Asian countries in 2017. These paperless trade systems aim at enabling the electronic exchange and mutual recognition of trade data and documents. Asia-Pacific Member States are preparing for implementation of a Framework Agreement on Facilitation of Cross-Border Paperless Trade in Asia and the Pacific.[14]

Like single windows for trade, one-stop centres allow investors, including foreign investors that engage in trade, to complete all regulatory and licensing procedures necessary for business establishment. As a result, they reduce the costs and time required to establish businesses. They also aim to prevent informal trade by supporting the formalization of small-scale cross-border traders. This has important gender implications as many of them are women. In addition, these one-stop shops allow Governments to advertise sectors of high priority to investors across the globe, and screen these investors in an effective yet low-cost manner. Challenges to their effective implementation relate to technical capacity, budgetary constraints and, above all, inter-agency coordination, which calls for policy coherence at national and regional levels.

The speed of implementation of the TFA commitments and other trade-facilitating measures varies considerably across countries (see figure 5).[15] Developed economies have the highest implementation rate (78.5 per cent), while LDCs, LLDCs and

---

11   United Nations Conference on Trade and Development, International Trade Centre and United Nations Economic Commission for Europe, "Repository of NTFC cases across countries" (2018). Available from http://unctad.org/en/DTL/TLB/Pages/TF/Committees/default.aspx.

12   United Nations Conference on Trade and Development, "National Trade Facilitation Committees: Beyond compliance with the WTO Trade Facilitation Agreement" (2017). Available from http://unctad.org/en/PublicationsLibrary/dtltlb2017d3_en.pdf.

13   International Trade Centre, United Nations Economic Commission for Europe and United Nations Conference on Trade and Development, "National Trade Facilitation Committees: Moving towards implementation", UNCTAD/DTL/TLB/2017/3 (Geneva, 2015). Available from http://www.intracen.org/uploadedFiles/intracenorg/Content/Publications/2014-2015-324%20-%20National%20Trade%20Facilitation%20Committees_Low-res.pdf.

14   The Economic and Social Commission for Asia and the Pacific, *Digital Trade Facilitation in Asia and the Pacific, Studies in Trade, Investment and Innovation* (United Nations publication, Sales No. E.18.II.F.10).

15   The Economic and Social Commission for Asia and the Pacific, "Trade Facilitation and Paperless Trade Implementation - Global Report 2017" (Bangkok, November 2017). Available from http://www.unescap.org/resources/trade-facilitation-and-paperless-trade-implementation-global-reports-2017.

Figure 5
Implementation of trade facilitation measures, 2017
(*Trade facilitation score*)

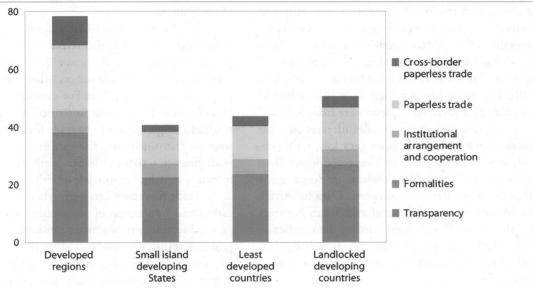

Source: UN Global Survey on Trade Facilitation and Paperless Trade Implementation, 2017; UNESCAP (2018).

SIDS achieve implementation rates significantly below the global average (between 40 and 50 per cent), indicating that these countries may need further technical assistance and capacity-building support to help them bridge the implementation gap.

4.3 Aid for Trade

As of 2015, almost $300 billion has been disbursed for Aid for Trade support, mainly in Asia (41.5 per cent) and Africa (38.7 per cent), with 27 per cent of the total going to LDCs. Regional and global programmes attracted almost 15 per cent of total disbursements. More than three quarters of total disbursements have gone to four sectors: transport and storage (28.6 per cent), energy generation and supply (21.6 per cent), agriculture (18.3 per cent), and banking and financial services (11.1 per cent).[16] Aid for Trade support could focus more on gender equality, by designing projects and programmes in which women have a higher presence, including in the informal sector.

In addition, Aid for Trade in support of the implementation of the TFA is becoming a greater priority for both developing countries and donors.[17] Moreover, a broad range of countries at all levels of development is undertaking actions to boost digital connectivity, ranging from supply-side issues such as ICT infrastructure and network coverage availability, to the demand-side issues that affect digital connectivity such as affordability and usage.

4.4 Trade finance

The importance of short-term financing of international trade, known as trade finance, is explicitly recognized in the Addis Agenda as an important means of implementation of the SDGs. Estimates show that if trade financing to small and medium-sized enterprises (SMEs) increases by 10 per cent, global trade

16 Organization for Economic Cooperation and Development, World Trade Organization, *Aid for Trade at a Glance 2017* (OECD Publishing, Paris, 2017). Available from https://www.wto.org/english/res_e/publications_e/aid4trade17_e.htm.

17 World Trade Organization, "Aid for Trade Global Review 2017 Monitoring Exercise" (2017). Available from https://www.wto.org/english/tratop_e/devel_e/a4t_e/a4tmonit_6gr_e.htm.

would grow by 1 per cent.[18] However, the gap in trade finance remains large, particularly in developing countries, with global unmet demand estimated at about $1.5 trillion.[19] The gap is especially pronounced for SMEs, including many women entrepreneurs. While SMEs comprise 44 per cent of proposed trade finance applications, they comprise 58 per cent of all the declined trade finance proposals in 2016. This figure has increased since 2014, when 53 per cent of all declined requests were from SMEs.[20]

Existing data shows that default rates on trade finance have historically been very low, with typically lower default rates and expected losses than other asset classes. Nonetheless, in some areas, trade financing data is incomplete. Data for Africa, the Middle East, and Central and South America remains limited, although existing data indicates that default rates remain low. Strengthening data collection on default and recovery rates is thus important.

The Basel Committee on Banking Supervision sets standards for the capital that commercial banks must hold against liabilities (see chapter III.F), including liabilities related to trade finance. The December 2017 Basel III reforms adjusted capital charges for banks' exposures to other banks, which are relevant for trade finance exposures. The reforms incorporated the removal of the Basel II sovereign floor rule which the Basel Committee on Banking Supervision announced in October 2011. Under the sovereign floor rule, the counterparty risk weight applied to a claim on a bank could not be lower than that of the risk weight applied to the Government of the country in which the bank was incorporated, resulting in higher risk weights for banks in countries that are poorly rated or do not have credit ratings.[21] Improving regulatory alignment across countries, encouraging greater collaboration between financial

institutions, and promoting standardization of trade finance instruments can help combat the decline in correspondent banking and enhance the provision of trade finance.

MDBs and export credit agencies, together with local, regional and international banks, can play an important, catalytic role in the provision of trade finance. The default rate on MDB trade finance portfolios is extremely low. For example, the Asian Development Bank, as an intermediary bank, has not had a single default in its trade finance portfolio over the last nine years. The vast majority of MDB trade finance activities (98 per cent) are guarantees to banks to reduce country-level risk.

Trade financing can be furthered with digitization and automation of transactions and due diligence. Electronic transactions can infuse efficiency, promote transparency—including through providing a trail of ownership to the transaction—and enhance efforts to build security around data and its accessibility. Digital platforms and fintech can lower barriers to enter the financial markets and increase productivity, and can also reduce costs of due diligence and KYC processes, thus helping to reverse the decline in correspondent banking.

4.5   Women in international trade

Women's participation in international trade supports several SDGs, but has been constrained by a number of challenges. The United Nations Conference on Trade and Development (UNCTAD) has developed the Trade and Gender Toolbox[22] to analyse and measure the potential impacts of trade on women and girls. Ex ante gender impact assessments of trade agreements, for instance, help Governments identify policy measures that redress anticipated negative impacts upon women, and scale up other measures that are expected to have positive impacts.

18   World Trade Organization, "Trade Finance and SMEs: Bridging the gaps in provision" (2016). Available from https://www.wto.org/english/res_e/booksp_e/tradefinsme_e.pdf.

19   Asian Development Bank, "2017 Trade Finance Gaps, Growth, and Jobs Survey" (September 2017). Available from https://www.adb.org/publications/2017-trade-finance-gaps-jobs-survey.

20   International Chamber of Commerce, *2016: Rethinking trade and finance* (October 2016). Available from https://cdn.iccwbo.org/content/uploads/sites/3/2016/10/ICC-Global-Trade-and-Finance-Survey-2016.pdf.

21   Basel Committee on Banking Supervision, *High Level Summary of Basel III reforms* (December 2017). Available fromhttps://www.bis.org/bcbs/publ/d424_hlsummary.pdf.

22   United Nations Conference on Trade and Development, "Trade and gender toolbox", UNCTAD/DITC/2017/1 (2017). Available from http://unctad.org/en/PublicationsLibrary/ditc2017d1_en.pdf.

The Toolbox methodology has already been applied to assess the impact on the well-being of women and gender equality in Kenya from the Economic Partnership Agreement between the EU and the East African Community.

Gender equality issues started to feature more strongly in recent FTAs than before. First, gender considerations were introduced in the preambles of some of the earlier trade agreements or addressed as cross-cutting issues. Gender-related capacity-building mechanisms were already in place in some of the FTAs as well. In more recent FTAs, gender equality issues are addressed in specific chapters devoted to gender, which greatly increase the visibility of such issues in trade instruments. Both the Canada-Chile FTA and the Chile-Uruguay FTA acknowledge the importance of gender mainstreaming and equality policies in fostering sustainable economic development. These FTAs include provisions for cooperation activities that benefit women in numerous areas—such as skills enhancement, financial inclusion, agency and leadership, entrepreneurship, and access to science, technology and innovation—and for the setting up of trade and gender committees to operationalize the relevant chapters of the agreements.[23] To date, gender provisions do not include aspects such as gender-related standards, application of dispute settlement mechanisms to trade and gender chapters, and harmonization of gender-related legislation between the parties.

The ITC-led SheTrades[24] initiative seeks to connect 1 million women-owned businesses to markets by 2020 and has identified seven global actions needed to unlock markets for women: (i) quality gender-disaggregated data on economic participation; (ii) integrating gender awareness into trade policies and trade agreements; (iii) opening up government procurement to women entrepreneurs; (iv) supporting supplier diversity in the private sector; (v) enabling market access for women in a wider array of sectors; (vi) enabling access to financial services; and (vii) overturning legal impediments to women's economic participation, including access and ownership of resources.

4.6 Voluntary sustainability standards

Voluntary sustainability standards (VSS) provide norms and metrics relating to production practices that reduce the negative impact of production upon environmental, social, ethical and food safety conditions in the producing countries. Reflecting the rapid growth of global demand for green and sustainable products, VSS-certified production has significantly expanded, particularly in the last decade. In 2015, about a quarter of the global coffee production was certified as complying with one or more VSS, such as Fairtrade International and UTZ, among others. Similarly, more than 16 per cent of global cocoa, 15 per cent of global palm oil and 14 per cent of global tea production in 2015 were certified as compliant with one or more VSS. Complying with VSS can reinforce the transformative impact of trade; for example, it enhances the marketability of agricultural, forestry and fishery exports of developing countries, and transforms on-the-ground production methods to more sustainable ones. It may also have gender impacts. For trade to play its full role in supporting markets for sustainable goods, however, it is important to ensure that VSS themselves do not become disguised forms of non-tariff barriers restricting trade. Ensuring that such standards are transparent, that they do not discriminate or restrict trade unnecessarily, and that they are based on relevant international standards, in line with WTO principles, can go a long way towards opening new trade opportunities, especially for small and medium-sized producers in developing and least developed countries.[25]

5. Bilateral and regional trade and investment arrangements

A large share of international trade today takes place under bilateral, regional or interregional FTAs. Thus,

---

23   United Nations Conference on Trade and Development, "The new way of addressing gender equality issues in trade agreements: Is it a true revolution?" UNCTAD Policy Brief No. 53, (October 2017). Available from http://unctad.org/en/PublicationsLibrary/presspb2017d2_en.pdf.

24   See https://shetrades.com.

25   The Economic and Social Commission for Asia and the Pacific, "Handbook on negotiating sustainability development provisions in preferential trade agreements" (Bangkok, forthcoming).

Figure 6
Intraregional goods trade, 2000–2016
(*Percentage of exports*)

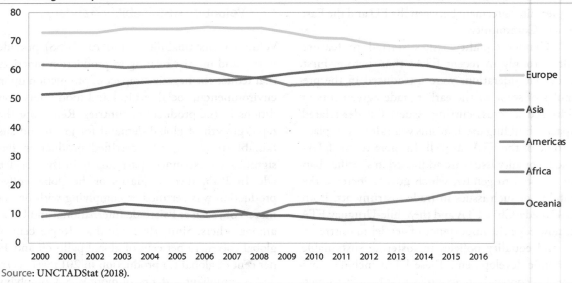

Source: UNCTADStat (2018).

trade in the Americas, Asia and Europe mainly takes place regionally, while in Africa, intraregional trade is lower than 20 per cent, with some growth (see figure 6).

5.1   Regional trade agreements

The process of harmonizing trade policy at the regional level is gaining momentum. In Africa, the African Continental Free Trade Area (AfCFTA) is scheduled for agreement in March 2018. There has been growing consensus that regional integration reduces trade costs within Africa and boosts regional value chains, and ultimately contributes to the achievement of the SDGs.[26,27] AfCFTA negotiations have largely completed a framework agreement and protocols on trade in goods, trade in services and dispute settlement, with a signing of the agreement by the African Union Heads of State and Government scheduled for 21 March 2018. The AfCFTA includes modalities to eliminate tariffs on

90 per cent of products over five years for non-LDCs and 10 years for LDCs. The remaining 10 per cent of products comprises sensitive products whose tariffs are to be liberalized over a longer period and excluded products, which will not initially be subject to liberalization. The AfCFTA is estimated to have the potential to increase intra-African trade by approximately 50 per cent in 2022 compared to the 2010 level.[28]

In other regional agreements, following the withdrawal of the United States of America from the Trans-Pacific Partnership, the 11 remaining member countries continued the negotiation process on the renamed Comprehensive and Progressive Agreement for Trans-Pacific Partnership (CPTPP). Covering 13 per cent of world gross product (WGP), the CPTPP was signed in March 2018. Negotiations on the Regional Comprehensive Economic Partnership (comprising 30 per cent of WGP)[29] of the Association of Southeast Asian Nations (ASEAN)

26   *Economic Report on Africa 2015*, (United Nations publications, Sales No: E.15.II.K.2).

27   Ibid.

28   United Nations Economic Commission for Africa, "ECA urges Africa to push ahead with Continental Free Trade Area", 1 December 2016. Available from https://www.uneca.org/stories/eca-urges-africa-push-ahead-continental-free-trade-area.

29   The Economic and Social Commission for Asia and the Pacific, "The Asia-Pacific trade and investment agreement database", Briefing note 10, (2018). Available from https://artnet.unescap.org/databases/aptiad-briefing-notes.

countries with Australia, China, India, Japan, New Zealand and the Republic of Korea, and are ongoing, as are negotiations between the European Union and Mercosur.

An increasing number of regional trade agreements have started to include provisions on social development (e.g., gender equality), but more generally on core labour standards. Labour provisions figure in about 30 per cent of all trade agreements made in 2017, compared to only 7 per cent two decades ago. Today, 70 per cent of trade agreements between developed and developing countries contain labour provisions. Recent research finds that trade-related labour provisions may help ease labour market access for women and reduce the gender wage gap. Research suggests that such provisions have not been used for protectionism, nor do they distort trade flows.[30] Others argue that labour provisions undermine the comparative advantage of lower-wage trading partners and could undermine their ability to raise standards through economic development, particularly if it hampers their ability to trade.[31] Further analysis suggests that there is no unambiguous evidence that trade agreements with labour provisions cause better labour market outcomes, although the two may be correlated.[32]

5.2 Investment agreements

The number of international investment agreements (IIAs) continues to grow amid greater complexity, albeit at a lower speed. In 2017, countries concluded 14 new IIAs, out of which there were 8 bilateral investment treaties (BITs) and 6 treaties with investment provisions (TIPs).[33] Three main types

of TIPs can be distinguished: (i) TIPs that include obligations commonly found in BITs, including substantive standards of investment protection and investor-state dispute settlement (ISDS) provisions; (ii) TIPs that include limited investment provisions; and (iii) TIPs that establish an institutional framework between the parties to promote and cooperate on investment.[34]

Countries terminated at least 16 BITs in an attempt to renegotiate their treaties to recalibrate the balance between the State and foreign investors. These terminations reflect a recent debate on how trade and investment can be made more inclusive and sustainable to ensure a more direct contribution to achieving the SDGs.[35] By end-2017, the cumulative number of IIAs stood at 3,326 treaties.

The number of new treaty-based ISDS cases continues to expand. The disputes can be costly for countries. In the Addis Agenda, Member States of the United Nations recognized that the goal of protecting and encouraging investment should not affect their ability to pursue public policy objectives. Member States further committed "to craft trade and investment agreements with appropriate safeguards so as not to constrain domestic policies and regulation in the public interest".[36]

To align IIAs with the SDGs, countries have embarked on a reform process to create a new generation of IIAs. Their focus concentrates on five areas: (i) safeguarding the right to regulate; (ii) reforming investment dispute settlement; (iii) promoting and facilitating investment; (iv) ensuring responsible investment; and (v) enhancing systemic consistency and modernizing existing stock of old

---

30   Celine Carrère, Marcelo Olarreaga and Damian Raess, "Labor Clauses in Trade Agreements: Worker protection or protectionism?" Development Policies, Working Paper No. 200 (FERDI, 2016). Available from http://www.ferdi.fr/sites/www.ferdi.fr/files/publication/fichiers/p200-ferdi-_c.carrere-m.olarreaga-d.raess_.pdf.

31   World Trade Organization, "Labour standards: consensus, coherence and controversy". Available from https://www.wto.org/english/thewto_e/whatis_e/tif_e/bey5_e.htm, (accessed 15 March 2018).

32   Alberto Posso, "Preferential Trade Agreements with labour provisions and labour market outcomes: evidence from Asia and the Pacific - Labour Provisions in Asia-Pacific free trade agreements Part II", Background Paper No.2/2017 (The Economic and Social Commission for Asia and the Pacific, 2017). Available from http://www.unescap.org/sites/default/files/DA9-02-2017%20Labour%20provisions%20in%20PTAs%202%20-%20Alberto%20Posso.pdf.

33   Examples of TIPs are investment chapters in economic partnership agreements and free trade agreements, regional investment agreements and framework agreements on economic cooperation.

34   World Investment Report 2016 (United Nations publication, Sales No. E.16.II.D.4).

35   Asia-Pacific Trade and Investment Report 2017 (United Nations publication, Sales No. E.17.II.F.22).

36   Addis Ababa Action Agenda of the Third International Conference on Financing for Development (Addis Ababa Action Agenda) (United Nations publication, Sales. E.16.I.7), para. 91.

Figure 7

International investment agreements signed, 2000–2017

(*Number of new BITs and TIPs signed and cumulative number of IIAs signed, minus those discontinued*)

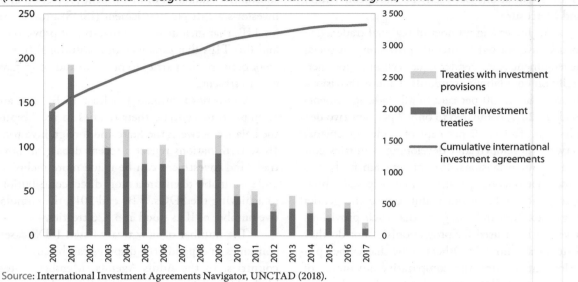

Source: International Investment Agreements Navigator, UNCTAD (2018).

generation treaties.[37] The African Union is finalizing a sustainable-development-oriented Pan African Investment Code, which aims to bring more regulatory coherence to intra-African investment. It would include standards—including on corporate social responsibility, human rights, natural resources and corruption—and structures—including ISDS and counterclaims by the State.

The impact of IIAs on investment flows is unclear. While IIAs cannot compensate for an otherwise substandard business and investment environment, they aim to send a positive signal to the investors that host countries party to IIAs are serious about attracting and protecting investments. Still some studies suggest that investors consider determinants of FDI—such as rapid economic growth potential, a minimum level of development, stable

political and economic climate, and an overall conducive business climate—to be more important than IIAs. [38, 39]

6. Domestic enabling environment for trade

At the domestic level, the Addis Agenda calls for policy actions that are complementary to trade policy changes and support households and businesses in capturing economic opportunities arising from trade. Strengthening the network of trade and investment supportive institutions (TISIs) that facilitate international business transactions can contribute to improving the international competitiveness of MSMEs, which in turn can help address the challenges facing equitable distribution of trade gains. These TISIs, such as chambers of commerce,

37   United Nations Conference on Trade and Development, "UNCTAD's Reform Package for the International Investment Regime", 18 December 2017. Available from http://investmentpolicyhub.unctad.org/Publications/Details/1183.

38   The Economic and Social Commission for Asia and the Pacific, *Handbook on policies, promotion and facilitation of FDI for sustainable development in Asia and the Pacific*, ST/ESCAP/2786 (Thailand, 6 November 2017). Available from http://www.unescap.org/sites/default/files/FDI%20Handbook-low.pdf.

39   United Nations Conference on Trade and Development, "The Impact of International Investment Agreements on Foreign Direct Investment: An Overview of Empirical Studies 1998–2014", Working Draft of IIA Issues Note (September 2014). Available from http://investmentpolicyhub.unctad.org/Upload/Documents/unctad-web-diae-pcb-2014-Sep%2024.pdf.

business associations and export promotion agencies, play a critical role in enabling MSMEs to access market information and networks and to improve their capacity to comply with international standards—necessary aspects of conducting business in international markets. It is estimated that each additional dollar invested in a national trade promotion organization would generate $87 worth of exports and $384 of additional GDP per capita.[40]

7.   Trade, technology and incomes

The WTO World Trade Report 2017[41] states that while the overall effects of trade on the volume of employment tend to be positive but minor, trade can offer opportunities for better paying jobs in many cases. While trade does play a role in increasing wage inequality, other factors, such as technological progress, are important determinants as well (see chapter III.G).[42]

Empirical evidence shows that international trade induces increases in the skill premium (the ratio of the wages of high-skilled workers to the wages of low-skilled workers), as well as skills upgrading in both developed and developing economies. The available evidence from developing economies also shows that trade affects employment composition through the adoption of new technologies. This comes about both by giving exporters incentives to invest in more productive technology and by making imports of technology-intensive capital goods cheaper. New technologies are complementary with high-skilled labour and often replace low-skilled labour.

However, the gains from trade are not shared equally within countries, leading to widespread economic and social disparities in some countries (see also section 4.5 on trade and gender). Removing trade barriers will change the distribution of gains and losses from trade, as firms and individuals adjust to new competitive pressures. In this process, the economy may experience aggregate net gains from trade, but the costs are often highly concentrated by sector, job type or geographic region. Shifts to the production structure—for example, by importing more technology-intensive capital goods—may also affect a country's terms-of-trade and ability to economically diversify in the long run. Overall, a broad set of policies would be needed to address these impacts, including in trade, education, training, housing, and regional development strategies. In other words, the requirements are part and parcel of sustainable development strategies.

40   International Trade Centre, "Investing in Trade Promotion Generates Revenue" Doc. No. TS-2016-4.E (Geneva, 4 February 2016). Available from http://www.intracen.org/publication/Investing-in-Trade-Promotion-Generates-Revenue/.

41   World Trade Organization, "World Trade Report 2017: Trade, technology and jobs" (2017). Available from https://www.wto.org/english/res_e/publications_e/wtr17_e.htm.

42   International Monetary Fund, World Bank and World Trade Organization, "Making trade an engine of growth for all: The case for trade and for policies to facilitate adjustment" (2017). Available from https://www.wto.org/english/news_e/news17_e/wto_imf_report_07042017.pdf.

Chapter III.E
Debt and debt sustainability

1. Key messages and recommendations

At a time when Governments are faced with large financing needs to implement the 2030 Agenda for Sustainable Development, and as global financial conditions are set to tighten, many countries are constrained from raising resources due to their already high debt burdens. Risks for a renewed cycle of debt crises and economic disruption are growing, posing a significant challenge to the achievement of the Sustainable Development Goals (SDGs). Despite a more favorable global economic outlook, emerging debt challenges in developing countries have intensified since the publication of last year's report. Debt-service indicators among developing countries have deteriorated in a widespread manner, and vulnerabilities have increased across developing countries, in particular in several countries that previously benefitted from debt relief under the Heavily Indebted Poor Countries (HIPC) and Multilateral Debt Relief (MDRI) initiatives. Many natural-resource-producing countries have seen rapid debt accumulation as Governments have attempted to cushion the shock from falling commodity prices. Strains are also evident in several countries experiencing conflicts or political unrest, and in some small island developing States (SIDS), which remain vulnerable to disasters.

Recent debt shocks highlight a need for enhanced measures to manage vulnerabilities, including through improving debt management capacities in many developing countries. The international community has long offered technical assistance in public debt management, including at the subnational level and going beyond central government liabilities. It also develops analytical tools to advise Governments of emerging vulnerabilities. The effectiveness of the tools, however, depends on central authorities having comprehensive information on the financial obligations of all units and levels of government. *Debtors need to improve their capacity to monitor and analyse debt developments, which will require better and broader data collection. Creditors have a role to play in these efforts by making terms and conditions of lending public, straightforward and easy to track.*

The 2017 Atlantic hurricane season underlined not only the vulnerability of SIDS to natural catastrophes, but also that innovative instruments, such as state-contingent debt instruments that reduce or delay debt-servicing payments in times of crisis, could lessen financial stresses. The International Monetary Fund (IMF) has recently investigated several proposals for such instruments. *The international community could consider actions to help realize the potential of this market, including through developing model contracts and common standards, providing technical support, and, more ambitiously, by increasing the use of such instruments in official lending.* An additional proposal from the Economic Commission for Latin America and the Caribbean (ECLAC) is being investigated by a task force of regional institutions that would swap discounted external debt of Caribbean countries for climate adaptation investments. *Additional detailed analysis of this proposal is warranted with a view to piloting implementation in a limited number of countries on a trial basis. Additional tools could also be explored to ensure that developing countries affected by disasters are not left to deal with growing debt burdens in the longer run.*

Changes in emerging and developing countries' debt compositions may render future insolvencies more complicated to address, with nontraditional development partners gaining increased prominence.

There are also growing obligations to new plurilateral[1] development finance institutions, although there is not yet a global understanding of whether those debts will enjoy the same seniority of payment as debt of traditional multilateral and regional development lenders. The Paris Club provides a forum for official creditor coordination, but does not currently include all countries. *There is thus a need to re-examine official creditor cooperation mechanisms to address these issues.* While improved bond contracts—including those that benefit from enhanced collective action clauses—should make borrowers less subject to litigation from distressed debt funds (so-called vulture funds), only 27 per cent of outstanding emerging market bonds have these enhanced clauses. *The international community should continue to consider ways to strengthen the treatment of the main components of sovereign debt in workouts. In this context, the international community should continue to strengthen the market-based approach through expanded use of enhanced clauses in debt contracts. It should also explore complementarities and incongruities of existing initiatives to specify principles and guidelines for debtor and creditor responsibilities in borrowing by and lending to sovereigns, in line with the commitment in the Addis Ababa Action Agenda (hereafter, Addis Agenda) to work towards a global consensus.*

2.   Debt trends

The cyclical upturn of the global economy in 2017-2018, described in chapter I, as well as continued monetary policy support and regulatory enhancements, have led to a decline in global near-term financial stability risks (see also chapter III.F).[2] However, this generally benign global environment masks increased debt risks and vulnerabilities in both developing and developed countries, particularly as monetary policy normalization continues and interest rates rise in global markets.

First, leverage continues to rise in the private nonfinancial sector in both developed and developing countries. Private sector debt—one of the triggers for the 2008 crisis—has continued to increase in the aggregate, with deleveraging uneven across sectors and countries. Second, the search for yield in global markets has allowed several developing countries to return to markets and issue sovereign bonds in 2017, leaving them vulnerable to debt rollover and interest rate risks, especially in the context of rising global interest rates. Third, commodity prices remain low, are only slowly recovering, and thus continue to weigh on balance sheets in commodity-exporting economies.[3] A renewed downturn in commodity prices would leave these economies vulnerable to fiscal and corporate debt risks.

Consequently, there is no reason for complacency about the stock of developing-country external debt. Many countries exceed threshold indicators jointly developed by the IMF and the World Bank for analyses of low-income-country debt sustainability (see figures 1 and 2).[4] Eighteen low-income developing countries were judged by the IMF and the World Bank to have high risk or already be in a state of debt distress (see figure 3), and ratings have been broadly deteriorating. As of end-2017, three countries have seen their rating downgraded relative to 2013, with only three upgrades. Fragile States, African post-HIPC countries, and commodity exporters were most likely to have a weaker debt assessment. Risks in SIDS also remain high, due in large part to their susceptibility to natural disasters.

1   The term "plurilateral creditor" refers to official lenders with more than one shareholder that extend non-commercial credit to other sovereigns and that do not have universal/open memberships, unlike established multilaterals such as the African Development Bank, Asian Development Bank, European Bank for Reconstruction and Development, Inter-American Development Bank and World Bank.

2   International Monetary Fund, *Global Financial Stability Report, October 2017*: Is Growth at Risk? (Washington, D.C., October 2017). Available from https://www.imf.org/en/Publications/GFSR/Issues/2017/09/27/global-financial-stability-report-october-2017.

3   United Nations, Report of the Secretary-General on external debt sustainability and development, 31 July 2017, A/72/253. Available from https://undocs.org/A/72/253.

4   For countries deemed to have policies and institutions of "medium" quality, the thresholds as revised in 2017 are external debt in excess of 40 per cent of gross domestic product (GDP) and debt servicing above 15 per cent of exports. See International Monetary Fund. *Review of the debt sustainability framework in low-income countries: Proposed reforms* (2017).

Figure 1
External debt of low- and middle-income countries, 2000–2017
(*Percentage of GDP*)

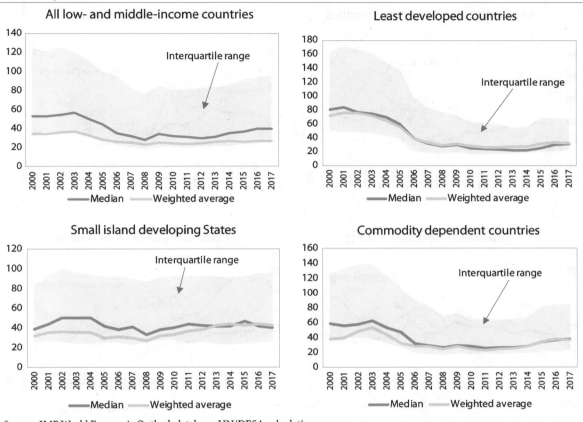

Source: IMF World Economic Outlook database, UN/DESA calculations.
Note: Commodity dependent developing countries as defined by UNCTAD, State of Commodity Dependence 2016. Available from http://unctad.org/en/PublicationsLibrary/suc2017d2.pdf.

Moreover, the composition of debt is changing. As noted above, many developing countries, including least developed countries (LDCs), have increasingly tapped international financial markets to raise resources. The share of private creditors in public and publicly guaranteed debt has doubled in LDCs, from 8 to 16 per cent of total external public debt, and increased from around 41 to 61 per cent in all developing countries (see figure 4). Increased market-based financing—both domestic and international—can be beneficial, but carries risks. In addition to not embedding concessional interest rates, market-based instruments typically have shorter maturities than official loans. "Bullet repayments"[5] increase rollover

risk, which could be further exacerbated by tightening global financial conditions.

The changing creditor landscape has also resulted in the increasing prominence of non-Paris Club (NPC) bilateral and plurilateral creditors. Between 2015 and 2016, South-South Cooperation drove a more than twofold increase in new bilateral loan commitments to low- and middle-income countries, reaching $84 billion.[6] In many cases, lending by NPC bilateral and plurilateral creditors has caused their share in total external debt to exceed the share of traditional Paris Club and multilateral creditors. This has implied a welcome unlocking of new financing, but often on less con-

5   A bullet repayment is payment of the face value of a bond on its maturity date, rather than amortized payments.
6   World Bank (2017). International Debt Statistics 2018. Available from https://data.worldbank.org/products/ids

Figure 2
External debt service of low- and middle-income countries, 2000–2017
(*Percentage of exports*)

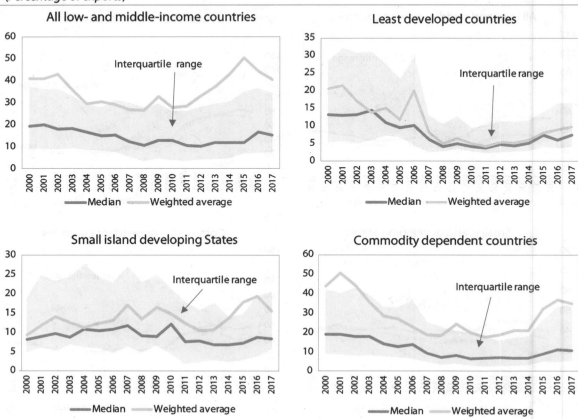

Source: IMF World Economic Outlook database, UN/DESA calculations.
Note: Commodity dependent developing countries as defined by UNCTAD, State of Commodity Dependence 2016. Available from http://unctad.org/en/PublicationsLibrary/suc2017d2.pdf. Debt service includes interest and amortization of short-term debt on an original maturity basis outstanding at the end of the previous year, plus the portion of long-term debt outstanding at the end of the previous year maturing during the current year. Thus, countries whose financial sectors hold substantial gross short-term external obligations will show large debt-servicing ratios, which do not necessarily imply unsustainability.

cessional terms. As these creditors are not integrated into existing mechanisms for creditor coordination (e.g., the Paris Club, which has long-standing principles to govern official sector involvement in debt restructurings), any restructuring that may be necessary could be more complicated.

Governments have also increasingly issued domestic debt in recent years, which reduces exchange rate mismatches and is welcome from a financial market development perspective. However, domestic debt often carries higher interest costs and specific risks. Countries where non-resident investors have a significant presence in the domestic debt market can be vulnerable to capital flight and associated exchange-rate pressures if non-resident investors with short-term investment horizons hold a significant amount of domestic debt and lose confidence in the Government's solvency or economic policies. Moreover, fiscal stress can transmit to domestic financial systems to the degree that banks have invested in local government bonds.

Finally, contracts for non-standard borrowing have been making increasing use of credit enhancements to shift lenders' risks to borrowers. For example, several countries—natural resource producers in particular—have issued debt that includes collateralization provisions. The terms of these provisions are often complex and in many cases non-transparent. They may commit the debtor to

Figure 3
Debt risk classification of low-income countries, 2007–2017
(*Percentage of total*)

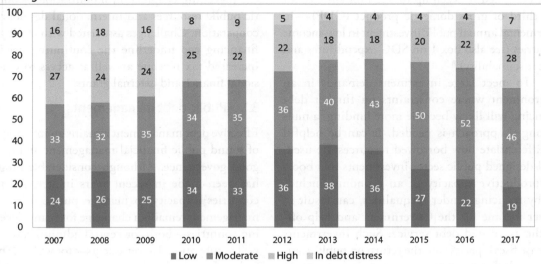

Source: IMF (LIC DSF database).
Note: Published debt sustainability analyses only, latest available per year. Coverage is of low-income developing countries eligible to draw from the Poverty Reduction and Growth Trust at IMF..

Figure 4
Composition of external public and publicly guaranteed debt
(*Share of total*)

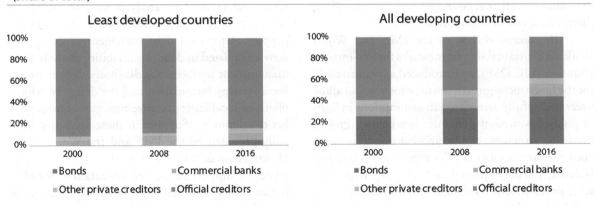

Source: World Bank, International Debt Statistics, UN/DESA staff calculations.

selling commodities to the creditor at below-market prices for some time or to selling specified public assets, although the terms of the loan may appear favourable up front. In cases of insolvency, such collateralization could complicate the restructuring, as these creditors would assert their rights to the assets or exports securing the loan, which could disrupt government operations.

3. Borrowing sustainably to advance sustainable development

Countries face pressing demands for additional public investment in the SDGs. A recent assessment of 26 low-income countries found that existing fiscal space is likely insufficient to undertake the spending needed to achieve the SDGs.[7] Investment needs have been estimated to reach up to $224 billion—about one third of gross domestic product (GDP)—in incremental annual public investment in low-income countries (see also box 1 on SDG expenditures and debt sustainability).[8]

To meet large investment demands in an environment where constraints on further debt financing will likely become more binding, a multipronged approach is needed. It can be helpful to differentiate how borrowed resources are used. Well-designed public sector investments that boost the productive capacity of an economy, including by reducing gender inequalities, can result in higher income for the Government and help offset the associated debt service. Such investments increase fiscal space when the return on public capital exceeds financing costs. Nonetheless, countries that are approaching debt sustainability limits will need to exercise prudence in implementing investment, since the near-term costs can be prohibitive, especially if additional borrowing risks are fuelling a debt crisis. In such cases, debt financing should be confined to projects with clear and large returns that would not tip the country's debt indicators into distressed levels or trajectories.

The recent review of the IMF and World Bank debt sustainability frameworks for low-income countries (LIC DSF) has introduced a "realism tool" for the investment-growth nexus, which would allow users to carefully assess growth assumptions in light of public investment dynamics (see below). Project financing structures can be another option in some countries and sectors if risks can be managed and isolated, possibly through risk sharing structures with development banks and private investors, as appropriate. However, it is critical that any such structure is fully transparent; contingent liabilities can greatly exacerbate debt crises, particularly when their realization occurs as a surprise.

External borrowing is of course not the only source of investable public resources, as indicated in the preceding chapters on mobilization of domestic public resources and international development cooperation. Challenges associated with closing the financing gap underline the continuing need for increased tax revenue as well as access to concessional finance and external grants.

3.1   Public debt management

Effective debt management remains an intrinsic part of sound public financial management and overall good governance. Although considerable progress has been made in recent years in strengthening countries' capacity to manage public debt, debt management remains a challenge for many developing countries—both for central administrations as well as subnational governments—for which continued international technical support is required, and given. As interest grows in the potential of subnational finance to contribute to the SDGs, capacity development support in public debt management will become even more important.

Technical assistance in public debt management can usefully be classified as either "upstream," which refers to debt analysis or assessment, or "downstream," which consists of implementation support. Upstream debt management comprises activities related to debt sustainability analysis; debt management performance diagnosis; debt management strategy formulation and the design of reform plans; or local currency government securities market development. Support in these areas is principally provided by the IMF and the World Bank. Downstream debt management technical assistance relates to support in the implementation of policy recommendations, debt data recording and validation, debt operations, and debt reporting and statistics. Organizations involved in providing technical assistance increasingly cooperate to ensure a holistic approach.

---

7   Anja Baum and others, "Can they do it all? Fiscal space in low-income countries", IMF WP/17/110 (Washington, D.C., 2017). Available from https://www.imf.org/en/Publications/WP/Issues/2017/05/05/Can-They-Do-It-All-Fiscal-Space-in-Low-Income-Countries-44889.

8   Guido Schmidt-Traub, "Investment Needs to Achieve the Sustainable Development Goals", SDSN Working Paper (2015). Available from http://unsdsn.org/wp-content/uploads/2015/09/151112-SDG-Financing-Needs.pdf.

> **Box 1**
>
> **SDG expenditures and debt sustainability**
>
> The relationship between the Sustainable Development Goals (SDGs) and debt sustainability is explored in ongoing research by the United Nations Conference on Trade and Development (UNCTAD)[a] which estimates the cost to government budgets of achieving SDGs 1–4[b] by 2030 for a sample of low-income, middle-income and upper-middle-income countries. The UNCTAD SDG model projects the evolution of general government gross public debt if the additional cost is covered by borrowing on commercial terms, on concessional terms or with grant financing covering half the borrowing requirement. These alternative scenarios are compared to a baseline business-as-usual scenario in which government expenditure and public debt follow current trends.[c]
>
> The SDG scenario shows that the increase in public debt is likely to be unsustainable in all three cases if additional expenditures are fully funded through debt issuance on commercial terms. If external grants cover 50 per cent of the additional fiscal expenditures, the growth of debt would be more manageable, but still high and likely unsustainable in all three cases.
>
> The resource gap to fully fund the eradication of extreme poverty and hunger and provide quality education and universal health care, while simultaneously stabilizing public debt levels, is significant. Progress in domestic resource mobilization, improved resource allocation in national budgets, and efficient public debt management would help to reduce the gap. The model shows, however, that such improvements would clearly be insufficient on their own, and that the SDGs cannot realistically be financed fully on commercial terms. In the light of large investment needs related to the 2030 Agenda for Sustainable Development, the SDGs will not be achieved without substantial support from the international community for what are essentially high-return investments in international prosperity and development.
>
> a   A more detailed description of this research can be found on the online annex of the Inter-agency Task Force on Financing for Development, available from https://developmentfinance.un.org/debt-and-debt-sustainability.
>
> b   SDG 1, no poverty; SDG 2, zero hunger; SDG 3, good health and well-being; SDG 4, quality education.
>
> c   The scenarios exclude the possibility of debt crisis due to a loss of creditor confidence owing to the size of the increase in public debt. They also assume that additional spending has no impact on the baseline rate of economic growth, and no increase in tax revenues. The model does not capture the impact on long-term productivity growth of improvements in human capital associated with the accomplishment of the covered Sustainable Development Goals (SDGs).

Different tools are available to boost debt management capacity. They include the Debt Management and Performance Assessment provided by the World Bank, the Medium-Term Debt Management Strategy tool provided by the IMF and the World Bank, and recording and reporting systems, such as the Commonwealth Secretariat Debt Recording and Management System and the Debt Management and Financial Analysis System of UNCTAD. Institutions, including the IMF, keep these tools under review and adapt them to changing needs.

UNCTAD and the Commonwealth Secretariat continue to be the major providers of downstream technical assistance in public debt management. In 2017, they supported over 100 countries in total. A key objective is to ensure the availability of reliable and timely debt data that is essential for prudent risk analysis and the elaboration of government strategies aimed at ensuring sustainable debt levels. The IMF and the World Bank, with the generous financial support of several bilateral donors, have provided a range of public debt management technical assistance and training activities to over 25 developing countries during the past fiscal year (July 2016-June 2017). The IMF Statistics Department also provides technical assistance on the compilation of government debt statistics.

The need for Governments to take a comprehensive approach to their nation's debt and asset management has also underlined the importance of improving debt management by subnational units of government, and by other elements of the public sector. Anecdotal evidence suggests that many subnationals are confronted with significant challenges in managing their public debt portfolios, although a number of subnationals have made substantial progress in improving debt management, in some cases with the support of international technical assistance. Coordinated assistance from both central Governments and the international community is needed to build the required level of capacity at the subnational level. The successful cooperation of UNCTAD and the Government of Argentina in establishing a capacity-building programme for its provinces is an example of such cooperation. In addition, the management of the assets and liabilities of state-owned enterprises, and of the Government's contingent liabilities can be of first-order importance in containing overall costs and risks.

3.2 Reform of the debt sustainability framework for low-income countries

Achieving debt sustainability is a major responsibility of the upstream side of sovereign debt management. The IMF and World Bank developed the LIC DSF to support this aim. Following an extensive review, and responding to changes in the debt landscape noted above, the IMF and the World Bank Executive Boards approved comprehensive reforms to the LIC DSF in September 2017.

Staff analyses and extensive consultations with debtors, creditors and civil society organizations identified several areas for improvement, showing a need to (a) ensure that the LIC DSF incorporates more country-specific information; (b) reflect the evolving financing landscape, including risks emanating from increased market financing and contingent liabilities; and (c) send important early warning signals without unnecessarily constraining countries' borrowing for development.

Against this backdrop, the framework has introduced a series of new features while maintaining its basic architecture including (i) a revised approach to assess country debt carrying capacities using an expanded set of variables in addition to the World Bank's Country Policy and Institutional Assessment indicators; (ii) methodological improvements to the framework's accuracy in predicting debt distress; (iii) tools to help shed light on the plausibility of underlying macroeconomic projections, including public investment dynamics, fiscal adjustments and their impact on growth dynamics; (iv) stress tests tailored to specific country circumstances, including on natural disasters and contingent liabilities; (v) streamlined debt thresholds and standardized stress tests; and (vi) a revised total public debt benchmark and tools for assessing risks associated with market-financing conditions.

The new LIC DSF is expected to become effective in the second half of 2018; a guidance note was published in February 2018 to provide operational and technical guidance on its implementation.[9] The IMF and World Bank will continue to conduct extensive outreach, and provide training opportunities on the new framework, both internally and to country authorities. Priority will be given to countries with weak capacity.

The IMF debt sustainability analysis for market access countries has been developed to monitor risks for countries that typically rely on financial markets for funding. A review of this framework has been initiated.

3.3 Transparency of debt reporting

Effective sovereign debt management requires full information on the terms and conditions of debt, contingent liabilities and domestic arrears, where they are present. These data need to provide broad coverage of the public sector, including subnational governments, social security funds and public corporations. Also, to inform debt projections, data should be available on debt contracts that have been signed but for which funds have not yet been disbursed.

Unfortunately, the full data set is often not available, with key data gaps arising from (i) countries reporting only the direct and guaranteed debt of the central administration; (ii) confidentiality clauses that prevent disclosure of key information; (iii) complex lending terms, particularly on collateralized lending; and (iv) poorly understood contingent liabilities related to potential banking sector stress, loss-making public enterprises or public-private partnerships, among others.

Building a fuller picture of developing countries' indebtedness and potential vulnerabilities will require actions from creditors as well as debtors. Debtor governments should build capacity to collect, analyse and publish debt data for a perimeter that extends beyond the central Government, disclose undisbursed portions of agreed loans, improve

---

9   International Monetary Fund, "Guidance Note on the Bank-Fund Debt Sustainability Framework for Low Income Countries", 14 February 2018. Available from http://www.imf.org/en/Publications/PolicyPapers/Issues/2018/02/14/pp122617guidance-note-on-lic-dsf.

accounting of contingent liabilities, keep track of arrears to suppliers, and attempt to limit use of confidentiality agreements in debt contracts they negotiate. They should also better monitor granting of officially guaranteed commercial debt, including those guaranteed by export credit agencies, as default on these loans can give rise to official arrears. Creditors should limit use of confidentiality clauses in debt contracts. Moreover, for collateralized loans tied to natural resource shipments, terms should be kept simple with compliance easy to monitor. A platform to publish comprehensive official and private sector lending is warranted.

4.　Natural disasters, shocks and debt sustainability

The devastating impact of the 2017 Atlantic hurricane season put the spotlight on the vulnerability of developing countries to natural disasters and their wide-ranging consequences. Hurricane Irma destroyed infrastructure and homes across Barbuda. Reconstruction costs estimated by the World Bank and Caribbean Development Bank estimated would equal 15 per cent of Antigua and Barbuda's annual GDP. Hurricane Maria swept over Dominica, causing loss of life and unprecedented destruction estimated at 226 per cent of GDP. As climate change is expected to make such events more frequent and more intense, there is need for the international community to address these risks, and for official sector creditors, in collaboration with countries at risk, to work on pre-emptive and reactive policies to provide appropriate support in times of crisis.

In terms of pre-emptive measures, it is important that countries receive sufficient support to finance successful adaptation to climate change. Countries at risk should build sufficient policy buffers in good times to support recovery, including through overall prudent debt management. However, they often face pressures on their fiscal positions from recovery expenditures and already high debt burdens, limiting their ability to invest sufficiently in climate adaptation. Despite existing exceptions for SIDS, many environmentally vulnerable countries have per capita incomes that make them ineligible to access concessional financing windows. A review of such eligibility and graduation criteria should be considered by the international community, as discussed in chapter III.C.

Most countries also cannot self-insure to the degree necessary. The use of state-contingent debt instruments, which are structured to automatically pay less or postpone payments to creditors during difficult times, could increase the resilience of sovereign balance sheets. There has been increasing international interest in how they might be designed (see box 2). Efforts are warranted to advance such analyses, including encouraging both the private and official sectors to experiment in issuing such instruments.

If a severe natural disaster does hit, provision of timely support is critical. Governments and international institutions have devised a number of quick disbursing loan facilities and insurance programmes to address sudden needs for international funds, as discussed in chapter III.F. There may also be a need to seek debt relief from private and official creditors. Prompt and constructive engagement with creditors can support an orderly and efficient debt restructuring to take place. In this context, steps have been taken and proposals made to address the financial constraints of environmentally vulnerable and highly indebted countries, aiming to ensure debt sustainability while explicitly accounting for climate change adaption needs and the impact of natural disasters. Grenada's 2015 debt restructuring introduced a "hurricane clause," which allows for a moratorium on debt payments in the event of a natural disaster. ECLAC has proposed a debt-for-climate adaptation swap for the Caribbean, involving discounted purchases from official and private creditors by the Green Climate Fund and channelling them to a Caribbean resilience fund to receive the freed national funds from the participating countries for disbursement to selected climate adaptation investments. A task force comprising several regional institutions was formed in December 2017 to advance work on the proposal.[10] In view of the systemic nature of the challenge that poses risks to the long-term debt sustainability in affected regions and the scale of climate

---

10　Economic Commission for Latin America and the Caribbean, "ECLAC establishes task force for Caribbean's Debt Swap Initiative", 27 November 2017. Available from　https://www.cepal.org/en/news/eclac-establishes-task-force-caribbeans-debt-swap-initiative.

Box 2
State-contingent debt instruments

There has been a renewed interest in the role that state-contingent debt instruments (SCDIs) can play in reducing risks to sovereign balance sheets. Such instruments are designed to link a country's debt obligation to its ability to pay, and can thus provide insurance against risks such as a deep recession, commodity price decline or natural disaster. Instruments include GDP-linked bonds, which would provide stability over the economic cycle; commodity-linked bonds, which could link interest payments to specific commodity prices; and "extendibles," which would provide an automatic maturity extension if a natural disaster occurs. [a] In response to growing interest, the IMF developed an associated toolkit to simulate debt and financing need impacts under varying SCDI designs.

Proponents of SCDIs have made a strong case for these instruments over recent decades. Their arguments note that GDP-linked bonds, which link the repayment obligations of a sovereign to economic growth, can stabilize the debt-to-GDP ratio and generate policy space during recessions that can be used to support recovery. Insofar as the debt stabilization benefits of such instruments reduce the probability of sovereign debt crises, the default risk premium on all the sovereign debt should fall. In debt restructurings, SCDIs could provide an important role in facilitating an orderly debt exchange, providing downside insurance to the sovereign while giving upside benefits to the creditors when the recovery is successful.

While the theoretical benefits are clear, critics point out that advocates fail to consider practical complications associated with issuing such instruments in financial markets. The IMF examined these constraints, finding that (i) liquidity and novelty premiums could be high when SCDIs are first issued; (ii) there may also be stigma associated with such "first-movers;" (iii) significant issuance could lead to a reduction in the supply of conventional bonds; (iv) SCDIs could transfer "excessive" risk to the private sector; and (v) issuance could increase the risk of "moral hazard" (meaning the borrower takes excessive risk knowing relief will be provided).

Despite these challenges and constraints, there is scope for greater use of SCDIs, especially by small open economies that are vulnerable to terms-of-trade shocks and natural disasters. Official sector actions could help realize the potential of this market, including through developing model contracts and common standards, providing technical support to debt management and statistic offices, and, more ambitiously, by underwriting or subsidizing their issuance. Public creditors should also consider increasing the use of state-contingent instruments in their own lending, building on existing experience such as countercyclical lending contracts by the Agence Francaise de Développement.

a International Monetary Fund, "State-contingent debt instruments for sovereigns", IMF Policy Paper, 22 May 2017. Available from https://www.imf.org/en/Publications/Policy-Papers/Issues/2017/05/19/pp032317state-contingent-debt-instruments-for-sovereigns.

---

change adaptation needs, the international community could also consider a greater use of global risk pooling mechanisms (see also chapter III.F).[11]

5. Resolving unsustainable debt situations

As the Addis Agenda notes, scope exists to improve the arrangements for resolving sovereign insolvency crises.[12] Recent developments reported above may further challenge these arrangements.

5.1 Official creditor involvement in debt restructurings

A more fragmented official creditor base could pose coordination challenges in future debt restructurings. Effective official creditor coordination will remain essential, given what are referred to as first-mover and free-rider problems.[13] The Paris Club has extensive experience in negotiating debt relief on behalf of a large group of official creditors in

---

11   See, for example, United Nations Conference on Trade and Development, "Environmental vulnerability and debt sustainability in the Caribbean: do we have enough tools to address catastrophic risk?", Policy Brief 62. Available from http://unctad.org/en/PublicationsLibrary/presspb2017d11_en.pdf.

12   *Addis Ababa Action Agenda of the Third International Conference on Financing for Development (Addis Ababa Action Agenda)* (United Nations publication, Sales. E.16.I.7), para. 99. Available from http://www.un.org/esa/ffd/wp-content/uploads/2015/08/AAAA_Outcome.pdf.

13   A "first-mover" refers to the first creditor to restructure, who in turn gets the most favourable deal; the "free-rider" is a less cooperative creditor who benefits from concessions given by other creditors.

ways that overcome these problems. Further expansion of the Club would provide one way to address this challenge in the new environment and thereby strengthen the international financial system. Alternatively, official creditors would need to develop other coordination mechanisms.

International practice has been not to restructure debts owed to the multilateral institutions and to the IMF, except in exceptional circumstances, such as those addressed by the Multilateral Debt Relief Initiative of 2005. However, there is thus far no experience in restructuring debts owed to new development finance institutions, and it is unclear whether these creditors will demand senior treatment on par with established multilateral creditors (such as the World Bank) that other official bilateral creditors may not accept. A further complication is the case of public sector entities that have purchased and hold the sovereign bonds of other countries. In these circumstances, there could be a lack of clarity about whether the bondholder is a private or an official creditor. Even where this distinction is clear, the existence of official and private creditors in the same voting pool (e.g., in a bond with collective action clauses) could complicate restructurings.

Against the backdrop of a more challenging official sector landscape, it would be helpful to look back at prior experiences of official sector actions to identify workable approaches for the future. In this context, and as part of its commitment to assemble a comprehensive database on debt restructurings, the IMF is examining ways to present comparable information on both private and official sector involvements (building, for the latter, on the database of Paris Club debt treatments). The effort is expected to be completed by end-2018.

5.2   Private creditor involvement in debt restructurings

Lacking sufficient political support to develop a proposed comprehensive sovereign debt workout mechanism, the international community has focused on encouraging contractual improvements to facilitate restructuring of insolvent obligations to private cred-

itors. In addition, to further encourage cooperative behaviour, a number of "soft-law" approaches have suggested principles and guidelines for debtor and creditor interaction.

In October 2014, the IMF endorsed key features of enhanced collective action and pari passu clauses in international sovereign bond contracts. These features are meant to reduce issuers' vulnerability to holdout creditors in case of a debt restructuring. Between October 2014 and end-September 2017, 245 of the 338 international bond issuances (approximately 87 per cent of the nominal principal value of new internationally issued sovereign debt) included such enhanced collective action and modified pari passu clauses. However, with only about 27 per cent ($294 billion out of $1.1 trillion) of the outstanding stock of international sovereign bonds having the enhanced clauses, a significant stock without these provisions remains and will decline only gradually.[14] Moreover, the enhanced clauses only apply to bonds; a significant portion of developing countries also have borrowed from banks, to which these clauses do not apply.

While an aim of the contractual reforms was to reduce the ability of non-cooperating bondholders to undermine voluntary restructurings, investors in distressed debt have a role to play in resolving unsustainable borrowing situations. Distressed debt investment funds can provide liquidity in secondary markets for sovereign bonds. However, a subset of these funds that buys the distressed debt at a large discount with the intent to recover the full face value through litigation has made restructurings extremely difficult. Thus, recent legislative efforts have been made to curtail this type of investing, including the Law on Deterring the Activities of Vulture Funds, adopted in Belgium in 2015. A spread of such legislation to other jurisdictions could help to further discourage disruptive behaviour and should aim to strike the right balance between further discouraging disruptive behaviour and preserving secondary-market liquidity.

In the absence of "hard" law oversight of workouts from sovereign insolvency, a number of forums

---

14   International Monetary Fund, "Third Progress Report on Inclusion of Enhanced Contractual Provisions in International Sovereign Bond Contracts" (Washington, D.C., 2017). Available from https://www.imf.org/en/Publications/Policy-Papers/Issues/2017/12/15/pp113017third-progress-report-on-cacs.

have sought to specify principles and guidelines that, while not mandatory, could, through voluntary adoption, become accepted standards that courts might choose to enforce. Indeed, the Addis Agenda committed Member States to working towards a global consensus on guidelines for debtor and creditor responsibilities in borrowing by and lending to sovereigns, building on existing initiatives.

Such initiatives began with the "Principles for stable capital flows and fair debt restructuring" of the private sector Institute of International Finance (IIF), originally issued in 2004, last updated with an addendum to the principles in 2012;[15] this was followed by the Human Rights Commission's "Guiding principles on foreign debt and human rights"[16] in 2011, the UNCTAD "Principles on promoting responsible sovereign lending and borrowing"[17] (noted in para. 97 of the Addis Agenda), the General Assembly resolution on basic principles on sovereign debt restructuring processes[18] that has been adopted into national law by two countries, and the Group of Twenty's (G20) "Operational guidelines for sustainable financing".[19]

While the IIF initiative focused on recommendations to debtor governments, the other initiatives focused on the responsibility and accountability of borrowers and lenders alike. The UNCTAD Principles also focus on the safeguarding of the public interest in sovereign debt financing and contracting. The G20 guidelines emphasize best practice and are concerned with the sustainability of financing tools and practices. These different foci and emphases provide ample opportunity for the exploration of complementarities as well as incongruities, in line with the commitment in the Addis Agenda to work towards global consensus.

---

15   The Principles and the Addendum may be found in Institute of International Finance, "Report on implementation by the Principles Consultative Group" (2017). Available from https://www.iif.com/system/files/32370132_pcg_report_2016-vf.pdf.

16   A/HRC/20/23.

17   United Nations Conference on Trade and Development, "Principles on promoting responsible sovereign lending and borrowing", UNCTAD/GDS/DDF/2012/Misc.1.

18   A/RES/69/319.

19   Welcomed by G20 Finance Ministers, Baden Baden, March 2017. Available from http://www.bundesfinanzministerium.de/Content/DE/Standardartikel/Themen/Schlaglichter/G20-2016/g20-operational-guidelines-for-sustainable-financing.pdf?__blob=publicationFile&v=2.

Chapter III.F
Addressing systemic issues

1. Key messages and recommendations

The Addis Ababa Action Agenda (hereafter "Addis Agenda") emphasises the importance of the coherence and consistency of the international financial and monetary and trading systems in support of development. To achieve the Sustainable Development Goals (SDGs), Member States of the United Nations need not only increased financing, but also fit-for-purpose national and international institutions that facilitate economic stability and sustainable development.

The 2008 world financial and economic crisis highlighted regulatory gaps and misaligned incentives in the international financial system. Reforms to financial system oversight proposed in the aftermath of the crisis have aimed to address these concerns. The Financial Stability Board (FSB) and the financial regulatory standard-setting bodies monitor implementation of post-crisis regulatory reforms, as well as the impact of reforms on financial intermediation, including for small and medium-sized enterprises (SMEs) and long-term financing. *Member States should implement agreed financial regulatory reforms, while being watchful of unintended consequences as well as new regulatory gaps that may result from financial innovation.*

Post-crisis prudential financial measures, along with international macroeconomic policy coordination, have helped support a more stable international economic environment. Yet, as noted in chapter I, the world remains vulnerable to financial and economic volatility. After nearly a decade of loose monetary policies in many countries, rising global interest rates could lead to capital flight from developing countries, resulting in currency volatility, increased risk of debt distress, and real-sector economic impacts. Continued efforts are needed to further reduce systemic risks and promote a strong, stable and sustainable global financial and monetary system. *Countries with systemically important economies should continue to develop mutually coherent macroeconomic and financial policies.*

At the same time, the world is increasingly challenged by disasters that cause humanitarian emergencies and reverse development progress. A number of initiatives taken over the past decade increased the availability of quick-disbursing international financial resources for use during economic and financial crises and after disasters. To facilitate stocktaking of these efforts, the 2017 ECOSOC Forum on Financing for Development Follow-up invited the Inter-agency Task Force on Financing for Development (hereafter, "Task Force") to prepare an inventory of existing quick-disbursing instruments that can assist countries, which is included as an annex to this chapter.

Some quick-disbursing instruments are part of the multilayer global financial safety net (GFSN) for addressing economic crises. While the GFSN has been strengthened at the national, regional and global levels in recent years, *Governments should continue to work to remove gaps in GFSN coverage, ensure adequate levels of financing, increase its flexibility and strengthen its countercyclicality.* The development of new regional institutions and bilateral instruments has expanded the availability of resources for many countries; however, many of the instruments are untested in practice. *The Task Force recommends continued efforts to improve coordination between different elements of the GFSN, ensuring the combined responses would be adequate and agile enough to meet the depth of possible challenges.*

The inventory also describes programmes to pool risks related to disasters to be able to better manage them. Currently, the international community is serving like an "insurer of last resort" for emergencies through an ad hoc system of voluntary responses, but in some cases this financial response is slow or insufficient. These ex post measures also do not incentivize disaster risk reduction. *Contributors to disaster response should work to realign their financing from ex post to ex ante provision of risk-pooling funds and instruments, improving efficiency, predictability and speed of response. An increased focus on preparedness should include developing instruments that build incentives for risk reduction into their design and facilitate "building back better".* Expanding and diversifying risk pools can reduce the costs of protection and improve their sustainability. Insurance-like instruments can be a useful complement to pooled funds; although to effectively diversify risks, a sufficient number of countries need to participate. *To increase coverage, the Task Force recommends that donors assist least developed and other vulnerable countries in participating in sovereign risk pools.*

The United Nations is also working to make itself fit for purpose for the 2030 Agenda for Sustainable Development, exemplified by a proposal of the Secretary-General for system-wide reforms to enhance United Nations institutional coherence with sustainable development, including achievement of gender parity at all levels. A central component of these reforms is a restructuring of the United Nations development system (UNDS), including proposals for revamping the Resident Coordinator system and introducing a Funding Compact. *Adoption of UNDS reforms can help promote institutional coherence, increase the system's capacities, and enhance its partnership approach at country-level to help realize the ambition of the sustainable development agenda.*

2.   Macroeconomic stability

As discussed in chapter I, the synchronized upturn in growth provides an opportunity for policymakers worldwide to address risks in the economic and financial systems as well as impediments to long-term investment (see chapter III.B) that hold back progress towards the SDGs. Continuation of the global growth trend in 2018 looks likely, but significant risks to the forecast remain. As noted, expected increases in interest rates in systemically important economies can have spillover effects on exchange rate stability, capital flows and ultimately growth in developing countries. As noted, social and environmental factors—for example, inequality and climate change—impact both the global macroeconomic environment and the financial system, and should be included in the stability agenda. Greater global macroeconomic policy coherence would help mitigate downside risks and reduce spillovers. The world has several systems in place that aim to promote macroeconomic stability and help mitigate some of the impact of risks. These include early warning systems, macroeconomic policy coordination, and global standards for regulation of the financial system. There are also tools available at the national level to help mitigate some of the residual risks.

The global early warning system

The main international process for monitoring vulnerabilities in the global financial system is jointly undertaken by the International Monetary Fund (IMF) and the FSB, the latter primarily focused on financial markets and institutions. The main mechanism of the FSB for identifying and assessing risks and vulnerabilities in the financial system is the Standing Committee on Assessment of Vulnerabilities (SCAV).[1] The SCAV focuses on macrofinancial-related vulnerabilities and risks arising from structural weaknesses in the financial system, such as misaligned incentives, amplification mechanisms or other forms of potential market

---

[1]   SCAV members include the International Monetary Fund (IMF), the Bank for International Settlements, the Organization for Economic Cooperation and Development and the World Bank, as well as members from forums of securities regulators (through the International Organization of Securities Commissions), banking regulators (through the Basel Committee on Banking Supervision) and insurance regulators (through the International Association of Insurance Supervisors).

stress. Its work focuses on the potential for international spillovers across financial systems that may be difficult to contain at a domestic or regional level. Where policy actions are deemed to be required to address vulnerabilities, the SCAV draws attention to them in relevant forums, FSB standing committees, and standard-setting bodies, as appropriate.

The IMF and the FSB also jointly conduct semi-annual early warning exercises (EWE) that consider a range of scenarios, including tail risks that may be less likely but potentially more disruptive.[2] The EWE does not attempt to predict crises, but rather seeks to identify vulnerabilities and triggers that could precipitate systemic crises, and suggests risk-mitigating policies.[3]

The IMF employs a comprehensive approach to detecting risks that make countries vulnerable to crises. As part of this assessment, Fund members are evaluated twice per year for underlying vulnerabilities in their fiscal, external and domestic non-financial sectors, and for potential price volatility in financial markets.[4] Quantitative toolkits tailored to each of three country groups—advanced economies, emerging markets and developing economies—are used to inform the assessment. In addition, countries are assessed for susceptibility to events that might spill over from other markets or countries, as well as for weaknesses in expected policy implementation that could impede an adequate response to an emerging crisis owing to political instability or gridlock.

Fund staff also analyse the transmission mechanisms from climate risks to financial stability, and help identify good practices for macroprudential stress tests reflecting climate risks. Various financial sector assessment programmes, from small island developing States (SIDS) to major jurisdictions, have included stress tests for effects of disasters on financial institutions.

Capital account management and macro-prudential regulations

One potential source of instability of special concern to developing countries resides in the capital account of the balance of payments. Large and volatile capital flows can give rise to systemic risks through many channels, with potentially substantial impact on the asset prices, exchange rates, debt sustainability and financial stability, often impacting the real economy. Historically, many developing countries—indeed, developed countries as well, in the early post-war decades—limited the flow of funds into and out of their economies, particularly short-term investments, out of concern for their destabilizing volatility. Over time, however, more and more countries removed restrictions on capital flows in expectation of greater financial inflows. While capital-account liberalization can deliver benefits through increased capital inflows, historically it has often been followed by rapid credit expansion and financial crises. The Addis Agenda notes that when dealing with risks from large and volatile capital flows, necessary macroeconomic policy adjustment could be supported by macroprudential and, as appropriate, capital-flow management measures.

In 2017, the IMF examined how macroprudential policies could help increase resilience to large and volatile capital flows[5] as a follow-up to its 2016 review on experience with its policy framework on capital-account policies.[6] The paper finds

2   The early warning exercises (EWEs) are not published, but IMF country, regional, and global surveillance activities follow up on EWE findings and policy recommendations.

3   Following discussion at the IMF Executive Board and with the Financial Stability Board (FSB), the EWE findings are presented to senior officials during the IMF-World Bank Spring and Annual Meetings; International Monetary Fund, "IMF Annual Report 2017: Promoting Inclusive Growth" (Washington, D.C., 2017), p. 34.

4   See International Monetary Fund, "Assessing Country Risk: Selected Approaches—Reference Note", 1 June 2017. Available from https://www.imf.org/en/Publications/TNM/Issues/2017/06/01/Assessing-Country-Risk-Selected-Approaches-44959.

5   Macroprudential policy options, mainly applied to banks, include countercyclical capital requirements (eased in economic downturns, increased during booms); capital requirements that differentiate risk by financial sector; measures to contain liquidity and exchange rate mismatches on bank balance sheets; and caps on permitted loan-to-value and debt-to-income ratios. They can also include tools traditionally associated with other policy fields, such as monetary policy (e.g., reserve requirements) and fiscal policy (e.g., levies imposed on wholesale funding).

6   See the discussion in the 2017 report of the Inter-agency Task Force on Financing for Development.

that macroprudential policies, in support of sound macroeconomic policies and strong financial supervision and regulation, can play an important role in helping countries harness the benefits of capital flows while mitigating systemic financial risks and improving the capacity of the financial systems to safely intermediate cross-border flows.[7] The IMF is building a new macroprudential database that will deepen understanding of how macroprudential measures can increase resilience to systemic risks associated with capital-flow volatility. Going forward, it will also continue to engage with its members in dialogue on capital flow issues.

3. Financial regulation

When the 2008 world financial and economic crisis struck, it became clear that regulatory frameworks were insufficient to address systemic risks in the financial system. A significant portion of the financial sector had exposure to assets that were much riskier than most financial sector analysts or regulators understood, especially in the housing sector in certain developed countries. The response was to strengthen regulations on risk-taking by financial institutions (while giving financial support to prevent bankruptcy to some large financial institutions with systemic implications), while also taking steps to strengthen consumer protection.

Now, almost a decade after the reform process was initiated, policy development for the agenda endorsed by the Group of Twenty (G20) is largely complete. The FSB, which brings the major regulatory authorities together in one forum, has concluded that the "G20 reforms are building a safer, simpler, fairer financial system".[8] The remaining gaps in implementation, the risk of reform fatigue or even reform rollback, combined with new and emerging risks to financial stability, underscore the importance of dynamic and effective implementation of financial regulation to ensure the regulatory framework keeps pace with a changing financial

system, mitigates crisis risks, and aligns with the sustainable development agenda.

Robust regulatory frameworks are essential for the stability of the international financial system, and a prerequisite for implementing the 2030 Agenda for Sustainable Development. To achieve the SDGs, the international financial system needs to intermediate credit towards sustainable development in a stable manner, balancing the goals of access to credit with financial stability. Ultimately, stability and sustainability are mutually reinforcing: long-term investment should contribute to a more stable financial and monetary system; without a stable system, the development agenda risks being derailed by future crises. At the same time, regulations create incentives—including incentives on the allocation of capital, with potential unintended consequences on access to credit for implementation of the SDGs, such as to underserved SMEs (see section 3.1 below), trade finance (see chapter III.D), long-term financing for infrastructure (see chapter III.B), and flows to developing countries. However, there have not yet been full evaluations of these impacts. Concerns have been compounded by low levels of global investment, with many companies spending their earnings on dividends and stock buybacks, rather than investing in productive capacity (see chapter III.B).

The FSB has been monitoring whether updated regulations constrain access to credit; it has found that, overall, higher financial resilience is being achieved without impeding the supply of credit to the real economy. Cross-border banking exposures have declined (see figure 1), driven particularly by declining cross-border exposure of European banks. However, cross-border bank claims in all other regions have continued to increase. Some emerging market and developing economies continue to report concerns about the reduction in global banks' activity in their domestic markets. To date, this decline does not seem to have significantly impacted their overall credit growth.

7   International Monetary Fund, "Increasing Resilience to Large and Volatile Capital Flows—The Role of Macroprudential Policies", IMF Policy Papers (Washington, D.C., 2017). Available from https://www.imf.org/en/Publications/Policy-Papers/Issues/2017/07/05/pp060217-increasing-resilience-to-large-and-volatile-capital-flows.

8   See the FSB chair's letter to the G20, available from http://www.fsb.org/2017/07/fsb-chairs-letter-to-g20-leaders-building-a-safer-simpler-and-fairer-financial-system/.

Figure 1
Cross-border banking exposures, 2000–2017
(Billions of United States dollars, percentage)

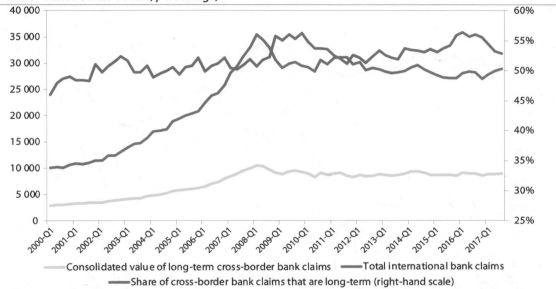

Source: BIS, UN/DESA calculations based on BIS data.

Figure 2 shows that total cross-border bank claims on developing countries have continued to rise, although the shares that are long-term have decreased, and trends vary across countries. Continued monitoring and analysis, including of liquidity during periods of stress, is needed in order to determine if countries are experiencing unintended consequences. Going forward, the FSB expects to increasingly focus on monitoring regulatory implementation by national authorities, and evaluating the effects of the reforms, using its framework for post-implementation evaluation published in July 2017.[9] The framework will guide analyses of whether reforms are achieving their intended outcomes, and help identify material unintended consequences that should be addressed. The FSB is currently evaluating trends in the financing of infrastructure investment including, to the extent possible, the effects of financial regulatory reforms on this financing.

3.1 Regulating financial institutions

One of the main aims of banking regulations is to ensure that commercial banks hold sufficient capital and liquidity to cover potential losses in the bank's portfolio and absorb liquidity shocks, and thus better withstand financial and economic stress. Various complementary requirements were agreed by the Basel Committee on Banking Supervision (BCBS) since 2009, including boosting the ratio of banks' capital to its risk-weighted assets (i.e., its loans portfolio, with higher risk weightings for riskier assets in order to incentivize banks to reduce risky activities); increasing banks' capital relative to total assets (leverage ratio); assuring banks have enough high-quality liquid assets to meet potential short-term net cash outflows (liquidity coverage ratio); and requiring banks to maintain a sustainable funding profile—that is, relying primarily on sources of funding that are generally stable, like some retail deposits, in contrast to those that are more volatile, like some unsecured wholesale funding (net stable funding ratio). As may be seen in figure 3 and figure 4, higher levels of additional capital and liquidity coverage were gradually attained and the shortfalls measured against the new standards were largely eliminated. In addition, a countercycli-

---

9   Financial Stability Board, "Implementation and Effects of the G20 Financial Regulatory Reforms, 3rd Annual Report" (Basel, 3 July 2017). Available from http://www.fsb.org/wp-content/uploads/P030717-2.pdf.

Figure 2
Cross-border banking exposures to developing countries, 2000–2017
(*Billions of United States dollars, percentage*)

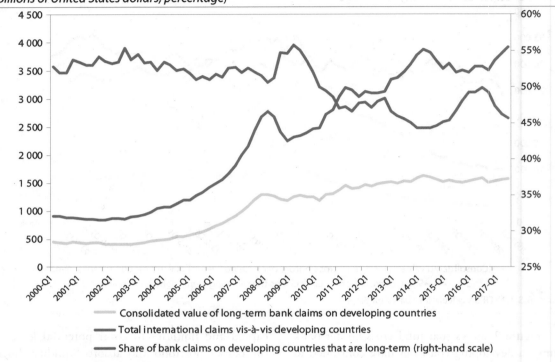

Consolidated value of long-term bank claims on developing countries
Total international claims vis-à-vis developing countries
Share of bank claims on developing countries that are long-term (right-hand scale)

Source: BIS, UN/DESA calculations based on BIS data.

cal factor, which increases capital requirements during boom times and reduces them during times of economic bust, was added to the regulators' toolkit and is currently being phased in.[10]

Final standards were adopted by the BCBS in December 2017 to reduce excessive variability in banks' risk-weighted assets.[11] With respect to the standardized approach for credit risk,[12] which is used by the majority of banks in countries that apply Basel standards, the reforms improve the granularity and risk sensitivity of the risk weights to take into account more information about the underlying asset and/or counterparty. Notably, the BCBS introduced a lower risk-weight for loans to SMEs, in recognition of the important role they play in generating growth and jobs, and in contributing to sustainable development. These reforms will take effect from January 2022.[13]

Other areas of reform also reflect progress on the FSB agreed agenda. For example, the latest

10   For an explanation of the policy and current countercyclical positions, see Bank for International Settlements, "Countercyclical capital buffer (CCyB)", 18 February 2018. Available from https://www.bis.org/bcbs/ccyb/.

11   For details, see Bank for International Settlements, "Governors and Heads of Supervision finalise Basel III reforms", press release, 7 December 2017. Available from https://www.bis.org/press/p171207.htm.

12   The standardized approach is the simplest approach to estimating credit risk, as banks apply risk weights based on the type of borrower and the type of credit exposure.

13   With regard to the internal-ratings-based approaches for credit risk, which are used by the largest and most complex banks, the December 2017 reforms to take effect from January 2022 remove the ability to use advanced approaches for exposure to financial institutions and mid- and large-sized corporates and specify a number of input parameters. The reforms also remove the use of internal model approaches for operational risk. In addition, the reforms introduce an output floor that limits the extent to which banks can lower their capital requirements relative to the standardized approaches, which will be phased in from 2022 to 2027. See Bank for International Settlements, "Basel III: Finalising post-crisis reforms" (December 2017). Available from https://www.bis.org/bcbs/publ/d424.pdf.

progress report showed that almost all FSB member jurisdictions have substantively implemented the principles and standards on the deferral and use of compensation tools to more effectively align the compensation of employees with the long-term interests of their firms in order to reduce excess risk-taking.

To remove the problem of financial institutions being "too big to fail," recovery and resolution standards have been developed to ensure no financial institution is so big that it cannot be resolved; additional loss-absorbency standards have been developed as well. Global systemically important banks (G-SIBs) will need to meet standards about the total loss-absorbing capacity they will need to hold. Should a systemically important institution fail, it would need to be wound up, or "resolved," in an orderly fashion across many countries, with the goal of avoiding a ripple effect throughout the global financial system. While reforms in this area have progressed, further work is required to build effective resolution regimes and to operationalize resolution plans for cross-border firms.

In addition, the International Association of Insurance Supervisors (IAIS) is working to develop an activities-based approach to systemic risk in the insurance sector, rather than a size-based approach. This may have significant implications for the assessment of systemic risk in the insurance sector and hence for the identification of global systemically important insurers (G-SIIs) and for related policy measures. Thus, the FSB, in consultation with the IAIS and national authorities, has decided not to publish a new list of G-SIIs for 2017. The policy measures set out in the FSB 2016 communication on G-SIIs, as updated in February 2017 as concerns the higher loss-absorbency standard, will continue to apply to the firms listed in the 2016 communication.

Figure 3

Implementation of Basel III risk-based capital and leverage ratios, 2011–2016
(*Billions of euros, percentage*)

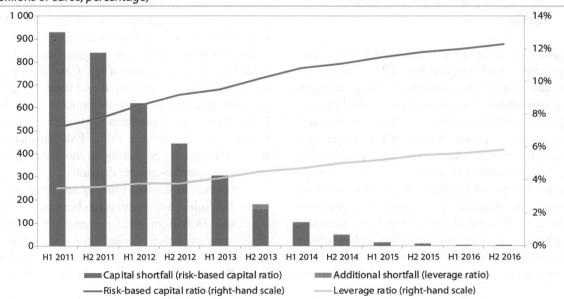

Source: September 2017 BCBS Basel III Monitoring Report.
Note: Data for Group 1 banks that are internationally active and have Tier 1 capital of more than €3 billion. The September 2017 survey included 105 such banks. The capital ratio is based on CET1 capital and is weighted by risk-weighted assets, leverage ratio is weighted by leverage-ratio exposure. The bars show shortfalls for total capital at the target level.

Figure 4
Implementation of Basel III liquidity and stable funding ratios, 2011–2016
(Billions of euros, percentage)

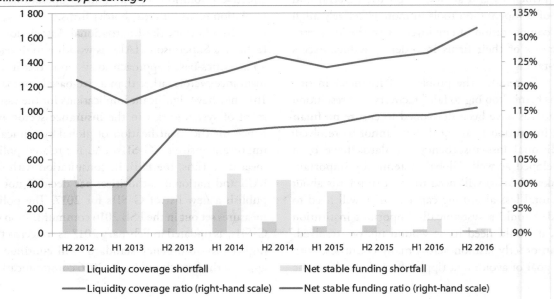

Source: September 2017 BCBS Basel III Monitoring Report.
Note: Data for Group 1 banks that are internationally active and have Tier 1 capital of more than €3 billion; the consistent time series includes 87 banks for the liquidity ratio and 91 banks for the stable funding ratio. Liquidity ratio is weighted by total net cash outflows; the stable funding ratio is weighted by the required amount for stable funding.

3.2   Regulating derivatives and shadow banking

Shadow banking, which falls outside the regulatory framework for regular banks,[14] and derivatives can also pose systemic risks to the global economy. Implementation of reforms agreed in the FSB with regard to over-the-counter derivatives is now well progressed, although this has taken longer than originally intended due to the scale and complexity of the reforms and other challenges. The main criticism of derivatives markets was that they were opaque, with insufficient knowledge of counterparty exposures. Central clearing (which has increased markedly in interest rate derivatives and, to a lesser extent, credit default swaps) is simplifying much of the previously complex and opaque web of deriva-

tives exposures, and the central counterparties supporting that clearing are more resilient. In addition, more collateral is in place to reduce counterparty credit risks within the system. Progress has also been made in improving transparency. Central clearing frameworks, as well as margin and interim capital requirements, have been implemented in most FSB jurisdictions, while platform trading frameworks have been implemented in half of FSB jurisdictions. The FSB is currently evaluating incentives for central clearing of over-the-counter derivatives.

Reforms to shadow banking are being implemented. While much progress has been made, as of June 2017, 14 FSB jurisdictions were behind schedule in implementation of at least one area of shadow banking reform.[15] The shadow banking work of the FSB examines non-bank credit intermediation

---

14   The FSB defines shadow banking as "credit intermediation involving entities and activities (fully or partly) outside of the regular banking system" (see http://www.fsb.org/what-we-do/policy-development/shadow-banking/). Some authorities and market participants prefer to use other terms such as "market-based finance" instead of "shadow banking" for this segment of activities.

15   Financial Stability Board, "Implementation and Effects of the G20 Financial Regulatory Reforms, 3rd Annual Report" (Basel, 3 July 2017).

involving bank-like activities, such as maturity/liquidity transformation and/or leverage, that can become a source of systemic risk. Such non-bank credit intermediation involving bank-like activities tends to be more active in advanced economies. This risk can be compounded where non-bank activities have links to the banking system. While non-bank financing can be a welcome source of diversification of credit supply, it can become a source of systemic risk if it is involved in bank-like activities. To address risks to financial stability, the FSB has been working to "transform shadow banking into resilient market-based finance"[16] through system-wide oversight and developing policy recommendations. The recommendations focus on addressing banks' involvement in shadow banking, liquidity or maturity mismatches, leverage in the system, incentive problems and opaqueness associated with shadow banking, notably securitization.

The aspects of shadow banking generally considered to have contributed the most to the 2008 world economic and financial crisis have declined significantly and are considered by the FSB to generally no longer pose financial stability risks.[17] Since the crisis, however, assets held in collective investment vehicles that are susceptible to runs (such as open-ended fixed income funds, credit hedge funds, real estate funds and money market funds) have grown or remain relatively large. Such collective investment vehicles grew by 11 per cent in 2016, slower than the compounded annual average assets growth of about 13 per cent a year since end-2011.[18] The considerable growth has been accompanied by a relatively higher degree of credit investment as well as some liquidity and maturity transformation. In January 2017, the FSB published its policy recommendations to address structural vulnerabilities

from asset management activities, which are currently being operationalized by securities regulators.

As referenced in chapters III.B and III.G, an emerging class of technology firms are engaging in financial intermediation outside the normal perimeters of banking regulation. At the same time, traditional financial institutions are digitalizing services, which may also significantly accelerate the speed and volume of financial transactions. Together, these technology-enabled financial innovations, often called "fintech," mean that regulators may need to complement their focus on financial institutions and markets with increasing attention to financial activities, as these services are increasingly provided by a diverse group of firms and market platforms.[19] Regulation will also need to consider the impact of virtual currencies (see chapter III.A). Regulatory innovation will be important, and Member States should share lessons learned, including those from so-called regulatory sandboxes and other innovation facilitators. With the blurring of boundaries among entities, activities and jurisdictions, policymakers may wish to consider whether new common standards and legal principles are warranted to assure that the activities align with national and international priorities.

4. Shocks financing instruments

The Addis Agenda urged Member States, international institutions, and all relevant stakeholders to work to prevent and reduce the risk and impact of financial crises, as well as to better prevent and manage risks from disasters. Member States committed to promoting innovative financing mechanisms to allow countries to better prevent and manage risks and develop mitigation plans. To help take stock, the 2017 ECOSOC Forum on Financing for Develop-

---

16   See http://www.fsb.org/what-we-do/policy-development/shadow-banking/.

17   Financial Stability Board, "Assessment of shadow banking activities, risks and the adequacy of post-crisis policy tools to address financial stability concerns," 3 July 2017. Available from http://www.fsb.org/2017/07/assessment-of-shadow-banking-activities-risks-and-the-adequacy-of-post-crisis-policy-tools-to-address-financial-stability-concerns/.

18   Financial Stability Board, "Global Shadow Banking Monitoring Report 2017", 5 March 2018. Available from http://www.fsb.org/2018/03/global-shadow-banking-monitoring-report-2017/.

19   For a deeper discussion on the potential regulatory responses to fintech, see D. He et al. "Fintech and financial services: initial considerations", International Monetary Fund Staff Discussion Note, SDN/17/05 (June 2017); and Financial Stability Board, Financial Stability Implications from FinTech: Supervisory and Regulatory Issues that Merit Authorities' Attention" (June 2017).

ment Follow-up requested "an inventory of domestic and international financial instruments and funding modalities, and existing quick-disbursing international facilities and the requirements for accessing them".[20]

There are diverse types of shocks, which can broadly be classified as those resulting from economic or market activity and disasters. For both types of shocks, the financial responses can be characterized by availability, predictability, speed, cost and volume.[21]

Predictability and speed are critical in shocks response, as slow responses can cost lives. Households could, for example, experience unrecoverable health impacts or be forced into ruinous asset sales.[22] Businesses can face bankruptcy, with unrecoverable impacts on employment. While national responses can be organized relatively quickly, there are insufficient financial means in many cases, necessitating a call on international resources. Yet provision of international resources can take weeks if not months to be agreed. For disaster response, most international emergency efforts remain on an ad hoc and voluntary basis and, as reported in chapter III.C, many calls for humanitarian contributions go without sufficient donor commitments or timely disbursements. The delays to disbursement ultimately raise the costs of shocks response.

This underscores the advantages of preparing for crises in good times with both prevention and establishing quick-disbursing financial facilities for response. Prevention efforts need to take place at the local, national and international levels. In relation to economic shocks, this entails strengthening macroeconomic policy frameworks and financial regulations nationally, and cooperating to reduce risk and volatility arising from the international financial architecture, as discussed above. For disasters, cli-

mate change mitigation and adaptation and disaster risk reduction and preparedness are critical, including the development of institutional frameworks and financing mechanisms.

In relation to financial facilities, countries still mostly rely on national self-insurance models as opposed to multi-country risk pooling, thus not taking advantage of the benefits of diversification. Domestic instruments should be part of the response; however, they are too numerous to list in an inventory, as they differ in each country. Some examples include fiscal reserves, foreign exchange reserves, and national insurance programmes. Experience shows that the effectiveness of any shocks response is significantly enhanced when a country has an already operating social infrastructure in place, as setting up ad hoc disbursement systems is slow, prone to errors and susceptible to corruption. Social protection systems for all, which were agreed to in both the Addis Agenda and 2030 Agenda for Sustainable Development, provide a permanent infrastructure that reduces costs in cases of shocks. Chapter III.A includes a discussion of many types of domestic financing modalities, including a specific section on financing for national systems of social protection, including floors.

In terms of international facilities, as shown in the inventory, many international institutions offer some quick-disbursing instruments, and some institutions have resources that can be tapped in the case of both economic shocks and disasters. However, different programmes and instruments were created to meet different needs. Each facility in the inventory has a unique combination of the five characteristics (availability, predictability, speed, cost and volume). The causes and responses to economic shocks and disasters are sufficiently different to warrant separate analysis.

---

20   "Information note by the President of the Economic and Social Council on arrangements for the 2017 Economic and Social Council Forum on Financing for Development follow-up" (E/FFDF/2017/3, para.7). A version of the requested inventory covering international financing instruments is included as an annex to this chapter, while a more detailed version is available from https://developmentfinance.un.org/inventory-quick-disbursing-international-instruments.

21   "Availability" refers to whether countries have access to the finance or eligibility for the instrument, while "predictability" is about whether financing is provided under unambiguous conditions, for example without negotiation, and in response to specific events.

22   Daniel Clarke and Ruth Vargas Hill, "Cost-benefit analysis of the African Risk Capacity Facility", IFPRI Discussion Paper 01292 (International Food Policy Research Institute, September 2013).

4.1   International instruments for addressing economic shocks

The multilayered GFSN provides resources for addressing economic shocks. Figure 5 shows its constituent components, including IMF resources, those of regional financial arrangements (RFAs), and bilateral financial arrangements. The GFSN, however, needs to be more comprehensive, coherent and coordinated to be effective in serving its purpose. Many countries, including some large emerging markets and those that could act as transmitters of shocks, continue to lack adequate access to predictable and reliable funding. Improvements to the GFSN would be more effective if agreed in advance of crises rather than in the midst of them.

Figure 5 also shows that countries in a position to do so have built substantial stocks of foreign exchange reserves, which can be drawn upon in a crisis, but maintaining such self-insurance is costly. One initiative that spread during the 2008 world economic and financial crisis was the creation by many central banks of bilateral swap lines, which are promises of two nations to swap up to predetermined amounts of their currencies as needed over a specific time period. These swap lines were highly effective because of their predictability once established, speed of disbursement, low cost and relatively high volumes of resources. While some swap lines were discontinued once the crisis subsided, as shown in the annex to this chapter, many are currently in effect, although coverage is far from universal.

The IMF has taken steps to help reduce remaining gaps in the GFSN, including, in May 2017, strengthening its quick-disbursing instruments the Rapid Credit Facility and Rapid Financing Instrument. In July 2017, it introduced a new Policy Coordination Instrument, which is a non-financing tool designed to signal commitments to reforms and catalyse financing from other sources. In November 2017, IMF staff presented a blueprint for a future liquidity backstop. To enhance crisis prevention, staff developed a proposal for a new facility, called the Short-term Liquidity Swap (SLS), to provide members with very strong policies with predictable and renewable liquidity support against potential, short-term, moderate capital flow volatility. The SLS was designed as a revolving credit line, and included several other innovative features. However, the proposal was not adopted by the IMF's Executive Board. The IMF also discussed a possible role for a new Time-Based Commitment Fee in response to concerns about prolonged use of high-access arrangements on a precautionary basis, but this proposal was also not adopted.

Additional options for GFSN reform could build on regional reserve pooling. Synchronization among the IMF, RFAs, multilateral development banks, and other sources of quick-disbursing funds and facilities has begun, with a number of efforts at coordination and learning among the different facilities. In 2017, the IMF proposed a new framework for more structured collaboration with RFAs. However, more can be done to prepare joint strategies and share experiences, especially as most RFAs have yet to be seriously tested with a crisis. Further sharing of lessons among RFAs and wider preparation on how future activity might be coordinated are warranted.

It is an open question whether the total value of the GFSN as shown in figure 5 and listed in the inventory is sufficient to respond not only to limited national crises, but also to multi-country, systemic crises. While IMF resources have increased significantly since the 2008 crisis, they are lower today than they were before the mid-1990s, both as a share of world gross product and as a share of gross global capital flows. In the previous crisis, multilateral development banks stepped in with additional countercyclical financing in a limited number of countries. However, that is not their primary mission, which is more focused on long-term infrastructure and financing policy change, and they are increasingly under capital constraints.

One additional option that would increase anti-crisis liquidity involves IMF special drawing rights (SDRs). Indeed, the previous allocation of SDRs was made in the wake of the 2008 crisis. Following a note prepared for the G20 in 2016 that outlined initial considerations on a greater role for the SDR in the smooth functioning of the international monetary system, a high-level external advisory group of prominent academics, former policymakers, and market practitioners was convened by the IMF to advise on this issue. IMF staff are currently ana-

Figure 5
Evolution of the global financial safety net, 1995–2016
(*Billions of special drawing rights*)

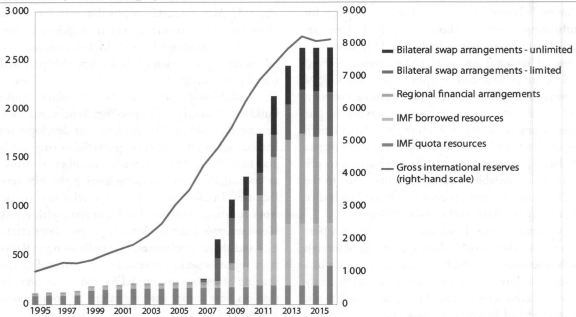

Source: IMF, "Collaboration between regional financing arrangements and the IMF", IMF Policy Paper (Washington, D.C., July 2017). Available from https://www.imf.org/en/Publications/Policy-Papers/Issues/2017/07/31/pp073117-collaboration-between-regional-financing-arrangements-and-the-imf.
Notes: Unlimited bilateral swap arrangements are estimated based on known past usage or, if undrawn, on average past maximum drawings of remaining central bank members in the network. Two-way arrangements are only counted once. Limited bilateral swaps arrangements include all those with an explicit value limit and excludes Chiang Mai Initiative Multilateralization (CMIM) arrangements. Two-way arrangements are only counted once. Regional financial arrangements are based on explicit lending capacity/limit where available, committed resources, or estimated lending capacity based on country access limits and paid-in capital; and includes CMIM arrangements. Prudential balances are not included in the calculation of IMF resources, quota resources are only for countries in the Financial Transaction Plan.

lysing the potential scope for a broader role for the SDR for IMF Executive Board consideration in 2018.

A notable feature of each of the international facilities discussed thus far is that they would all increase the external debt of the country drawing on them, which is of particular concern in some SIDS (see chapter III.E). The Task Force identified several policy options for providing relief of these obligations in the event of a shock, and particularly recalls its 2017 discussion of the possibility of official lenders introducing state-contingent debt instruments, which would tie a sovereign's net payment obligations to its payment capacity (see chapter III.E). State-contingent debt instruments could be a useful complement to the GFSN because they are highly predictable and speedy, while not changing perceived creditor priority.

4.2   International instruments for addressing disasters

The international community is collectively committed to sustainable development and provides significant resources to respond to disasters. Yet the international system's overall financial response to disasters remains insufficient and inefficient. The inventory of quick-disbursing instruments identifies many innovations in financial instruments for addressing non-market-triggered emergencies in the last 15 years. In addition to new funds—such as the United Nations Central Emergency Response Fund (CERF), a grant-making facility started in 2006 to fund very early responses to humanitarian emergencies and to support humanitarian response activities within an underfunded emergency—there has also been ad hoc institutional collaboration. Institutional pooled funds and insurance-like instruments can play complementary roles, and greater provision of international resources to both of these types of instruments could bring many benefits and greater efficiency compared to the current practice of ex post disaster response.

Disaster risk is increasing and economic losses are rising. The IMF estimates that the average annual cost of natural disasters in low-income countries is equal to 2 per cent of gross domestic product, or four times the impact on larger economies. While many disasters are sudden, disaster risk can often be modelled. Where the probability of a disaster is not known, or the scale overwhelms efforts at risk management and the response capacity of the affected country, it is important that there be resources available to respond quickly, such as through the CERF and other forms of pooled funding. Global loan or grant funds will be less costly to operate than regional or subregional funds owing to greater diversification and scale. The international community could more rigorously assess the overall level and terms of international support for emergencies, not least because crises are likely to grow in number and intensity because of global climate change.[23] Shifting to more pooled funding could simplify and speed emergency response.

When disaster risk is not made explicit to public and private investors, hidden contingent liabilities often only become evident in the event of a disaster, when it is too late. Clarification of incentives of relevant stakeholders and quantification of the cost associated with inaction or late action can help promote disaster risk reduction. Current international financing instruments do not sufficiently clarify who bears the risks of disasters. The human cost is of course borne by residents, with households often uncertain about the level of financial assistance that might be available in the case of a disaster. National Governments bear much of the risk, but in some cases, policymakers with limited fiscal space may

have low incentives for long-term investment in disaster risk reduction and resilience when they are also facing a multitude of immediate needs related to poverty, hunger and other aspects of the sustainable development agenda. Donors providing development assistance respond to requests for humanitarian and disaster relief after emergencies; in doing so, they are implicitly acting like insurers of last resort, but without the benefits of predictability and speed that insurance-like instruments provide.

Appropriately designed insurance contracts have been used in the private sector for centuries to help clarify the burden of risk, share burdens fairly and set incentives for risk reduction.[24] Where sufficient information is available on the probability of a disaster occurring, insurance-like programmes can be a complement to pooled funds. International risk pooling, whether in multiple-country insurance, loan, or grant facilities, is one of the great advantages of international cooperation. In an insurance scheme, by grouping together well-diversified risks into a single risk pool, the cost of insuring against those risks (and thus the premiums that participants have to pay) can be greatly reduced. Well-designed parametric insurance,[25] with parameters relevant to different national contexts, can improve the efficiency of the resources that are available because of their speed and incentive for early recognition of the severity of intensive disasters. The contracts can also be designed to align incentives for prevention of emergencies by requiring policymakers to undertake disaster risk management, such as creating early warning systems, retrofitting, enforcing building codes and preparing contingency plans in advance.[26] While the resources provided by insurance after a disaster might not be sufficient to address all economic losses, these techniques can be applied at the sovereign level to help improve the incentive structure and increase the efficiency of emergency response. Successful sovereign risk insurance facilities have been operating for many years in the Caribbean (Caribbean Catastrophe Risk Insur-

23   Intergovernmental Panel on Climate Change, *Climate Change 2014: Impacts, Adaptation, and Vulnerability*, Fifth Assessment Report, Working Group II (2014).

24   David Jenkins and Takau Yoneyama, *The history of insurance* (London, Pickering & Chatto, 2000).

25   Parametric insurance is an insurance contract that disburses automatically once an event trigger has occurred.

26   These incentives can contribute to disaster risk reduction, but disaster risk management also requires dedicated financing.

ance Facility) and in sub-Saharan Africa (African Risk Capacity).

Many of the innovative instruments and facilities for sovereign insurance for disasters operate regionally, which constrains the diversification of the risk pool, given that hazards can cross borders and often impact several countries in a region together. For insurance to be effective and sustainable it requires diversification to manage risk. This requires involvement of sufficient numbers of participants with different risk profiles. The involvement of more countries in sovereign risk insurance programmes would increase their diversification, sustainability and efficiency. This could be done either through a global risk facility or through public or private reinsurance. However, it would require strengthening (and in some cases creating) regional facilities.

Not all countries are able to afford the necessary insurance premiums, especially least developed countries with limited revenue-raising capacity. Donors have been reluctant to pay the premiums for various reasons, including "moral hazard" concern, even though ex ante insurance would, in many contexts, be more efficient than the current ex post disaster response. Donor subsidies, conditional on the at-risk poor country agreeing to undertake effective disaster risk management, could boost participation in the insurance scheme, further diversifying risks and increasing efficiency. Partial payment of premiums by the insured can be used to further align incentives. Such an arrangement would prove beneficial to the entire system and provide a strong contribution towards risk-informed sustainable development.

5.   Institutional and policy coherence at the United Nations

The General Assembly recognized the need for significant institutional adjustments to the UNDS to effectively respond to the 2030 Agenda for Sustainable Development in its quadrennial comprehensive policy review.[27] To that end, the Secretary-General has presented a vision, paired with concrete measures for change, in his June and December 2017 reports on repositioning the UNDS. The reports are part of the broader reform agenda of the Secretary-General, which includes the peace and security architecture and Secretariat management.

At the heart of the reports is the proposal to build a new generation of United Nations country teams to be more responsive to sustainable development needs on the ground, led by an empowered and independent Resident Coordinator, and supported by a revamped regional approach and other measures at global level to better support in-country sustainable development results. A system-wide strategic document was developed by the United Nations Development Group in tandem with the reports. The Secretary-General also proposes to strengthen Member States' horizontal guidance and oversight of the UNDS, and to agree a Funding Compact to ensure better quality, quantity and predictability of resources, with commensurate commitments from the UNDS to increasing transparency and accountability.

The overarching reform package seeks to achieve greater coherence and accountability and generate integrated action and enhanced synergies across the UNDS. The Secretary-General has already taken immediate discretionary steps in this direction, including the revitalization of the United Nations Development Group and the creation of a Joint Steering Committee to advance collaboration of development and humanitarian efforts.

United Nations engagement and coherence with non-United Nations partners will be critical to contributing effectively to sustainable development efforts at the country level. Acknowledging the proliferation of development actors, the Secretary-General is actively pursuing a stronger system-wide approach to partnership. Leveraging and harnessing the complementary strengths of international financial institutions, civil society, philanthropic actors and the private sector is critical to mobilizing the means of implementation for the 2030 Agenda for Sustainable Development. This will maximize the reach and impact of the UNDS at country, regional and global levels.

As Governments look to mobilize partners and investments of all kinds—public and private, local to global—the UNDS also needs to step up its own capacities as well as the scale and approach of its

27   A/RES/71/243.

partnership engagements to realize the ambition of the sustainable development agenda.

6.   Global economic governance

From the beginning of the Financing for Development process in Monterrey, Mexico, in 2002, Governments committed to a package of global economic governance and policy reforms and have expended sincere efforts to implement them. While there have been achievements in governance reforms since then, along with the creation of new mechanisms of intergovernmental coordination through the G20, the Addis Agenda recognized the need to further broaden and strengthen the voice and participation of developing countries in international economic decision-making and norm-setting. There have also been complementary efforts to develop new regional and cross-regional institutions of international cooperation.

At the IMF, a member country's quota determines its maximum financial commitment to the IMF, its voting power, and has a bearing on its access to IMF financing. IMF Governors agreed in December 2016 to work towards completing the Fifteenth General Review of Quotas by the 2019 Spring Meetings and no later than the 2019 Annual Meetings, a process that began in 2010 after the agreement on the last reforms to IMF governance. The Executive Board's first progress report on the Fifteenth Review was submitted to the IMF Board of Governors in October 2017. The World Bank also agreed in 2010 to a reform of shareholding, which was to be fully phased in by March 2017. The shareholding of developing countries in the International Bank for Reconstruction and Development, the World Bank's main lending arm, grew from 38.1 per cent in 2010 to 38.8 per cent as at the end of June 2017.[28] In a 2015 review of shareholding, it had been decided that an agreement on further reform would cover both a selective capital increase in order to rebalance shareholding among member countries and a potential general capital increase to address the financial needs of the World Bank Group. The World Bank Executive Board September 2017 progress report called on the Board to bring these discussions to a successful conclusion by the 2018 Spring Meetings.

To address impediments to further reforms of global institutions, in April 2017, the G20 established an Eminent Persons Group (EPG) on Global Financial Governance, which will conduct a high-level review of the global financial architecture, including the optimal role of the international financial institutions. The EPG recommendations will cover the mandates, coherence, transparency, and accountability issues at international financial institutions related to attaining strong, sustainable balanced and inclusive growth, assuring financial stability, and financing global public goods. The EPG will present its conclusions in a report to the G20 finance ministers and central bank governors by the time of the IMF/World Bank 2018 Annual Meetings.

Stronger efforts are also being made to improve the diversity of international institutions, their gender diversity in particular. The United Nations Secretary-General launched a road map for achieving gender parity at all levels of the Organization in September 2017. It seeks to increase the recruitment and advancement of women — particularly in middle to senior management levels, where the gaps are the greatest and a glass-ceiling persists. In January 2018, the United Nations reached full gender parity, far in advance of the targets in the strategy, in the 44-member United Nations Senior Management Group, which brings together leaders of United Nations departments, offices, funds and programmes. The IMF is also making progress towards enhancing diversity at both at the Executive Board and among staff. The Executive Board issued its first report to the Board of Governors on the Executive Board's gender diversity in July 2016, calling on member countries to consider gender diversity when nominating candidates for Executive Directors and their staff. Female representation on the Board in 2017 reached 2 of 24, an increase from 1 of 24 in 2015.[29]

---

28   See https://unstats.un.org/sdgs/indicators/database/?indicator=10.6.1; and World Bank Group, "International Bank for Reconstruction and Development subscriptions and voting power of member countries", July 2017. Available from http://siteresources.worldbank.org/BODINT/Resources/278027-1215524804501/IBRDCountryVotingTable.pdf.

29   International Monetary Fund, "IMF Annual Report 2017" (Washington, D.C., 2017).

Annex:

Inventory of quick-disbursing international instruments

Institution	Facilities	Jurisdiction eligibility	Access type/conditions
Central bank swap lines			
National central banks	Developed country bilateral swaps with developing countries (examples)	Australia/China, Australia/Indonesia, Australia/Republic of Korea	Australian dollar swaps
		ECB/China	Euro swaps
		Japan/India, Japan/Malaysia, Japan/Thailand, Japan/Indonesia, Japan/Philippines, Japan/Singapore, Japan/Republic of Korea	Yen swaps
		United States/Mexico[a]	US dollar swaps
People's Bank of China	China bilateral swap lines	China/Albania, China/Argentina, China/Armenia, China/Belarus, China/Chile, China/Egypt, China/Hungary, China/Indonesia, China/Kazakhstan, China/Republic of Korea, China/Malaysia, China/Nigeria, China/Pakistan, China/Qatar, China/South Africa, China/Sri Lanka, China/Suriname, China/Thailand, China/Turkey, China/Ukraine, China/United Arab Emirates	Renminbi swap lines
Quick-disbursing multilateral loans			
Multilateral and regional financing arrangements			
IMF	Flexible credit line	189 Member States	Precautionary facility for only very strong performers who meet ex ante qualification criteria
	Precautionary and liquidity line		Precautionary facility for strong performers who meet ex ante qualification criteria
	Rapid financing instrument		Support for urgent balance of payments needs without formal adjustment programmes and designed for situations where a full-fledged economic programme is either unnecessary or not feasible.
	Rapid credit facility	70 PRGT-eligible Member States	Concessional support for urgent balance-of-payments needs without formal adjustment programmes and designed for situations where a full-fledged economic programme is either unnecessary or not feasible.
	Stand-by arrangement	189 Member States	Facility for all countries facing external financing needs, and includes high access precautionary arrangements (HAPAs), a type of insurance facility against very large potential financing needs

Institution	Facilities	Jurisdiction eligibility	Access type/conditions
	Extended fund facility		Augmentation of this existing facility is possible in case of shocks to a country already experiencing serious payments imbalances because of structural impediments, or with slow growth and an inherently weak balance-of-payments position
	Standby credit facility	70 PRGT-eligible Member States	Concessional facility for countries facing an immediate or potential balance-of-payments need, can be used as precautionary instrument
	Extended credit facility		Augmentation of this existing concessional facility is possible in case of shocks to a country with a protracted balance-of-payments problem
Fondo Latinoamericano de Reservas (FLAR)	Liquidity, contingency and treasury credits	Bolivia (Plurinational State of), Colombia, Costa Rica, Ecuador, Paraguay, Peru, Uruguay, Venezuela	On approval of Executive President
	Balance-of-payments (and debt restructuring) loans		On approval of Board of Directors, within 32 days
Chiang Mai Initiative Multilateralization (CMIM)	CMIM precautionary line	ASEAN +3 countries	Decision within two weeks of request, 30 per cent of total access available as quick disbursing
	CMIM stability facility		Decision within two weeks of request, 30 per cent total access available as quick disbursing
BRICS Contingent Reserve Arrangement (CRA)	Precautionary instrument	Brazil, Russian Federation, India, China, South Africa	Potential short-term BoP pressures; 30 per cent of total access on request
	Liquidity instrument		Short-term BoP pressures; 30 per cent on request
European Union Balance of Payments Facility	Loans	9 European Union member states outside the euro area	For countries experiencing or threatened by difficulties regarding their balance of payments; economic policy conditions will be set that must be met before funds are released
European Stability Mechanism (ESM)	Loans	19 States in the euro area	Conditional upon the implementation of macroeconomic reform programmes
	Precautionary credit lines		To support sound policies and prevent crisis situations from emerging
	Recapitalization of financial institutions		Both direct recapitalization by lending to the private sector, and indirect recapitalization through loans to the sovereign
Eurasian Fund for Stablization and Development (EFSD)	Financial credits	Armenia, Belarus, Kazakhstan, Kyrgyzstan, Russian Federation, Tajikistan	In support of anti-crisis and stabilization programmes
Arab Monetary Fund (AMF)	Short-term liquidity facility	22 AMF member states	For countries with a track record of structural and economic reforms that face temporary liquidity shortage due to unfavourable developments in global financial markets
Multilateral development bank lending			
World Bank	Deferred drawdown option	IBRD-eligible countries	Precautionary instrument agreed pre-shock and available for drawdown on cyclical/financial or catastrophe reasons

Institution	Facilities	Jurisdiction eligibility	Access type/conditions
	Immediate response mechanism	IDA-eligible countries	For countries in crisis, but requires prior inclusion of contingent emergency response components in selected IDA projects and adoption by the recipient of an IRM Operations Manual
	Special development policy financing	IBRD-eligible countries	Offered to countries that are approaching crisis or are in a crisis with substantial structural and social dimensions and that have an urgent and extraordinary financing need
	Crisis response window	IDA-eligible countries	Additional financing available in two stages for large economic crises, natural disasters or public health emergencies
Inter-American Development Bank (IDB)	Development sustainability contingent credit line	IDB borrowing members	Precautionary facility to support countries facing exogenous systemic economic shocks or exogenous country-specific economic shocks
	Deferred drawdown option	Middle-income IDB borrowing members	Optional precautionary facility used with policy based loans and available for any general financing need
	Contingent credit facility for natural disaster emergencies	IDB borrowing members	Covers urgent financing needs that arise immediately after a natural disaster, until other sources of funding can be accessed; requires active integrated disaster risk management programme
	Contingent credit line for natural disasters	IDB borrowing members	Covers urgent financing needs that arise immediately after a natural disaster, until other sources of funding can be accessed, but with a relatively low limit on resources
Asian Development Bank (ADB)	Precautionary financing option	Middle-income ADB countries	Delayed disbursement of a countercyclical support facility
African Development Bank (AfDB)	Emergency Liquidity Facility (discontinued)	AfDB regional members	For urgent financing needs, available for public and private sector clients – discontinued in December 2010
Corporación Andina de Fomento (CAF)	Contingent credit line for financial emergencies	17 States in Latin America and the Caribbean	Precautionary facility available for natural and economic shocks
Quick-disbursing grants			
IMF	Catastrophe Containment and Relief Trust	Either PRGT-eligible members with per capita income below IDA cutoff, or small States with per capita income below twice the IDA cutoff	IMF debt repayments relief and possible IMF debt stock relief for countries hit by a catastrophic disaster
World Bank	Pandemic Emergency Financing Facility	IDA-eligible countries	Donor funded facility with 'insurance' window covering outbreaks of six viruses; cash window for the containment of other diseases
United Nations[b]	Central Emergency Response Fund	193 Member States	Fast, predictable and flexible funding to United Nations agencies for humanitarian crisis response; rapid response window and underfunded emergencies window
	Peacebuilding Fund Immediate Response Facility	Member States on the agenda of the Peacebuilding Commission, those declared eligible by the Secretary-General	Fast, flexible and risk-tolerant financing to United Nations efforts supporting political solutions aimed at preventing the lapse and relapse into conflict

Institution	Facilities	Jurisdiction eligibility	Access type/conditions
Insurance/re-insurance			
African Risk Capacity (ARC)	ARC Insurance Company, Ltd	African Union members	Drought insurance for African Governments, paid by government premiums; reinsures risk
Caribbean Catastrophe Risk Insurance Facility (CCRIF)	CCRIF SPC	Anguilla, Antigua & Barbuda, Bahamas, Barbados, Belize, Bermuda, Cayman Islands, Dominica, Grenada, Haiti, Jamaica, Nicaragua, St. Kitts & Nevis, St. Lucia, St. Vincent & the Grenadines, Trinidad & Tobago, Turks & Caicos Islands	Insures Caribbean Member States against hurricanes, earthquakes and excessive rainfalls
Pacific Catastrophe Risk Assessment and Financing Initiative	[In development]		

a   Expired swaps: United States/Brazil, United States/Republic of Korea, United States/Singapore.

b   For a full list of multi-donor trust funds and other facilities, see Annex 1 of United Nations Development Program", Financing the United Nations Development System: Pathways to Reposition for Agenda 2030" (Dag Hammarskjöld Foundation and the United Nations Multi-Partner Trust Fund Office, September 2017). Available from http://mptf.undp.org/document/download/18649.

Chapter III.G
Science, technology, innovation and capacity-building

1. Key messages and recommendations

Science, technology and innovation (STI) are key means of implementation of the Sustainable Development Goals (SDGs). Expectations about the contribution of STI have increased in recent years as fast-evolving technologies are rapidly changing the development landscape. They open new possibilities to address long-standing development challenges across the SDGs—from poverty and hunger, access to health care and education, to low-carbon energy, combatting climate change, and financial inclusion. They are also changing the development finance landscape, creating opportunities across the action areas of the Addis Ababa Action Agenda (hereafter, Addis Agenda).

Advances in information and communication technologies (ICTs) are at the heart of this technological change. They have vastly increased digital interconnectedness, digital data storage and analytics capabilities at declining cost. Artificial intelligence (AI) in particular, which allows machines and computers to learn to solve problems on their own, could have transformative effects across many sectors of the economy, making it essential that innovations are in the public interest and guided by the 2030 Agenda for Sustainable Development and the Addis Agenda.

Indeed, the transformative power of technology raises complex ethical, socioeconomic and human rights challenges and risks. The rapid pace of technological change puts great adaptive pressure on economies and societies, while our understanding of their socioeconomic implications tends to develop more slowly than technology itself. Both access to and the capacity to adapt and take advantage of tech-

nological developments are very unevenly distributed within and between countries. Skills requirements are changing rapidly, which may further increase the digital skills divide. Women and girls, people with disabilities, older persons, indigenous peoples and people living in rural areas may face additional barriers in accessing and using technology.

One often identified risk is that technological change could lead to job losses and increased polarization in labour markets. *To ensure that technology dividends are shared broadly, countries should put in place policies to support lifelong learning and skills acquisition for all.* At the same time, the significant increase in self-employment and new forms of employment call for *adapted and strengthened employment and social protection policies. To address continued gender disparities and enhance inclusion of marginalized groups, such policies should emphasize the equitable participation of women and all social groups in decent jobs.*

In development finance, new technologies can help overcome weak contract enforcement, improve administrative procedures, increase access to financial services for those currently underserved and address data gaps. But opportunities will only be available to those who are connected. *Wide access of individuals and businesses to new technologies, platforms and payment systems is critical, and Governments need to adjust their regulatory frameworks in order to close access gaps while managing risks. Policymakers also need to be proactive in addressing emerging risks to privacy, financial stability, and financial integrity.*

Harnessing technological dividends and sharing them equitably are critical challenges for policymakers. National innovation strategies need to be broad and coordinated with industrial, macroeconomic, educational, social and STI policies, which should support the inclusiveness of these strategies. To help developing countries absorb, develop, integrate and scale up the deployment of key technologies and innovations for the SDGs, *international collaboration and support for science, technology and innovation remains critical and needs to be scaled up, particularly for the poorest and most vulnerable countries*.

2. New and emerging technologies and the SDGs

New and emerging technologies have the potential to significantly reshape our economies and societies. Due to their potential to disrupt industries and markets, these technologies are sometimes described as being part of a fourth industrial revolution (following mechanization, mass production and the digital revolution) and have the potential to accelerate SDG implementation through their rapidly declining costs and improving performance. This is particularly true for ICTs, whose reliance on open standards and platforms facilitates both widespread deployment and the convergence of several key and mutually reinforcing technologies. AI in particular—which allows machines and computers to address "non-routine" tasks and solve problems on their own—has the potential to become a "general purpose technology" impacting many sectors of the economy.[1]

These technologies and their applications offer new opportunities for economic prosperity, social inclusion, and environmental sustainability, with great potential to contribute to achieving the SDGs.[2] This can be seen in the emergence of innovation-driven entrepreneurs in developing countries that base their business model on specific aspects of the SDGs.[3] For example, agricultural biotechnology can improve productivity and natural-resource-use efficiency, with significant benefits to small farmers. Biological nanotechnology applications are already starting to have an impact on the diagnosis, treatment and prevention of disease. Biotechnology and synthetic biology have enormous potential for addressing the environment, climate crisis and loss of biodiversity through more advanced biofuels and "cleaner" agriculture—that is, agricultural processes with less input of chemical fertilizers and pesticides, and/or a reduction of carbon dioxide through artificial leaf technology. Nuclear and isotopic techniques to track and quantify carbon, water and nutrient movement and dynamics are also used to increase agricultural productivity, resilience, and the sector's greenhouse gas emissions. In Sudan, the application of climate-smart agriculture has allowed hundreds of women, many of whom are refugees or internally displaced persons, to start small-scale farms and home gardens in extremely arid areas. Table 1 presents a wide range of promising emerging technologies across the 17 SDGs, as identified by a group of 158 scientists for the 2016 Global Sustainable Development Report.[4]

The pace of technological change has accelerated significantly. In some areas, such as digital technologies, which are characterized by very low marginal costs and wide distribution through platforms and networks, performance, cost and applicability across sectors is improving at exponential rates. Technologies are also diffused much more rapidly across borders than in the past. For example, the adoption of the steam engine by develop-

1   Matthias Bruckner, Marcelo LaFleur and Ingo Pitterle, "The impact of the technological revolution on labour markets and income distribution", Frontier Issues (New York, United Nations Department of Economic and Social Affairs, 31 July 2017). Available from https://www.un.org/development/desa/dpad/wp-content/uploads/sites/45/publication/2017_Aug_Frontier-Issues-1.pdf. The United Nations Interagency Task team on science, technology and innovation (STI) for the Sustainable Development Goals (SDGs) has also begun exploring the impacts of exponential technological change, automation technologies and artificial intelligence on the SDGs.

2   United Nations, Report of the Secretary-General on science, technology and innovation for development (A/72/257). Available from http://undocs.org/A/72/257.

3   United Nations, Science, technology and innovation as catalysts of the SDGs (TD/B/C.II/36). Available from http://unctad.org/meetings/en/SessionalDocuments/ciid36_EN.pdf.

4   United Nations, Global sustainable development report, 2016 edition. Available from https://sustainabledevelopment.un.org/content/documents/2328Global%20Sustainable%20development%20report%202016%20(final).pdf.

Table 1:

Emerging technologies crucial for achievement of the Sustainable Development Goals (SDGs) by 2030

Clusters	Emerging technologies crucial for achievement of the SDGs by 2030	Opportunities in all SDG areas	Potential threats
Bio-tech	Biotechnology, genomics, proteomics; gene-editing technologies and custom-designed DNA sequencing; genetically modified organisms; stem cells and human engineering; bio-catalysis; synthetic biology; sustainable agriculture technology.	Food crops, human health, pharmaceuticals, materials, environment, fuels.	Military use; irreversible changes to health and environment.
Digital-tech	Big Data technologies; Internet of Things; 5G mobile phones; 3-D printing and manufacturing; cloud computing platforms; open data technology; free and open-source; massive open online courses; micro-simulation; E-distribution; systems combining radio, mobile phone, satellite, GIS, and remote sensing data; data sharing technologies, including citizen science-enabling technologies; social media technologies; mobile Apps to promote public engagement and behavioural change; pre-paid system of electricity use and automatic meter reading; digital monitoring technologies; digital security technology.	Employment, manufacturing, agriculture, health, cities, finance, absolute "decoupling," governance, participation, education, citizen science, environment, global data sharing, social networking.	Unequal benefits, job losses, skills gaps, social impacts; global value chain disruption; concerns about privacy, freedom; data fraud, theft, cyber-attacks.
Nano-tech	Nano-imprint lithography; nano technology applications for decentralized water and wastewater treatment, desalination, and solar energy (nanomaterial solar cells); promising organic and inorganic nanomaterials, e.g., graphene, carbon nanotubes, carbon nanodots and conducting polymers graphene, and others.	Energy, water, chemical, electronics, medical industries; high efficiencies; resources saving; CO_2 mitigation.	Human health (toxicity), environmental impact (nanowaste).
Neuro-tech	Digital automation, including autonomous vehicles (driverless cars and drones); IBM Watson; e-discovery platforms for legal practice; personalization algorithms; artificial intelligence; speech recognition; robotics; smart technologies; cognitive computing; computational human brain models; meso-science powered virtual reality.	Health, safety, security (e.g., electricity theft), higher efficiency, resource saving, new types of jobs, manufacturing, education.	Unequal benefits, de-skilling, job losses and polarization, widening technology gaps, military use, conflicts.
Green-tech	**Circular economy:** technologies for remanufacturing, product life-cycle extension and recycling; multifunctional infrastructures; technologies for service integration of centralized and decentralized systems. **Energy:** modern cook stoves; off-grid electricity; mini-grids based on intermittent renewables with storage; battery technology; heat pumps; desalination; small and medium-sized nuclear reactors; biofuel supply chains; solar photovoltaic, wind and micro-hydro technologies; salinity gradient power technology; water-saving cooling technology; LED lamps; advanced metering. **Transport:** integrated public transport infrastructure, electric vehicles, hydrogen-fuelled vehicles and supply infrastructures. **Water:** mobile water treatment technology, wastewater technology, advanced metering infrastructure. Buildings: sustainable building technology, passive housing. **Agriculture:** sustainable agriculture technology; bio-based products and processing, low-input processing and storage technologies; horticulture techniques; irrigation technologies; bio-organometallics. **Other:** marine vibroseis, artificial photosynthesis.	Environment, climate, biodiversity, sustainable production and consumption, renewable energy, materials and resources; clean air and water; energy, water and food security; development, employment; health; equality.	New inequalities, job losses; concerns about privacy, freedom and development.
Other	Assistive technologies for people with disabilities; alternative social technologies; fabrication laboratories; radical medical innovation; geo-engineering technologies (e.g., for iron fertilization of oceans); new mining/extraction technologies; deep sea mining technologies.	Inclusion, development, health, environment, climate change mitigation, resource availability.	Pollution, inequalities, conflict.

Source: UN/DESA, Global Sustainable Development Report 2016.

ing regions took 120 years. Current technologies are clearly spreading within much shorter periods of time. Frontier off-grid renewable energy technologies, for instance, are already allowing some developing countries to rapidly accelerate electrification in rural areas.[5]

At the same time, the transformative power of new technologies raises challenges and risks. Their rapid diffusion puts great pressure on societies and individuals to adapt, and also risks leaving behind those that do not have access to the required skills or infrastructure. Many developing countries struggle to employ new technologies with the same degree of intensity and versatility as developed countries.[6] In the area of ICT, the digital divide remains stark: estimates show that almost half of all households globally still do not have access to the Internet. In least developed countries (LDCs), 85 per cent of households lack Internet access.[7] The gender gap in Internet use has not narrowed globally between 2013 and 2017, and has, in fact, widened noticeably in Africa and in LDCs. Broadband connectivity in developing countries, when available, tends to be relatively slow and expensive, limiting the ability of businesses and people to use it productively.

There are also ethical, socioeconomic and human rights questions that have to be carefully considered in the context of new technologies, from autonomous trading agents in finance to biomedical technology. For example, research has recently found that machine learning algorithms acquire biases from text data reflected in day-to-day culture. More diversity in computer science professions and greater priority for girls and marginalized groups in science, technology, engineering and mathematics (STEM) education can help address these concerns.

The disruption caused by technological change has perhaps been most acutely perceived in labour markets, which have seen job polarization and widening inequalities in many countries. Section

3 below explores impacts, challenges and risks of new technologies for employment and the changing nature of jobs in both developed and developing countries. New technologies are also changing the development finance landscape, from greater financial inclusiveness due to fintech to the regulatory challenges posed by crypto-currencies. Section 4 provides a panorama of their impact across the action areas of the Addis Agenda.

The promise that new technologies hold for sustainable development will be realized only if risks are addressed and benefits distributed equally. It is up to policymakers—both national and international—to create an environment that encourages and facilitates the absorption of technologies, their productive use for sustainable development, and the emergence of new and innovative firms.[8] The concluding section 5 addresses national action and international cooperation for STI.

3. Impact of new technologies on labour markets and jobs

New technologies are affecting the functioning of labour markets and the international division of labour, with new types of employment replacing traditional patterns of work and sources of income. The ability of countries and enterprises to exploit new digital resources will become a key determinant of their competitiveness, but the jobs created will likely require different skills.

The overall effects of digitalization remain uncertain. Some experts argue that computers and robots might be able to perform a significant portion of work at some future point, leading to widespread unemployment; others strongly disagree, underlining the job-creating potential of new technologies. There is, however, broad agreement that innovation may result in temporary job losses. Effects will be context specific, differing greatly among countries and sectors. A key determinant for countries to

5   Sustainable Energy for All, *Global Tracking Framework. Progress toward Sustainable Energy 2017.* The World Bank and the International Energy Agency: Washington, D.C. Available from http://www.se4all.org/sites/default/files/eegp17-01_gtf_full_report_final_for_web_posting_0402.pdf.

6   Marcelo LaFleur, Kenneth Iversen and Lars Jensen, "Globalization of Knowledge and Technology. 2", Frontier Issues (New York, United Nations Department of Economic and Social Affairs, forthcoming).

7   International Telecommuncations Union, ICT Facts and Figures 2017. Available from https://www.itu.int/en/ITU-D/Statistics/Documents/facts/ICTFactsFigures2017.pdf.

8   *Technology and innovation report* (United Nations publication, forthcoming).

ensure a successful transition will be the strength of their institutions and policy frameworks, which will need to ensure an adequate supply of skilled workers with strong cognitive, adaptive and creative skills necessary for "working with the machines".[9]

3.1 Labour market trends

So far, there is no evidence that technological change has led to a significant increase in joblessness and aggregate unemployment levels. Global employment continues to expand in line with the labour force, with global unemployment rates falling to 5.7 per cent in 2016.[10] In advanced economies—where technological disruption in the near term is feared the most and costs of digitalization have declined dramatically—job destruction rates have fallen,

mostly for reasons related to population ageing (see figure 1).

Nonetheless, there is evidence of a shift in types of employment, which is already observed in increases in inequality, with wage and income growth concentrated at the upper end of the income distribution and job polarization (see figure 2). As jobs are being destroyed in manufacturing and parts of services sectors, employment in both low- and high-skilled occupations has increased. Studies on robotization show that the risk of job loss is high for routine and manual jobs (i.e., those jobs that have a high share of repetitive tasks that can be easily replicated by a machine or software). In the absence of adequate opportunities to acquire new relevant skills, many of those who are at risk of job loss may

Figure 1
Inequality, job destruction and computer storage costs, 1984–2013

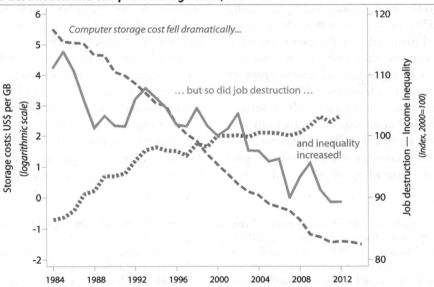

Source: ILO, database of labour statistics (2013); tenure rates: OECD, Labour Force Statistics; computer storage cost: Luke Muehlhauser, "Exponential and non-exponential trends in information technology", Machine Intelligence Research Institute (2014), available from https://intelligence.org/2014/05/12/exponential-and-non-exponential/.
Note: Job destruction rate is a weighted average of Australia, Belgium, Canada, Denmark, France, Greece, Ireland, Italy, Japan, Luxembourg, Netherlands, Sweden, United Kingdom and United States.

9   For a detailed discussion, see *Information Economy Report 2017: Digitalization, Trade and Development* (United Nations publication, Sales No. E.17.II.D.8). The STI Forum and related United Nations expert group meetings have also discussed the impacts of automation technologies on labour markets and employment since early 2016. An expert group meeting in Mexico City in December 2016 suggested a list of specific policy recommendations to address the impact of new technologies on labour markets and other issues.

10   International Labour Organization, *World Employment and Social Outlook: Trends 2017* (Geneva, International Labour Office, 2017). Available from http://www.ilo.org/global/research/global-reports/weso/2017/WCMS_541211/lang--en/index.htm.

be forced to accept lower-skilled and lower-paying jobs, putting further pressure on wages in the low-wage sector.[11] Men and women are differently affected by the changes, which may exacerbate existing gender inequalities in employment (see below). Job polarization also contributes to an increase in precarious forms of employment and long-term unemployment.[12]

While the digital economy has generated profits from larger markets and gains in productivity , the technological dividends have so far not been evenly distributed.[13] Together with the long-standing weakening of labour market institutions, these changes have contributed to the fall in the labour's share of income and a more skewed distribution of incomes (see figure 3).[14]

The key challenge going forward is to ensure that the productivity gains from digitalization are shared more fairly by strengthening labour market institutions (see next section) and by increasing employees' ability to work with new technologies. The skill-biased nature of digitalization is expected to further exacerbate skills and geographical mismatches.[15] Current education and training policies are ill prepared for this transition. With digitalization, cognitive abilities and complex problem-solving skills are becoming more important than physical strength or even technical skills.[16] Moreover, both new labour market entrants and current employees need continuous upgrading of skills and compe-

tencies. At the same time, the shift in the nature of employment towards more temporary, less secure jobs risks placing a greater burden on individual workers to acquire the right skills and competences at their own expense.[17] In many parts of the world, women are over-represented in informal occupations or the self-employed, constraining their opportunities for training, lifelong learning and skill acquisition. Providing strong policy support will be essential to ensuring the equal sharing of technological dividends from innovation.

3.2   Technology and institutional change

The technological revolution is impacting the world of work through shifts in the organization of production and a weakening of collective action. Currently, about 15-20 per cent of employees in advanced economies and 40-80 per cent of employees in developing countries are self-employed. Digitalization is expected to lead to a significant increase in self-employment (the "gig economy"), as firms will in-source more services through peer-to-peer networks. This will further weaken the capacity of trade unions and employers' associations to guarantee common labour standards and employment conditions through collective bargaining agreements.

At the same time, new technologies are predicted to improve the functioning of labour markets. AI and big data techniques are increasingly used to improve recruitment processes and could help cor-

---

11   Daron Acemoglu and Pascual Restrepo, "The race between machine and man: implications of technology for growth, factor shares and employment," NBER Working Paper No. 22252 (Cambridge: National Bureau of Economic Research, May 2016). Available from http://www.nber.org/papers/w22252.pdf; Daron Acemoglu Pascual Restrepo, "Robots and Jobs: Evidence from US Labor Markets," NBER Working Paper No. 23285 (Cambridge: National Bureau of Economic Research, March 2017). Available from http://www.nber.org/papers/w23285.

12   International Labour Organization. *World Employment and Social Outlook: Trends 2017.*

13   Dan Andrews, Chiara Criscuolo and Peter N. Gal, "The best versus the rest," OECD Productivity Working Papers, No. 5 (Paris, OECD, 2 December 2016). Available from http://www.oecd-ilibrary.org/economics/the-best-versus-the-rest_63629cc9-en.

14   International Labour Organization, *Non-standard Employment around the World: Understanding Challenges, Shaping Prospects* (Geneva: International Labour Office, 2016); Organization for Economic Cooperation and Development, *Economic Policy Reforms 2017: Going for Growth* (Paris, 2017); International Monetary Fund, "Understanding the downward trend in labor income shares" in *World Economic Outlook, April 2017: Gaining Momentum?* (Washington, D.C., 2017).

15   Pascual Restrepo, "Skill mismatch and structural unemployment," Massachusetts Institute of Technology Working Paper (Cambridge, 2015). Available from http://pascual.scripts.mit.edu/research/01/PR_jmp.pdf; Soloman Polachek and others (eds.) , *Skill Mismatch in Labor Markets* (Bingley, Emerald Group Publishing, 2017).

16   See http://reports.weforum.org/future-of-jobs-2016/skills-stability/.

17   International Labour Organization, *Non-standard Employment around the World.*

Figure 2
Changes in employment shares, 2000–2013 and 2013–2021
(*Percentage*)

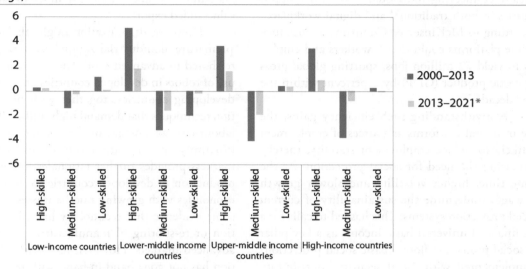

Source: ILO, Trends Econometric Models (November 2016).
Note: Change in employment shares expressed in percentage points.
* Forecasts after 2016.

Figure 3
Labour productivity and wage growth, 1999–2015
(*Index*)

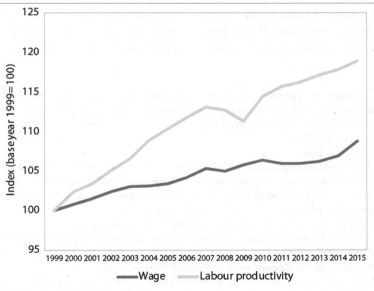

Source: ILO, *Global Wage Report* 2016/17 (2016).

rect skills and geographical mismatches.[18] Digital platforms such as LinkedIn and Monster.com are already connecting individuals with work opportunities in both traditional and digital workplaces. According to McKinsey & Company, for instance, online platforms could match workers and employers to yield 72 million jobs, spurring global gross domestic product (GDP) by 2 per cent within the next decade.[19]

Notwithstanding such efficiency gains, the rise in digital platforms as sources of employment is likely to reduce employment stability, thereby increasing the need for social protection. At the same time, higher volatility and slower growth in wages undermine the sustainability of current social protection systems. This has led to calls for a tax-financed universal basic income as a key pillar of social protection floors (basic social protection), complemented with social security contributory schemes. (see also chapter III.A and its discussion on social protection).

3.3   Effects of globalization

Exports of tradable manufacturing goods and integration into global supply chains have long been an engine of growth and job creation for developing countries. Participation in new digital platforms in sectors such as agriculture or tourism can enable small and medium-sized enterprises (SMEs) from developing countries to compete in well-defined market segments. They offer greater scope for functional upgrading in value chains where producers build trust and potentially move to sell higher value-added exports.[20]

However, digitalization might also speed up "premature deindustrialization" as activities are re-shored to advanced economies.[21] The increasing use of robots in developed countries and some large developing countries, together with new production techniques that demand high skills, will reduce labour-cost advantages of developing countries.[22] Proximity to innovation centres and consumer markets provides further rationales for re-shoring production to developed countries or to emerging economies with growing middle classes.[23] There is some evidence that technology has allowed retention or re-shoring of manufacturing activities in advanced markets. However, re-shoring of production has not gone hand-in-hand with re-shoring of employment.[24]

So far, most developing countries do not seem to be overly threatened by automation, owing to the uneven spread of such technologies across countries and industries. To date, the use of robots remains concentrated in just a few countries and sectors, such as automotive, computers and electronic equipment. In low-skill and labour-intensive sectors such as textiles, automation is not yet economically profitable; nor is it socioeconomically desirable in countries with high numbers of unskilled workers.

18   Ideal, "AI for Recruiting: A definitive guide for HR professionals." Available from https://ideal.com/ai-recruiting/; McKinsey & Company, "A labor market that works: connecting talent with opportunity in the digital age" (Washington, D.C., McKinsey Global Institute, 2015).

19   McKinsey & Company, ibid.

20   *Information Economy Report.*

21   Dani Rodrik, "Premature deindustrialization", *Journal of Economic Growth*, vol. 21, No. 1 (27 November 2015), pp. 1–33; International Labour Organization, *World Employment and Social Outlook: Trends 2015* (Geneva, International Labour Office, 2015). See also http://www.economist.com/news/special-report/21621158-model-development-through-industrialisation-its-way-out-arrested-development.

22   Morris Cohen and others, "Benchmarking global production sourcing decisions: where and why firms offshore and reshore", Stanford University Graduate School of Business Research Paper No. 16-28 (May 2016); UNCTAD, "Robots and Industrialization in Developing Countries", Policy Brief No. 50 (Geneva, October 2015). Available from http://unctad.org/en/PublicationsLibrary/presspb2016d6_en.pdf.

23   Koen De Backer and others, "Reshoring: Myth or Reality?", OECD Science, Technology and Industry Policy Papers No. 27 (Paris, Organization for Economic Co-operation and Development, 2016). Available from http://www.oecd-ilibrary.org/content/workingpaper/5jm56frbm38s-en.

24   Bruckner, LaFleur and Pitterle, "The impact of the technological revolution on labour markets and income distribution".

At the same time, moving up the value chain toward more skill-intensive industries may become harder if robot-based innovation leads to re-shoring and further concentration of such activities in a small number of countries that are technology leaders.[25] It may well be the case that the negative effects of robots are mostly felt in countries that do not use them.[26]

3.4 Structural and gender considerations

Digitalization and automation may also worsen ethnic and gender imbalances, although impacts differ between countries. In the United States of America, for instance, automation in the transportation industry could strongly impact African American, Hispanic and Native American workers, since they are overrepresented and earn better wages than their peers in non-driving occupations.[27] In ASEAN countries, women represent the majority in occupations that are likely to be automated, thus being more vulnerable to unemployment than men.[28] In Argentina on the other hand, female jobholders face an automation probability of 61 per cent, while for men it stands at 66 per cent.[29] Alternative employment opportunities may arise in the care sector, which is expected to expand further, not least because of ageing populations around the world. However, pervasive gender stereotypes perpetuate significant deficits of decent work in this sector and most care work continues to be unpaid, preventing the development of a larger, diversified care services market.

4. New technologies and Financing for Development: opportunities and risks in the action areas of the Addis Ababa Action Agenda

New and emerging digital technologies have the potential to alleviate key constraints and market failures that impede sustainable development finance, such as weak contract enforcement, cumbersome administrative procedures, and paucity of information and data. They can contribute to reducing inefficiencies and to cost savings across the action areas of the Addis Agenda, but they also raise new challenges and risks for policymakers and regulators, discussed below and throughout this report.

4.1 Domestic public finance

Fiscal policy can become more effective thanks to the greater ability of Governments to collect, process and act on information, through both improved public service delivery and tax collection. Digitalization increases efficiencies and saves costs in public financial management (PFM). Gains are accruing from the generation of more and better data, better data management systems and higher computer processing power, which can also lead to better policy design.[30] For developing countries alone, it is estimated that moving government payment transactions from cash to digital could save roughly one per cent of GDP annually with about half accruing directly to Governments, greatly improving fiscal balances.[31] In India, the country's national bio-

---

25   See the summary of the Inter-agency Task Force technical meeting on "The impact of new technologies on labour markets and the jobs of the future", available from https://developmentfinance.un.org/sites/developmentfinance.un.org/files/IATF%20Technical%20Meeting%20on%20Tech%20and%20Labour%20Markets_Summary_0.pdf.

26   *Trade and Development Report 2017* (United Nations publication, Sales No. E.17.II.D.5.).

27   Center for Global Policy Solutions, "Stick Shift: Autonomous Vehicles, Driving Jobs and the Future of Work", (Washington, D.C., 2017). Available from http://globalpolicysolutions.org/report/stick-shift-autonomous-vehicles-driving-jobs-and-the-future-of-work/.

28   Jae-Hee Chang, Gary Rynhart and Phu Huynh, "ASEAN in Transformation: How Technology Is Changing Jobs and Enterprises", Bureau for Employers' Activities, Working Paper No.10 (Bangkok, International Labour Organization, 2016).

29   Anton Estevadeordal and others (eds.), "Robot-Lución: The Future of Work in Latin American Integration 4.0", *Integration and Trade*, vol. 21, No. 42 (August 2017). Available from http://publications.iadb.org/handle/11319/8487.

30   Sanjeev Gupta and others (eds.), *Digital Revolutions in Public Finance* (Washington, D.C., International Monetary Fund, 2017). Available from https://www.bookstore.imf.org/books/title/digital-revolutions-in-public-finance.

31   Susan Lund, Olivia White and Jason Lamb, "The value of digitalizing government payments in developing countries", in Gupta and others, ibid.

metric identity programme combined with a concerted public effort to increase financial inclusion have allowed an increasing number of government transfer payments to be made directly to individuals, significantly reducing leakage.

Although still in its infancy, distributed ledger technology—popularly called blockchain—is increasingly being applied and piloted in PFM administration as data and transactions infrastructure. Blockchain technology can instil trust and ensure security through its decentralized features. Its ability to work with "smart contracts"[32] can automate transactions such as licensing, revenue collection and social transfers, significantly lowering costs. Estonia, for example, offers citizens a digital identity card based on blockchain, which allows citizens to access public, financial and social services as well as pay taxes.[33] Another area of interest is blockchain's ability to combat illegal activities through improved verification of authenticity and provenance throughout the supply chain (the mining industry provides a good example).[34]

On the resource mobilization side, the increased use of digital payments also provides better means of verifying economic outcomes of taxpayers and can help formalize and tax previously undocumented economic activities. However, digitization also brings new opportunities for tax-avoidance and profit shifting and other financial integrity issues such as money laundering and funding of terrorism.[35] Chapter III.A on domestic resource mobilization includes a detailed discussion of rules for the taxation of the digital economy and cross-border implications in particular. The United Nations Committee of Experts on International Cooperation in Tax Matters and the Organization for Economic Cooperation and Development have both started to look into how the international community can address these issues.

At the national level, Governments need to increase investments not only in their own capacities to take advantage of digitalization, but also in ensuring that all individuals and businesses have access to these systems, and be mindful of adoption costs that may exclude certain sections of society. The collection of ever more detailed data also increases the responsibility of Governments to protect citizens' privacy and to adopt regulatory frameworks that prevent abuse.

4.2 Private finance

Digitally enabled innovation in the financial sector (fintech) offers new business models for providing financial services and is at the heart of financial inclusion in many developing countries. Fintech includes start-ups that provide digitally based financial services, established telecoms firms, and online retailers that use ICT capabilities and customer bases to provide digital financial services, such as mobile-telephone-based money, payments and banking service. Fintech can help overcome traditional impediments to accessing financial services by large segments of the population in developing countries in multiple ways.

First, fintech allows businesses and organizations to reach a wide range of consumers without a large investment in physical infrastructure (other than for ICT, which has broader uses). With the cost and time of financial service provision significantly reduced, resources can be dedicated to expanding reach, which makes smaller transaction markets more attractive from a business perspective. This has implications for lowering the cost of remittance transfers, as discussed in chapter III.B. Second, fintech can reduce collateral requirements and cut monitoring costs, and provide alternative credit-scoring methods where borrowers lack credit history. Online marketplaces are able to extend loans to small and

---

32   Smart contracts can automatically pay out an entitlement when certain eligibility criteria are met and verified by the blockchain network.

33   Arvind Krishna, Martin Fleming and Soloman Assefa, "Instilling digital trust: blockchain and cognitive computing for government", in Gupta and others, *Digital Revolutions in Public Finance*.

34   See, for example, "Diamonds Are The Latest Industry To Benefit From Blockchain Technology", *Forbes* (10 September 2017) on how blockchains can be applied in the diamond and other industries.

35   Dong He and others, "Virtual currencies and beyond: Initial considerations", IMF Staff Discussion Note (Washington, D.C., International Monetary Fund, January 2016). Available from https://www.imf.org/external/pubs/ft/sdn/2016/sdn1603.pdf.

micro firms active on their platforms owing to the extensive data they are collecting. Fintech can facilitate registration of asset ownership; this can serve as a security measure, allowing more agents to access credit, and facilitate matching between different investors and project/business owners.[36] Improvements to the business environment, such as secure land tenure and property rights, can also raise investment levels. Digitalization can improve registration procedures, and a few initiatives are looking into how blockchain can be used to expand and simplify land and property registration.[37]

At the same time, private finance can be a key source of investment for STI infrastructure. The United Nations Conference on Trade and Development (UNCTAD) estimates the total investment required to build universal basic 3G coverage in developing and transition economies at less than $100 billion, and in LDCs at less than $40 billion.[38] These amounts could be attainable with an enabling framework for private investment and policies aimed at generating sufficient demand, and with government support to achieve universal connectivity, including in thinly populated and low-income areas.

4.3   Development cooperation

The main benefits of digital technologies in development cooperation are cost-savings and efficiency gains through timely and better targeted responses, reduced risk of fraud, and a better understanding of impacts, and thus better program and project design and implementation. As an example, biometric registration data of Syrian refugees in Jordan and Lebanon, collected by UNHCR, is then used by agencies to authenticate identity at ATMs and point of sale.[39] Blockchain technology can help improve humanitarian emergency response coordination, such as digitalizing payments to response workers under the Ebola crisis in Sierra Leone, which helped reduce strikes, fraud and traveling time for workers.[40] Satellite imagery, mobile phone data and AI technology can help identify, predict and target poverty interventions where information is missing, track the movement of displaced people or climate-related changes, and can augment existing monitoring tools.[41]

To the extent that technologies increase transparency and accountability in development cooperation, they could also help raise the general public willingness to provide support. As an example, through the International Aid Transparency Initiative (IATI), data systems and standards are already in place to track financial flows to development and humanitarian projects. Increasing numbers of publishers are adding results to their published projects and increasing traceability.

4.4   Trade

Increasing digitalization and globalization are creating new opportunities for trade. Digitalization helps small businesses and entrepreneurs in developing countries connect with global markets. It also creates new jobs and opens new ways of generating income, jobs and entrepreneurial opportunities. UNCTAD estimates show that some 100 million people are employed by ICT services globally, so far largely in developed countries. Cross-border business-to-consumer (B2C) e-commerce was worth about $189 billion in 2015, which corresponds to 7 per cent of total B2C e-commerce.[42] At the same

---

36   United Nations Development Programme, "Digitally enabled financial services: how digital technology drives financial inclusion", BPPS Strategic Policy Unit Paper (New York, forthcoming).

37   For example, the ongoing work of Bitland in Ghana, or Bitfury in Georgia. See "Bitcoin, blockchain and the fight against poverty", *Financial Times*, 22 December 2017.

38   *World Investment Report*. Geneva (United Nations publication, Sales No. E.17.II.D.3).

39   See: http://www.unhcr.org/en-us/cash-based-interventions.html and http://www.unhcr.org/en-us/596331dd7

40   Joe Abass Bangura, "Saving money, saving lives; a case study on the benefits of digitizing payments to Ebola response workers in Sierra Leone", Better Than Cash Alliance Case Study Series (New York, Better Than Cash Alliance, May 2016). Available from https://www.betterthancash.org/tools-research/case-studies/saving-money-saving-lives-a-case-study-on-the-benefits-of-digitizing-payments-to-ebola-response-workers-in-sierra-leone

41   See, for example, Joshua E. Blumenstock, "Fighting poverty with data", *Science*, vol. 353, Issue 6301 (19 August 2016), pp. 753-754.

42   *Information Economy Report: Digitalization, Trade and Development* (United Nations publication, Sales No. E.17.II.D.8).

time, changing trade patterns due to digitalization (such as re-shoring, discussed above) could also have negative impacts for developing countries, whose integration into the digital economy will be critical for their ability to compete in global markets.

Blockchain technology also has great potential in trade finance, which is characterized by a large number of stakeholders and mostly paper-based documentation. Potential benefits include simplified processes, reduced settlement times, errors, fraud and disputes, and increased trust between all parties to a transaction. A group of banks have partnered with blockchain service provider IBM on implementing a new blockchain-based global system for trade finance. Similarly, IBM has teamed with another set of banks to build and host a new blockchain-based system for providing SMEs with trade finance.[43] Digitization can also reduce the costs associated with know-your-customer and anti-money laundering rules, thus helping to counter some of the negative trends in correspondent banking.

4.5   Debt and systemic issues

The ability to collect more and better information can improve credit analysis and allow more agents to access credit. More generally, digitalization could enhance economic data collection, support early warning systems and improve risk preparedness. On the other hand, the provision of financial services outside existing supervisory and regulatory frameworks poses new challenges to the regulatory regime, which is currently structured around financial service-providing entities rather than activities. Regulators have already begun to address these issues in the context of cross-border transactions of virtual currencies. The Financial Action Task Force has called on countries to apply anti-money laundering measures to virtual currency exchanges.[44] If virtual currencies were used on a larger scale, they could raise new financial stability risks, and even reduce the effectiveness of monetary policy.[45]

4.6   Data

Digital technologies and the Internet are generating vast amounts of (financial and non-financial) data, raising questions regarding who owns data and how it can and should be used. Governments need to strike the right balance of addressing privacy concerns without stifling beneficial innovations. There is also a need for capacity development in data management and data and process standardization. Efforts to support sharing of best practices in policy and regulation should be strengthened. As an example, authorities and regulators in Kenya (where mobile money was pioneered) are often credited for having put in place appropriate legal and regulatory frameworks guiding the use of digital technologies.[46]

5.   National and international actions on science, technology and innovation

Technology is making rapid advances, with impacts felt across countries and sectors. To reap its benefits and to address the significant risks and challenges described above, appropriate policy frameworks need to be in place and complementary investments need to be made, both at the national level and through enhanced international support.

5.1   National innovation strategies

There is no single optimal system or policy blueprint for a national STI policy and innovation strategy, since the innovation context varies greatly between countries. Both public and private actors contribute to the innovation process, with Governments often the main funder of basic research, which is critical to the absorptive capacity of countries. Private actors play a more prominent role in development, demonstration and diffusion of technology. Even in these latter stages, public policy and public funding

43   Martin Arnold, "Banks team up with IBM in trade finance blockchain", *Financial Times*, 4 October 2017.

44   Dong He and others, "Fintech and financial services: Initial considerations", IMF Staff Discussion Note (Washington, D.C., International Monetary Fund, June 2017). Available from https://www.imf.org/en/Publications/Staff-Discussion-Notes/Issues/2017/06/16/Fintech-and-Financial-Services-Initial-Considerations-44985.

45   Dong He and others, "Virtual currencies and beyond".

46   Njuguna Ndung'u (2017). "Digitalization in Kenya; revolutionizing tax design and revenue administration", in Gupta and others, *Digital Revolutions in Public Finance*.

are often critical, and key components of a national innovation strategy.

Recent trends in national innovation strategies show that many Governments, particularly in developed countries, have focused their attention on improving the ability of firms to invest in research, development and innovation, rather than on public research, as a response to budgetary constraints.[47] This includes financing of business innovation and entrepreneurship, rationalizing public research spending, and strengthening ties between public and private research. Global public and private research and development (R&D) expenditure has remained relatively constant, growing only modestly between 2009 and 2015, from 1.64 to 1.70 per cent of GDP. While lower overall, R&D expenditure in developing countries grew at a faster rate, driven to a significant degree by China, which is now second only to the United States in R&D expenditures. In LDCs on other hand, only around 0.24 per cent of GDP is dedicated to R&D. Generally, absolute spending remains highly concentrated, both in terms of countries and firms (see figure 4).[48] The 200 largest global firms, which are concentrated in the United States, Japan and China, account for 70 per cent of all business R&D spending.[49]

Developing countries and their firms and entrepreneurs thus spend significantly less on R&D than developed countries, despite high potential returns associated with technological catch-up. One reason is that returns to innovation cannot be realized in the absence of key complementary factors, such as physical and human capital.[50] National innovation strategies thus need to be broad in order to address broader constraints to innovation, and be embedded in sustainable development and productive diversification strategies. Policies should also take into consideration gender equality throughout the policy process—from design to evaluation—and consider technology foresight and assessment as tools to ensure the inclusive application of STI for sustainable development.

Public leadership is particularly important in so-called mission-oriented innovation that aims to tackle grand structural challenges such as climate change. Indeed, the 2030 Agenda for Sustainable Development calls for transformative change in many areas, which requires public policy to target not only the rate but also the direction of innovation.[51] Many countries are already focusing innovation policies on specific socioeconomic sectors, such as agribusiness, biotechnology, the software industry and climate change. Examples include Inova Agro, a fund targeting the agribusiness sector in Brazil, FONSOFT in Argentina and PROSOFT in Mexico, which provides SMEs in the software industry with competitive funding. Some countries have also implemented taxes and other mechanisms to redirect funds from companies to support sectoral and general research activities. One example is a levy on palm oil producers in Malaysia that funds research in the sector.[52]

Another key constraint is that start-ups and SMEs often have difficulty accessing venture capital. Countries have set up targeted funds and are partnering with multilateral organizations and private venture capital firms to close this financing gap. Examples include the Islamic Republic

47 Organization for Economic Cooperation and Development, *OECD Science, Technology and Innovation Outlook 2016* (Paris, OECD Publishing, 2016). Available from http://www.oecd.org/sti/oecd-science-technology-and-innovation-outlook-25186167.htm.

48 Data from UNESCO Institute for Statistics. Available from http://data.uis.unesco.org.

49 Organization for Economic Cooperation and Development, *OECD Science, Technology and Innovation Outlook 2016*.

50 Xavier Cirera and William F. Maloney, *The Innovation Paradox. Developing-Country Capabilities and the Unrealized Promise of Technological Catch-Up* (Washington, D.C., The World Bank, 2017). Available from https://openknowledge.worldbank.org/bitstream/handle/10986/28341/9781464811609.pdf?sequence=4&isAllowed=y.

51 See, for example, Mariana Mazzucato, "Building the entrepreneurial state: a new framework for envisioning and evaluating a mission-oriented public sector, Levy Economics Institute Working Paper Collection, Working Paper No. 824 (Annandale-on-Hudson, New York, Levy Economics Institute, January 2015). Available from http://www.levyinstitute.org/pubs/wp_824.pdf.

52 For a longer and more detailed list of examples drawn from the UNESCO 2015 Science report, see the online annex of this report, and its section on STI and capacity-building, available from https://developmentfinance.un.org/science-technology-innovation-and-capacity-building.

Figure 4
Research and development expenditure, 2000–2015
(*Percentage of GDP*)

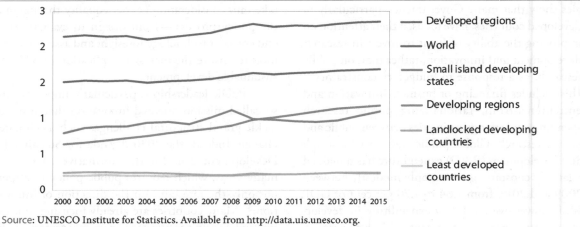

Source: UNESCO Institute for Statistics. Available from http://data.uis.unesco.org.

of Iran's Innovation and Prosperity Fund, which offers tax incentives and pays partial costs of commercializing knowledge and technology to SMEs, and Azerbaijan's State Fund for the Development of Information Technologies, which provides start-up funding through equity participation or low-interest loans.

5.2 Development cooperation for STI and capacity building, and actions by the UN system and others

National efforts to strengthen science, technology and innovation need to be complemented by international support. Official development assistance for scientific, technological and innovative capacity has increased significantly in recent years, amounting to $1.8 billion in 2016. However, much of the increase in recent years has not benefited the poorest and most vulnerable countries, which have seen STI-specific aid flows stagnate in recent years (see figure 5).

South-South cooperation on STI is an important complement to North-South cooperation. Several developing countries have built up significant STI knowledge, resources and capacity that are sometimes more affordable and appropriate for recipient countries.[53] Through the Development Cooperation Forum, Southern partners have called on South-South and triangular cooperation to take an even more prominent role in unleashing the transformative power of STI.[54] The BRICS countries (Brazil, Russia, India, China and South Africa) have intensified STI cooperation under the BRICS STI Framework Programme.

Several United Nations agencies have also invested considerably in enhancing capacity development for STI. Some agencies developed guidelines and e-learning tools (e.g., the Food and Agriculture Organization), created new training mechanisms, such as academies and virtual institutes (e.g., the International Labour Organization and UNCTAD), implemented pilot projects in volunteering and capacity-building (UNDP-UNV), and carried out

---

53   South-South and triangular cooperation for achieving the 2030 Agenda: building innovative and inclusive partnerships. United Nations Development Cooperation Forum. Summary document of the DCF Argentina High-level Symposium, 6-8 September 2017. Available from https://www.un.org/ecosoc/sites/www.un.org.ecosoc/files/files/en/dcf/dcf-argentina-summary.pdf.

54   ECOSOC Development Cooperation Forum, "Promoting sustainable development through triangular cooperation", DCF Policy Brief No. 19 (New York, DCF Secretariat, September 2017). Available from https://www.un.org/ecosoc/sites/www.un.org.ecosoc/files/files/en/dcf/brief%203_Triangular_cooperation_final_01_09_17.pdf.

technical assistance initiatives to enhance capacities in the field of technology and innovation (WIPO).[55] The United Nations Department of Economic and Social Affairs (UN/DESA) is implementing a four-year project for mobilizing STI in developing countries for the SDGs. UNCTAD continues to support the development of national capacities in the STI policy field through its science, technology and innovation policy (STIP) reviews, and is currently revising the framework with a view to incorporate SDG considerations into the STIP reviews. To prevent the evolving digital economy from leading to widening digital divides and greater income inequalities, UNCTAD launched the eTrade for all initiative in 2016.[56] The United Nations Educational, Scientific and Cultural Organization (UNESCO) continues to promote international scientific cooperation and capacity-building through several programmes, including GO-SPIN, which supports countries in developing STI policy instruments, as well as its STEM and Gender Advancement tools, which aim at improving measurement and policies for gender equality in STEM fields. The International Telecommunications Union (ITU) has a large capacity-building programme focusing on strengthening skills among its membership in a wide range of ICT-related topics. Through the ITU Academy, which has more than 10,000 users, and its Centres of Excellence network, it delivers face-to-face and e-learning courses to beneficiaries from all regions.[57]

5.3   Technology Facilitation Mechanism

Under the umbrella of the Technology Facilitation Mechanism (TFM),[58] the second STI Forum was held in New York on 15 and 16 May 2017. The Forum attracted more than 800 participants, representing a cross section of scientists, innovators, tech-nology specialists, entrepreneurs, policymakers and civil society representatives. The Forum explored policies and actions for advancing STI to achieve the six SDGs up for review at the 2017 High-level Political Forum and proposed recommendations for action detailed in the Co-Chairs' summary of the STI forum.[59]

The STI forum is organized by the United Nations Interagency Task Team on STI for the SDGs (IATT), which has been co-convened since September 2017 by UNCTAD and UN/DESA, and has 35 active members.[60] The IATT and its members will develop an initial demo version of the online platform of the TFM, which is envisaged as a gateway for information on STI initiatives, mechanisms and programmes around the world, and it is expected to connect suppliers and users of technologies that advance progress towards achieving the SDGs.

5.4   The Technology Bank for the Least Developed Countries

The Addis Agenda reiterated the call from the Istanbul Programme for the creation of a Technology Bank for the LDCs. On 23 December 2016 the United Nations General Assembly established the Technology Bank for Least Developed Countries. In September 2017, the United Nations and the Government of Turkey signed the Host Country Agreement and the Contribution Agreement, and in November, the Council of the Technology Bank adopted the programme of work and budget for 2018. During its first year of work, the Technology Bank, in collaboration with other United Nations entities, including UNCTAD and UNESCO, will focus on preparing STI reviews and technology needs assessments and on promoting digital access to research and technical knowledge in selected LDCs.

---

55   United Nations, Report of the Secretary-General on the state of South-South cooperation (A/72/297). Available from http://undocs.org/A/72/297. The World Intellectual Property Organization (WIPO) Technology & Innovation Support Center (TISC) initiative aims to assist local users to create, protect, own and manage their own intellectual property rights, strengthen the local technological base and increase technology transfer through Service Level Agreements with national IP Offices, see http://www.wipo.int/tisc/en/.

56   For more information, see https://etradeforall.org/.

57   See https://academy.itu.int/index.php?lang=en.

58   See https://sustainabledevelopment.un.org/tfm.

59   See E/HLPF/2017/4 of 31 May 2017. Available from http://www.un.org/ga/search/view_doc.asp?symbol=E/HLPF/2017/4&Lang=E.

60   Membership as of October 2017.

Figure 5
Official development assistance for scientific, technological and innovative capacity, 2000–2016
(*Billions of United States dollars*)

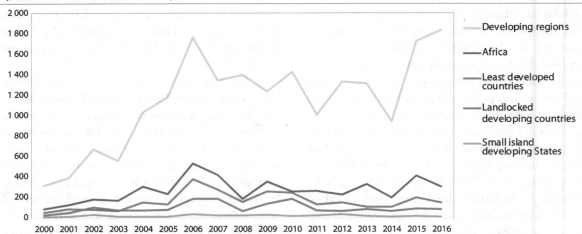

Source: OECD Creditor Reporting System and UN/DESA calculations.
Notes: Includes ODA commitments reported under education, medical, energy, agricultural, forestry, fishery, technological and environmental research, ICT and research and scientific institutions.

Chapter IV
Data, monitoring and follow-up

1. Key messages and recommendations

The range and depth of data demands to fully implement the monitoring frameworks for the Sustainable Development Goals (SDGs) and financing for development outcomes are unprecedented. The frameworks require data that is disaggregated by income, sex, age, race, ethnicity, migration status, disability, geographic location and other nationally relevant characteristics in order to cover all population groups and leave no one uncounted. Monitoring the implementation of the Addis Ababa Action Agenda (hereafter, "Addis Agenda"), requires data that are not included in the SDG indicators process, with a focus on policies and financial flows. The Inter-agency Task Force on Financing for Development (hereafter, "Task Force"), despite its limited resources, seeks to pull together the relevant data that exist; however, there is no central process for trying to bridge the data gaps that have been identified by the Task Force in its 2017 report.[1]

Significant efforts are required to strengthen national statistical capacities to provide the necessary data and statistics to monitor the progress in the implementation of the 2030 Agenda for Sustainable Development and Addis Agenda. Funding the modernization efforts of national statistical systems is essential. Support from multilateral and bilateral donors for all areas of statistics accounted for only 0.3 per cent of total official development assistance (ODA), which is far below what is needed. *Donors should consider increasing the ODA they provide to statistical systems.*

Challenges in data collection are particularly steep for gender-related data fields. Despite an increase in data availability to monitor progress towards gender equality, additional efforts are needed to fill the gaps. *To overcome these challenges, Member States could incorporate plans for developing integrated national systems for gender statistics into their broader strategies.* The Task Force has previously recommended that policies of Member States not simply be "gender-sensitive, but actively seek to advance the goal of gender equality". This will not be possible if policymakers do not make use of gender-disaggregated information. *Member States should strengthen efforts to produce sex-disaggregated data, but they also should popularize the use of gender statistics to improve policy design and implementation.*

Further progress is also needed on data on the financial sector and on financial vulnerabilities. Substantial progress was made by the participating economies during the first year of the second phase of the Data Gaps Initiative, despite some key challenges in the implementation of some recommendations. These challenges include compilation of government finance statistics beyond central government; sectoral accounts, including details on shadow banking activities; and sharing of granular data. *Overcoming these challenges is essential to providing data to policymakers to monitor financial sector risks, analyse fiscal conditions, and understand cross-border financial interconnectedness.*

Finally, this report highlights transparency and accountability as a critical issue across chapters. Efforts at transparency, whether related to tax matters, debt levels, or trade and customs data, will be more successful if the basis for information sharing is more consistent. This chapter highlights efforts to improve the use of the Legal Entity Identifier (LEI)

---

1   *Financing for Development: Progress and Prospects.* Report of the Inter-agency Task Force on Financing for Development 2017 (United Nations publication, Sales. No. E.17.I.5), page 121.

in financial sector data. *Public entities that issue securities could lead by example and obtain an LEI for themselves.* Chapter II.A discussed the preparation of registries on beneficial ownership. *Transparency efforts could be linked and made more interoperable, so that policymakers can have better data and make more effective decisions that move the world closer to achieving the SDGs.*

2. Strengthening data and statistical capacities

2.1 Progress on the Cape Town Global Action Plan for Sustainable Development Data

The Cape Town Global Action Plan for Sustainable Development Data provides a strategic framework calling upon Governments, policy leaders and the international community to modernize and strengthen national statistical systems, and provides a framework for the design and implementation of country-led statistical capacity-building activities necessary to achieve the 2030 Agenda for Sustainable Development. The Global Action Plan was included in the General Assembly resolution on the work of the United Nations Statistical Commission pertaining to the 2030 Agenda for Sustainable Development,[2] which notes that the Action Plan should inform discussions at the policy and decision-making levels on statistical gaps and capacity-building needs in relation to the implementation of the SDGs. The Global Action Plan recognizes that modernization of national statistical systems is essential to the implementation of the 2030 Agenda for Sustainable Development, and emphasizes the need for countries, the United Nations and all other entities to intensify support for statistical capacity-building, including improving the information technology base of statistical systems.

The High-level Group for Partnership, Cooperation and Capacity-Building is developing notes on implementation for the Global Action Plan, which will serve as a practical starting point to guide implementation of programmes and activities aimed at strengthening national statistical systems and developing their capacity to respond to the data needs of the 2030 Agenda for Sustainable Development. The purpose of the notes is to offer guidance for national and international initiatives aimed at addressing the objectives under the six strategic areas of the Global Action Plan. Country examples provide case studies to highlight activities that countries are undertaking to carry out the Global Action Plan in their national settings. The implementation of the plan will also be reviewed at the upcoming United Nations World Data Forum 2018, being held in Dubai, United Arab Emirates, from 22 to 24 October.

2.2 SDG indicator framework

In order to promote accountability to their citizens, Member States committed to a systematic follow-up and review of the implementation of the 2030 Agenda for Sustainable Development at the national, regional and global levels. Member States agreed to a set of global indicators, to be developed by the Inter-agency and Expert Group on Sustainable Development Goal Indicators (IAEG-SDGs),[3] to follow-up and review the goals and targets of the 2030 Agenda for Sustainable Development. The global indicator framework was adopted by the United Nations Statistical Commission at its forty-eighth session in March 2017, and subsequently adopted by the Economic and Social Council in June 2017 and the General Assembly in July 2017.[4]

The global indicator framework was developed by the IAEG-SDGs through an open and transparent process involving all stakeholders. It consists of 232 indicators, addressing all goals and targets of the 2030 Agenda for Sustainable Development. The indicators are currently classified into three tiers, based on the existence of established methodology and data availability. As of December 2017, the framework comprised 93 tier I indicators (those with regular data), 66 tier II indicators (those without regular data), and 68 tier III indicators (those with no internationally established methodology or standards). In addition, there were five indicators classified in multiple tiers, meaning that different

---

2   A/RES/71/313.
3   A/RES/70/1, para. 75.
4   A/RES/71/313.

components of those indicators were classified in different tiers. Significant progress has been made in the methodological development of many tier III indicators since April 2017, when many more (84) indicators were still being classified as tier III.[5]

A robust and high-quality indicator framework requires continued work over time, and the framework will be annually refined and comprehensively reviewed by the United Nations Statistical Commission in 2020 and 2025. The IAEG-SDGs continues to work in an open, inclusive and transparent manner to ensure that the indicator framework is fully implemented so that all goals and targets are appropriately reviewed and no individual or group is left behind.

It is expected that the SDGs will be integrated into national development plans and frameworks. The global indicators are supplemented by national and subnational indicators that guide countries' follow-up and review. Decisions on national indicators are driven by national priorities.

2.3   Funding for statistical capacities

To measure progress across the SDGs, national statistical systems need to produce accurate, reliable, easy-to-use, timely and disaggregated data and statistics. While data availability and quality have improved over the years, national statistical systems in developing countries still face significant capacity constraints to measure the SDGs and support their implementation. In some countries, institutional and legislative reforms are needed to ensure that the national statistical office can effectively lead the SDG monitoring and reporting processes. To fill data gaps, new institutional arrangements are required to enable private-public multi-stakeholder partnerships for the use of big data and non-traditional data sources.

Moreover, sufficiently disaggregated data are necessary for measuring progress and disparities across all population groups in order to leave no one behind. Aggregated data at the national level, and sometimes at the subnational level, often mask the developmental disparities among different population groups. National statistical systems need to find creative technological solutions to collect, integrate and better use granular data from multiple sources — including traditional surveys, censuses, administrative records and geospatial information. Better linking data from different surveys can provide new insights in a cost-effective way. Efforts can also be made to improve cross-country data comparability and make metadata publicly available. The creation of standardized approaches to the use of big data and non-traditional sources for SDG-related efforts can allow innovations to be shared, promote comparability and improve efficiency.

It is estimated that domestic and donor support to data and statistics for 77 of the world's lower-income countries will need to increase up to $1 billion per year to strengthen national statistical systems for SDG monitoring.[6] However, in 2015 (the last year for which data is available), countries received only $541 million in support from multilateral and bilateral donors — 0.3 per cent of total ODA — for all areas of statistics.[7] Countries in sub-Saharan Africa benefited most from the growth in ODA statistical support, followed by the countries in Central and Southern Asia and Latin America and the Caribbean (see figure 1). Support for data and statistics in least developed countries grew dramatically over this period, from $106.0 million in 2010 to $176.7 million in 2015. Continued and increased technical and financial support is needed to ensure that countries in developing regions are better equipped to monitor progress of their national development agenda.

2.4   Gender statistics, including data on time use and unpaid work

The Beijing Platform for Action states that statistics related to individuals should be "collected, compiled, analysed and presented by sex and age and reflect problems, issues and questions related to women and men in society".[8] The essential role of relevant,

---

5   Tier classifications are available from https://unstats.un.org/sdgs/iaeg-sdgs/tier-classification/.
6   Sustainable Development Solution Network (2015). Data for Development – A Needs Assessment for SDG Monitoring and Statistical Capacity Development.
7   Paris 21. Partner Report on Support to Statistics: PRESS 2017. Estimates include country-specific commitments to IDA borrowing countries and unallocated commitments to developing regions.
8   Beijing Platform for Action, para. 206 (a).

Figure 1

Total ODA dedicated to statistical capacity-building activities, 2010 and 2015
(*Millions of United States dollars*)

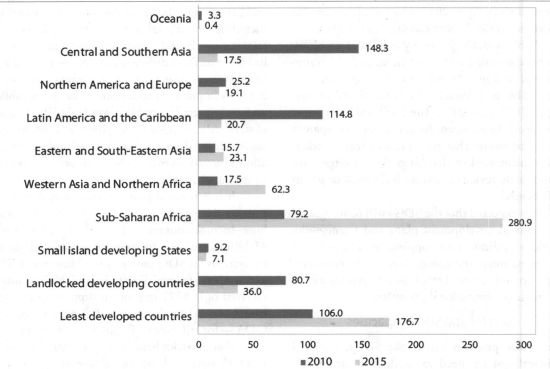

Source: SDG Indicator Database, UN/DESA.
Notes: Includes country-specific commitments only. Unallocated commitments to multiple countries and regions are excluded.

reliable and timely gender statistics—cutting across traditional fields of statistics, including education, health and employment as well as emerging ones, such as climate change—to ensure development and leave no one behind is also recognized in the 2030 Agenda for Sustainable Development.

Progress has been made on the availability of sex-disaggregated data for basic indicators on population, families, health, education and work, thanks to commitments by Governments to conduct decennial censuses, along with increases in the number of household surveys. Yet, gender statistics are still far from satisfactory, and many gaps exist

in terms of data availability, quality, comparability and timeliness. According to a 2018 assessment, sufficient and regular data is available for only 10 out of the 54 gender-specific indicators in the 2030 Agenda for Sustainable Development. Globally, less than one third of the data needed for monitoring the gender-specific indicators is currently available.[9] For example, high-quality data on causes of deaths, crucial for monitoring several SDG indicators under Goal 3 (good health and well-being), can only be produced by about 30 countries.[10] Less than half of all developing countries regularly produce information on labour force activities disaggregated by sex.[11]

9   *Turning promises into action: Gender equality in the 2030 Agenda for Sustainable Development.* United Nations Entity for Gender Equality and the Empowerment of Women (UN Women, 2018).

10   Prasanta Mahapatra and others, "Civil registration systems and vital statistics: successes and missed opportunities". *The Lancet,* vol. 370, No. 9599 (10 November 2007), pp. 1653–1663.

11   *The World's Women 2015: Trends and Statistics* (United Nations publication, Sales No. E.15.XVII.8).

A number of challenges on producing relevant and reliable gender statistics at the national level have been identified. First, there is a lack of national capacity in producing basic gender statistics and/or statistics that are sufficiently disaggregated. Often, gender statistics are not prioritized in regular statistical production. For many countries, it is necessary to integrate gender statistics in national statistical plans and strategies, including investing in improving basic gender statistics. Second, there is a lack of an integrated national system of gender statistics within countries. Given the cross-cutting nature of gender statistics, they are often collected by different producers within a country. These data are often not comparable across data sources and not shared with different producers. It is important to strengthen the links between producers of statistics in various fields at the national level. Third, there is a lack of standards for producing gender statistics for emerging areas. Statistical methods for producing relevant gender statistics are still lagging behind in many priority areas, such as individual-level poverty; quality of education and lifelong learning; and the different impacts of natural disasters and environment degradation on women and men. For some other areas, such as time spent on unpaid care and domestic work, statistical methods exist and data have been collected in 83 countries since 2000.[12] However, additional research is needed on innovative data collection approaches to reduce costs and the burden on respondents as well as to ensure a higher coverage and availability of time-use data across countries. Finally, there is a lack of recognition and knowledge of gender statistics by users. Gender statistics once produced should be properly communicated to all users including policymakers and the general public. Gender statistics can be a focus of efforts to improve the communications work of national statistical offices, such as the new project being launched by the United Nations Economic Commission for Europe to develop a strategic communications framework for such offices.

The 2017 ECOSOC Forum on Financing for Development Follow-up encouraged Governments to strengthen the collection of time-use data, time-use research on the unpaid care burdens of women and girls and the construction of satellite accounts to determine the value of unpaid care work and its contribution to the national economy. In addition to the need for innovative instruments to collect time-use data, other challenges exist in producing data on unpaid care and domestic work that accurately reflect gender inequalities. For example, evidence shows that women spend more time than men caring for family members. This activity often overlaps with domestic duties, making it difficult to capture it accurately in time-use surveys (see figure 2).[13] Furthermore, comparability of time-use data across countries remains a challenge owing to the different methods, definitions and classifications adopted by countries.[14] The United Nations Statistical Commission adopted in 2017 the International Classification of Activities for Time-Use Statistics[15] and plans for its operationalization, which will contribute to better harmonized data across countries in the near future. The UNECE Guidelines for Harmonizing Time-Use Surveys provides useful guidance in the design and implementation of time-use surveys, which can help improve international comparability.[16]

3. Monitoring the financial sector

The Group of Twenty (G20) Data Gaps Initiative (DGI) is a high-level effort to implement the regular collection and dissemination of reliable and timely financial statistics for policy use. It was initially launched to address data gaps revealed by the global financial crisis. The second phase of the initiative commenced in 2015 and is focused on monitoring risk in the financial sector; vulnerabilities, interconnections and spillovers; and data sharing. In addition

---

12   The Sustainable Development Goals Report 2017 (United Nations publication, Sales No. E.17.I.7).

13   Ibid.

14   *The World's Women 2015*.

15   See https://unstats.un.org/unsd/demographic-social/time-use/icatus-2016/.

16   See https://www.unece.org/fileadmin/DAM/stats/publications/2013/TimeUseSurvey_Guidelines.pdf - https://unstats.un.org/unsd/demographic-social/time-use/icatus-2016/.

Figure 2
Time spent unpaid on care and domestic, women and men, 2000–2016
(*Percentage of time spent per day*)

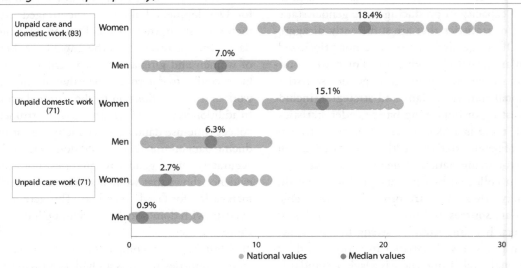

Source: SDG Indicator database, UN/DESA.

Notes: The figure reflects available data for 83 countries and areas over the period 2000-2016. Data disaggregated by unpaid domestic work and unpaid care work are only available for 71 countries. The number of countries and areas represented in each type of unpaid work is indicated in parentheses.

to the G20 economies, five non-G20 jurisdictions[17] with significant financial sectors are also participating in the DGI. The work is aimed at helping ensure financial stability in these large or important financial centres, thus benefiting the entire international community because of the reduced risk of financial crises that can spillover to affect smaller economies. The 2017 work programme of the initiative included four thematic workshops in 2017 (data sharing, data gaps on the insurance sector, institutional sector accounts and financial soundness indicators) as well as the annual Global Conference in June 2017.

To facilitate progress, a new monitoring framework for G20 economies was agreed at the Global Conference. Of the 20 recommendation areas, 12 are judged by the coordinating agencies to be complete or broadly on track. These include financial soundness indicators, data on derivatives, coordinated portfolio investment surveys, coordinated direct investment surveys, residential property prices indices, international data cooperation and communication, and promotion of data sharing. Areas where further work is needed include measures of

financial sector concentration, sectoral accounts data, household distributional information, cross-border exposures of non-bank corporations, and commercial property price indices.

To accelerate further progress with the most challenging recommendations, the 2018 work programme of the initiative includes three thematic workshops: on property price indices, sectoral account and securities statistics. The January 2018 workshop on property price indices discussed compilation practices and the use of residential and commercial property prices for policy purposes, as well as country-specific challenges. To advance work, participants agreed to be pragmatic, data-oriented, and to take account of available private source data. Representatives from several countries shared their experiences with digitalization and the use of big data to compile real estate price statistics.

A February 2018 workshop found that the G20 economies have made substantial progress in developing institutional sectoral accounts and balance sheets, with most economies being expected to disseminate these by 2021. The workshop also dis-

17   Hong Kong SAR, the Netherlands, Singapore, Spain and Switzerland.

cussed the templates to be used by the participating economies to report sector accounts data in the context of the DGI. The outcomes of discussions will be reflected in the final version of the templates. The workshop also discussed a planned handbook on the compilation of institutional sector accounts, which will present actual country practices, the main challenges encountered, and practices to address some of the challenges.

The DGI has important complementarities with the efforts to implement the LEI system globally. LEIs are unique identifiers for each business entity, which, in some countries, are mandated for automatically tracking financial transactions and counterparty exposures in large information databases in some markets. In May 2017, the Legal Entity Identifier Regulatory Oversight Committee, with membership from 50 countries, approved the collection of data on the ultimate and direct parents of entities with LEI, based on accounting consolidation and to be collected by the Global Legal Entity Identifier Foundation. This will provide an additional tool to increase transparency on group structures beyond the financial sector and allow the aggregation of data across corporate groups (including foreign affiliates), with the potential to show the financial interconnectedness between counterparties. Public entities that issue securities could lead by example and obtain an LEI for themselves. Expanded use of this technological solution will also bring down the cost per LEI, and consideration of potential business model changes may also facilitate use beyond financial institutions.